The Politics of Economic and Monetary Union

Integration and Idiosyncrasy

Erik Jones

ROWMAN & LITTLEFIELD PUBLISHERS, INC.
Lanham • Boulder • New York • Oxford

ROWMAN & LITTLEFIELD PUBLISHERS, INC.

Published in the United States of America
by Rowman & Littlefield Publishers, Inc.
4720 Boston Way, Lanham, Maryland 20706
www.rowmanlittlefield.com

12 Hid's Copse Road
Cumnor Hill, Oxford OX2 9JJ, England

British Library Cataloguing in Publication Information Available

Library of Congress Cataloging-in-Publication Data

Jones, Erik.
    The politics of economic and monetary union : integration and idiosyncrasy / Erik Jones.
        p. cm.—(Europe today)
    Includes bibliographical references (p.) and index.
    ISBN 0-8476-9034-2 (cloth)—ISBN 0-8476-9035-0 (paperback)
    1. Economic and Monetary Union. I. Title. II. Europe today (Rowman and Littlefield, inc.)

    HG925 .J66 2002
    337.1'4—dc21

                                                                    2002001814

Printed in the United States of America

⊗™ The paper used in this publication meets the minimum requirements of American
National Standard for Information Sciences—Permanence of Paper
for Printed Library Materials, ANSI/NISO Z.39.48–1992.

Contents

List of Tables and Figures vi

Preface vii

Abbreviations ix

Introduction: The End of the Beginning 1

1. Technology: Theory and Practice 17

2. Design: Interdependence and Accountability 35

3. Legitimacy: Delegation and Distributive Preferences 59

4. Symmetry: Mobilization and Adjustment 81

5. Motivation: Insulation and the Welfare State 101

6. Context: Ambition and Constraint 123

7. Determination: Power and Collective Action 143

8. Symbolism: Expectations and Idiosyncrasies 167

Conclusion: The Politics of EMU 183

References 193

Index 209

About the Author 214

Tables and Figures

Tables

2.1.   Three Clusters of Policy Rules behind EMU   42

2.2.   Economic Accountability Procedures   49

5.1.   European Current Account Performance, 1960–1973   109

5.2.   European Current Account Performance, 1983–2000   109

5.3.   Consistent Current Account Deficits   112

5.4.   Consistent Current Account Surpluses   115

6.1.   Euro-Dollar-Pound Exchange Rates, 1999–2001   131

7.1.   Macroeconomic Performance in France and Germany
       Compared   147

7.2.   Trade Dependence between France and Germany   152

7.3.   Import Penetration in France and Germany   153

7.4.   Sectoral Composition of German and French Employment   155

7.5.   German Economic Power Potential in a European Context   158

8.1.   Popular Attitudes toward Europe and the Single Currency   174

8.2.   Euro-optimists and Euro-pessimists   177

Figures

8.1.   Converging Expectations, Diverging Concerns   175

Preface

The controversy that has surrounded the creation of Europe's economic and monetary union is as hard to deny as it is to understand. When I first started working on the subject in the early 1990s, EMU was big and important but it was also technical and obscure. Outside of the economics profession, few people had a strong opinion on EMU because most had little idea as to what it entailed. However, that juxtaposition of importance, complexity, apathy, and ignorance changed rapidly. By the mid-1990s, EMU was one of the most hotly debated issues in European affairs. By the end of the decade, many regarded it as the culmination of the European project.

My objective with this book is twofold. To begin with, and in a small way, I hope that anyone who reads it will come away a little better informed about the mechanics of Europe's EMU project—how it was designed and how it is meant to work. There are already several excellent books on the technical aspects of EMU. Often, however, these books are written by economists for economists and other students of economics. This book is written with a larger audience in mind. My hope is to succeed in clarifying the issues at stake without sacrificing the sophistication of the analysis.

A more important objective is to situate EMU within the larger political discussions that surround it, both domestic and international. My general argument is that the controversy over EMU is not about EMU per se, but rather it is about the broader development of Europe's member states, the Union itself, and the world at large. EMU has always been a political issue, but in an instrumental sense and not in its own right. Thus Europeans can agree on what they can and cannot know about EMU— meaning they can come up with very similar formulas for estimating the costs and benefits—and yet they can still disagree about whether it is a good thing. Put another way, EMU is the egg and the controversy about EMU concerns the nest.

With any luck, this nesting of the controversy around EMU will not last far into the 21st century. Now that Europe's monetary union has come into being, national electorates and government officials should begin to incorporate the existence of the single currency into their larger agendas. Debates over the "grand alternatives" will continue to rage, but EMU will lie in the background rather than at center stage. Moreover, EMU's retreat back into popular obscurity can only be for the good. As with most technological innovations, the less excited we get about Europe's monetary union, the more use we will be able to make of it.

Many of the chapters of this book have been presented at conferences, seminars, and workshops during the course of writing. Some have also been published in preliminary form. Therefore, I would like to take this opportunity to acknowledge the placement of early editions of these arguments as follows:

- Chapter 3 appeared as "EMU and Europe's Democratic Deficit," in *The Coming of the Euro: Integration Theory and Economic and Monetary Union*, edited by Amy Verdun (Boulder, Colo.: Rowman & Littlefield).
- Chapter 4 appeared as "European Monetary Union and the New Political Economy of Adjustment," in *State of the European Union: Risks, Reforms, Resistance, and Revival*, volume 5, edited by Maria Green Cowles and Michael Smith (Oxford: Oxford University Press, 2000), 127–145.
- Chapter 7 appeared as "Franco-German Economic Relations: From Exchange and Convergence to Collective Action," in *France-Germany in the Twenty-First Century*, edited by Patrick McCarthy (London: Palgrave, 2001), 57–81.

In addition, my thinking about EMU has benefited greatly from a long and close association with a number of people. David Calleo and Patrick McCarthy deserve a special thanks for encouraging me to work and study in Brussels and for shielding me from the obsessive introspection that Europe's capital city can generate. Thanks are also due to Daniel Gros, Jeffry Frieden, Kathleen McNamara, and Francisco Torres for allowing me to borrow liberally from our collaborative work in pulling this argument together. Ronald Tiersky and Susan McEachern gave me the original stimulus, without which I never would have thought to write this volume. In addition, a number of friends and colleagues offered generous comments on the manuscript, without which it would certainly have suffered. Finally, my wife, Una, provided the encouragement necessary to keep me at the task and our sons, Isak and Jakob, the incentives to complete it.

Abbreviations

BEPGs	broad economic policy guidelines
ECB	European Central Bank
ECOFIN	Council of Ministers of Economics and Finance
ECSB	European System of Central Banks
ECSC	European Coal and Steel Community
EFC	Economic and Financial Committee
EMU	economic and monetary union
EP	European Parliament
EPC	Economic Policy Committee
euro-zone	collection of member states participating in the single currency (euro)
Eurogroup	group of Ministers of Economics and Finance of euro-zone member states
MEPs	Members of European Parliament
MPC	Monetary Policy Committee of the Bank of England
NATO	North Atlantic Treaty Organization
TEC	Treaty Establishing the European Community
TEU	Treaty on European Union

+

Introduction:
The End of the Beginning

The introduction of notes and coins for the new European single currency—the euro—marks the end of the beginning of economic and monetary union (EMU) in the European Union (EU). Gone for good are questions about whether EMU will actually happen. Clearly, it has. Now it is time to turn to questions about whether and for how long the euro will last.

My argument is that the politics of EMU is idiosyncratic and varies from country to country and from one situation to the next. This hyper-pluralism is both a weakness and a strength for European integration. It can explain why EMU was so difficult to create and why it is likely to prove surprisingly resilient. In a nutshell, it is hard to sell a single project to a multitude of different groups possessing different interests at different times in different contexts. Moreover, this is true whether that project is to create a monetary union or to disestablish one. By extension, and looking into the future, EMU is likely to succeed no matter what problems appear on the horizon. So long as the complaints about EMU vary across time and place, there should always be room for accommodation within the regime.

The optimism in my argument is not without qualification. It holds only so long as the politics of EMU remains idiosyncratic—varying from country to country and from one situation to the next. Should EMU succeed in crystallizing a politics uniquely its own from the collective idiosyncrasies of the participating member states, then basis for my optimism will necessarily give way. Europe's monetary union will not necessarily fail in a more coherent political environment, but the odds are greater that it might. Rather than benefiting from the inertia of Europe's hyperpluralism, EMU may inadvertently set the stage for a destructive political polarization.

1

The problem is finding relevant data to support a choice between these alternative futures, one of which is more optimistic than the other. EMU is massive in size and unprecedented in constitution. Never before have so many large advanced industrial economies joined in a common monetary regime—as opposed to growing up in one like the U.S. states. This problem is complicated by the difficulty of figuring out when EMU actually began. The introduction of the euro marks the end of the beginning. What marks the start?

By some accounts, EMU actually began on 3 May 1998 with the announcement of "irrevocably fixed" bilateral exchange rates between the currencies of eleven member states of the European Union.[1] The principal distinction between the EMU that exists now and the European Monetary System (EMS) that operated since 1979 is the notion that the bilateral exchange rates of participating countries are "irrevocably fixed." That distinction applied once the European Union announced the rules and levels for fixing intra-European exchange rates. Put another way, EMU started at the moment when saying "1.00000 Deutschemark is 1.12674 Dutch guilders is 6.24415 Austrian shillings" became equivalent to saying that "a Northern Irish pound is a Scottish pound is an English pound" or that "a (California) dollar is a (Texas) dollar is a (New York) dollar."[2]

Discussing the start of EMU is useful for focusing attention on the fact that a monetary union is a particular type of exchange rate regime and not a date marked on a diplomatic calendar or, necessarily, a large institutional infrastructure. The major innovation at the heart of Europe's economic and monetary union lies not in the buildings, paper notes, or coins that accompany it. Rather, more fundamentally, it lies in six-digit currency ratios and in the rules governing their cross-calculation. Take away either "irrevocably" or "fixed" as modifiers for intra-European exchange rates and the monetary union ceases to exist.

Too often, discussions of monetary integration skip over the central characteristics of a monetary union as a type of exchange rate regime— focusing instead on the ins and outs of convergence criteria or central bank independence. This is perhaps because the policy-relevance of regime characteristics lies only in the background or because exchange rate regimes are covered so extensively in introductory texts on international macroeconomics (and therefore we should already know enough about them). Alternately, the tendency to skip over the notion that a monetary union exists once exchange rates are irrevocably fixed derives from the belief that the only important debates are about the relative positions of business cycles, political symbolism, and economic governance, rather than monetary union per se.[3] Whatever the reasons, the tendency to skip over the fundamental characteristics of a monetary union as a type of exchange rate regime both assumes a simplicity that does not exist and reveals a complexity that cannot be tackled head-on. Bluntly, it misses the point.

Now that EMU has started, the facts that it consists of one currency and not several and that it is governed by an independent central bank and not a political council are important. But they are ancillary to the two questions at the heart of Europe's monetary integration process. To begin with, why do the countries of Europe want to fix their bilateral exchange rates? Second, how can they ensure that the bilateral exchange rates will remain fixed for all time—which is to say, irrevocably fixed?

The answers to such questions are anything but straightforward. Countries may choose to fix their exchange rates with one another on the basis of any number of considerations ranging from domestic economic welfare, to national prestige, to international leverage. Similarly, currency arrangements between countries can collapse for reasons equally as diverse as those for which they are created. National governments may choose to pull their currencies out of a monetary union as an assertion of pride, independence, or economic self-interest. Moreover, the reasons for joining a monetary union and for leaving one need not be the same or even similar. Countries may join for economic reasons and leave for more political reasons, or the reverse. Finally, different countries do not need to have the same reasons for joining or leaving the same monetary union. EMU may be an economic boon for one participant, offer domestic political advantages to another, and enhance the international prestige of a third. From this standpoint, it is hardly surprising that the process of building a system that would address all such contingencies stretches back into the late 1960s. EMU may have started with a simple announcement of irrevocably fixed bilateral exchange rates, but that does not mean it was easy.

EMU has been the most complicated and difficult task ever undertaken by the countries of Europe. A number of the continent's brightest economists and most powerful politicians have come up with sophisticated proposals to form a monetary union only to see them collapse repeatedly and spectacularly. Attitudes toward EMU have fluctuated as well, both across time and across countries. Some national governments have struggled to join and others have insisted on the right to remain outside. Professional economists have contested the foundational assumptions of their theoretical models. Public opinion has fluctuated for and against. The huge flows involved in world capital markets have supported efforts to bind Europe's currencies together, and they have undermined them. For all these reasons, it is not enough to announce that Europe's bilateral exchange rates are irrevocably fixed for EMU to begin. It is also necessary to understand what irrevocably fixing exchange rates entails.

The biggest challenge to understanding EMU is to sort out what is important from what is not, both to different participants and at different points in time. For those Europeans who first came up with the project in the late 1960s, this understanding was based on theoretical models, distant historical precedents, and loose analogies with existing exchange rate regimes. Thirty years later, we benefit from the direct experience of Europe's own successes and failures. The challenge of forming a monetary union has not gotten any easier, but our understanding of it is better informed.

The purpose of this introduction is to distill what I believe to be the crucial factors for the creation of EMU from the more than three decades of European monetary integration. In turn, these factors will constitute much of the basic conceptual vocabulary for the rest of the book. My analysis builds upon three assumptions:

- First, the choice for monetary union represents a choice for a particular type of exchange rate regime implying commitments in the present and in the future—exchange rates must be fixed, and the cross ratios must be irrevocable. The reasons that countries join or leave EMU may differ from place to place or time to time. However, the fact that a monetary union is a particular type of exchange rate regime (with all that entails) remains constant.
- Second, monetary integration—and all integration for that matter—requires that national governments choose for it to happen either through action or inaction. Changes in technology, markets, or ideas may make monetary integration more or less desirable, but they do not constitute integration in and of themselves.
- Third, the choices made by national governments are inherently political. Governments regard the choice for monetary integration from a self-interested rather than an altruistic perspective. Their calculus is subjective rather than objective.

Governments have not always been the most dynamic factors on the road to EMU. But the politics of creating and sustaining a monetary union is analytically distinct from the factors that make EMU more or less attractive. It is this politics that first culminated in the announcement of irrevocably fixed bilateral exchange rates between national currencies and ultimately led to the introduction of euro notes and coins. Whether EMU was really a good idea remains to be seen.

This introduction is divided into five sections. It begins with an overview of Europe's first attempt at monetary integration under the Werner Plan. The second section looks at the successes and failures of the EMS. The third follows the progress of the Maastricht Plan for EMU. The fourth outlines the rest of the book. The fifth concludes.

THE WERNER PLAN

Europe's first experience with monetary union started in 1969 and collapsed by the middle of the 1970s. The Werner Plan—so named because its patron was Luxembourg Prime Minister Pierre Werner—envisaged the creation of a European monetary union by 1980. The process of integration would take place in stages—with each step bringing the fluctuations in intra-European exchange rates ever closer to the ideal of being irrevocably fixed. Along the way, the participating member states would also begin to establish patterns of coordination in other fields of economic policymaking in order to facilitate the convergence of national currencies and to reap other cooperative advantages (for example, through lowering the indirect barriers to goods trade).[4]

The project fell apart even before it could begin. The closure of the gold window in 1971, the oil price shock in 1973, and the sharp global recession of 1975, made a mockery of European attempts to narrow the fluctuations of their bilateral exchange rates. Although Europe's heads of state and government brought forward institutions for fostering monetary integration—and, indeed, expanded those institutions to encompass currencies outside the European Community—they were unable to make any real progress. The European currency "snake" proved significantly less supple than the metaphor would imply. Countries joined and left the European monetary arrangement, only to join and leave again. By 1975, a group of "wise men" appointed by the European Council pronounced the Werner Plan a failure. They also noted that Europe's ambition to form a common currency was farther from realization in the middle of the 1970s than it had been at the start of the decade.[5]

Despite the initial pessimism of Europe's wise men, this early experience of monetary integration was not in vain. If nothing else, the failings of the Werner Plan underscored the importance of context and design to the creation of a monetary union. Such lessons were not wholly surprising and, at their core, they suggest the truism that forming a monetary union is easier under some circumstances than it is under others. They also indicate that while it is technically correct that a monetary union exists once exchange rates are pronounced "irrevocably fixed," simply announcing fixed exchange rates is insufficient to call a monetary union into being.[6] Both of these points were obvious from the late 1960s and they remain obvious today. However, recognizing that contingencies exist is only part of the problem. The other part is to appreciate such contingencies in their extremes. From that perspective, the difference between European understanding of monetary integration before and after the collapse of the Werner Plan is principally a matter of degree.

To illustrate this point it is necessary to flesh out the context within which Europe's statesmen and their advisers conceived and drafted the Werner Plan. International monetary conditions were propitious, with the prevailing Bretton Woods currency arrangement providing enough exchange rate stability to facilitate the creation of a monetary union in Europe while at the same time allowing enough turbulence to make a European monetary union worthwhile. The European Community was small, with only six member states, and it was relatively homogenous as an economic group. Finally, Europe's macroeconomic policymakers and their advisers shared a common set of beliefs about the role of the state in the economy derived from the widespread application of Keynesian economic thought. Thus the Werner Plan was not only to achieve monetary union in stages, but also to build upon the existing framework of the international monetary system and the larger consensus within which the liberal world economy was embedded.

Important differences existed even under such promising circumstances. France was more vulnerable to currency instability within the Bretton Woods system than Germany. Italy encompassed an important economic dualism between the prosperous regions of the north and the much poorer regions of the south. Finally, the implications of Keynesian analysis differed from country to country, and policy instrument to policy instrument—with the French directing their economy through credit rationing, the Belgians and the Dutch through indicative planning and concerted wage bargaining, and the Germans through increasingly rigid notions of absolute price stability.[7] Such differences coalesced around two competing perspectives of monetary integration as a process—one, called "monetarist," advocating irrevocably fixed exchange rates as an instrument for the promotion of economic convergence, and the other, called "economist," insisting on economic convergence as a precondition for irrevocably fixed exchange rates. Finally, each perspective had its own proponents. The French, Italians, and Belgians advocated the monetarist view. The Germans and the Dutch put forward the economist argument.[8]

The existence of two distinct camps should not be taken to indicate that Europe's reactions to the events of the early 1970s followed some underlying logic of states and markets. As various shocks struck Europe's economies, national approaches to monetary integration did not divide neatly. They splintered idiosyncratically. Hence the French struggled repeatedly to bind their currency with Germany's. The Italians and the British veered off on economic trajectories of their own. And yet the "monetarist" Belgians were more successful in stabilizing the short-term fluctuations of their Deutschemark exchange rates than their "economist" neighbors to the north. In such a context, the standards for successes and failures were national as well. Idiosyncrasy describes not just the movement, but the yardstick—a reality brought into sharp (if somewhat incredulous) relief by one Belgian finance minister's response to a Deutschemark appreciation with the assertion that the Belgian franc remained the stronger currency for not needing to move either up or down.[9]

The implications of the failure of the Werner Plan were clear. On the one hand, any project to form an economic and monetary union must be capable of withstanding the buffets of a suddenly more turbulent world economy. On the other hand, the principal challenge is to keep all participants on the same course rather than to address some fundamental schisms in economic thought. A monetary union is more than a technical arrangement. The Werner Plan demonstrated that monetary integration is, above all, a deeply practical venture.

THE EMS

Practical ventures require practical leadership. Soon after the collapse of "the snake" in the mid-1970s, European Commission President Roy Jenkins suggested that the European Community relaunch the project to create a monetary union. German Chancellor Helmut Schmidt and French President Valéry Giscard-d'Estaing made the suggestion a reality. Working bilaterally, and largely outside the institutional framework of the European Community, Schmidt and Giscard agreed to reconcile their national interests within a common framework for monetary cooperation. The ultimate objective of their efforts was to create the conditions under which a monetary union between France, Germany, and other European countries would be possible. However, the focus for their attention was the process rather than the end result.

The discussions between Schmidt and Giscard centered on the mechanical issues relating to intervention in support of a common exchange rate or parity grid. Such discussions often included other prospective participants such as the Belgians, Dutch, and Italians, as well as economic experts from national governments, the European Commission, and the academic community. Beneath the surface of such technical debates, however, lay a strong Franco-German will to assert leadership within Europe. The difficulty was to find sufficient means for reconciliation.[10]

The trade-off was between asymmetries: On the one hand, it is easier for the country with an appreciating currency to intervene in support of a common exchange rate. On the other hand, intervention by the country with the appreciating currency is more likely to be inflationary. The German currency tended to appreciate, making Germany the logical candidate to bear the burdens of intervention. However the German government feared inflation, which made it reluctant to intervene in currency markets. The situation for France was the reverse. France was more likely to see its currency depreciate and more accepting of inflation. Indeed, this contrast folded neatly into a simple dichotomy: The German currency tended to appreciate because the German government resisted inflation, and the French currency tended to depreciate because the French government accepted inflation. Germany, its currency, and its government were strong. France, its currency, and its government were weak.

The solution embodied in the European Monetary System was a compromise between German strength and French weakness. The Germans conceded to the creation of various financial mechanisms and institutional arrangements to facilitate intervention by countries whose currencies are depreciating. Meanwhile the French agreed to participate in institutions and practices that would shore up the government's ability to resist inflation. However, neither side of this compromise was successful. On the one hand, the institutions of the EMS did not actually facilitate intervention by governments in support of depreciating currencies. On the other hand, the institutions and practices of the European Monetary System were insufficient to bolster French resistance to inflation.[11]

The EMS was saved from collapse by a resurgence of French and German leadership during the winter of 1982–1983. The French government accepted the necessity of curbing its inflationary tendencies, and the German government conceded the importance of supporting French efforts within the EMS. Moreover, both governments agreed on the importance of the Franco-German partnership to the future of Europe—not only European monetary integration, but other forms of integration as well. The most dramatic display of this recognition came in the form of French President Mitterrand's 1983 address to the Bundestag in which he exhorted Germany's Social Democrats to express their support for the North Atlantic Alliance and its double-track strategy for dealing with the Soviets. A more lasting manifestation was the resurrection of the 1963 Elysée Accords outlining a pattern of cooperation between France and Germany punctuated with periodic bilateral summits and leading to the resuscitation of the West European Union. Thus the stabilization of the EMS became a cornerstone for the relaunching of Europe.[12]

This turnaround in the EMS yielded two important insights on the process of monetary integration—one related to "symmetry" and the other to "commitment." This first of these insights is that technical symmetry in the operations of the monetary arrangement is less important than the larger symmetry of roles played by different countries in the European system. The reason is simply that the technical asymmetries of the EMS cannot be overcome solely through a technical solution. The political will to work around the technical shortcomings of any monetary arrangement must exist as well. In turn, this will derives from a common interest—usually expressed as a trade-off. Thus, for example, Germany can assume a leading position in European monetary affairs so long as it is willing to acknowledge French leadership elsewhere and in some equally important area.[13]

The second lesson, relating to "commitment," operates predominantly in the domestic arena. Having agreed to make the commitment, the governments of Germany and France (or any participating country) could then use the strength of that commitment as a lever to force domestic change. Again, the logic applies outside the realm of monetary integration as well as inside. The German chancellor could rely on his country's commitment to Europe in order to overcome domestic opposition to NATO policy just as the French president could use French commitment to the EMS to enforce domestic economic austerity. In less cynical terms, the lesson of commitment is simply that monetary integration requires more than just appropriate international institutions. It also requires domestic adjustment.[14]

THE MAASTRICHT PLAN

The lessons of the EMS were applied with great success after 1983. While the European Community's heads of state and government had to realign their currency parities eleven times during the first five years of the EMS, they only had to do so three times after 1984, and not again between 1987 and 1992. Moreover, the EMS participants agreed to adjust the technical symmetry of the currency arrangement in 1987 and began taking on new members in 1988. Europe, it seemed, had finally come to grips with the process of monetary integration. European Commission President Jacques Delors' 1988 proposal to move beyond the process of monetary integration and toward the objective of monetary union was the end result.[15]

The plan to form an economic and monetary union in Europe signed at Maastricht in February 1992 incorporated all of the lessons of Europe's first two attempts at EMU. It was robust in that it provided a staggered entry date to allow for the possibility of unforeseen circumstances. It was appropriately designed in the sense that it bound would-be participants to accept a common economic philosophy and monetary constitution. It was roughly symmetrical in that it grew out of a larger Franco-German partnership that encompassed new institutional arrangements in other fields as well. And it implied a commitment to domestic adjustment with a new range of public indicators for sound economic performance in the form of explicit criteria for convergence.[16]

The Maastricht Plan was also almost immediately unsuccessful. During the late spring and summer of 1992, the larger Treaty on European Union ran into ratification troubles with a popular veto in Denmark and a close referendum in France. Moreover, these troubles coincided with a new and deep European recession—raising unemployment and worsening public finances. This combination of factors spilled over into currency markets first to rock and then to shatter the exchange rate mechanism (ERM) at the core of the EMS. In the autumn of 1993, the heads of state and government announced that the bands for currency fluctuations would have to be widened from ±2.25 percent to ±15 percent. With that declaration, the process of monetary integration appeared to move in reverse. Already by 1994 it became popular to ask whether the Maastricht Plan for EMU was dead and, if so, what Europe would do next.[17]

This early experience of the Maastricht plan for EMU underscored the importance of credibility and determination to the monetary integration project. Again, as with the previous teachings of experience, the lessons were important not as something new but rather as a matter of degree. For example, the notion of credibility initially grew out of the language of commitment under the EMS. The government of any country had to be credible in its commitment to the EMS if it was to convince national populations or capital markets to support the process of domestic adjustment. With the liberalization of capital markets in the late 1980s, however, credibility achieved a status all its own. No longer was it sufficient for a country to express commitment to the cause of monetary union for a domestic audience—that expression had to stand up to the scrutiny of giant mutual funds and footloose currency speculators. Where the domestic audience could foster or hinder a government's program for adjustment, the international audience could trigger hitherto unheard of flows of speculative capital. Where older conception of credibility was rooted in the reason of politics, the new logic of credibility derived from the potential irrationality of instant perceptions. The currency crises of the early 1990s may have started out as expressions of necessary readjustments. Soon, however, they assumed a life and raison d'être all their own.[18]

The determination to create EMU emerged as a grim acceptance on the part of political elites in national capitals across Europe—but particularly in France and Germany—of the longer term variability of popular attitudes and of the short-term volatility of market perceptions. Despite the popular malaise that grew out of the recession of the early 1990s and the repeated currency crises of 1992, 1993, and 1995, the heads of state and government continued to pursue EMU. Moreover, they responded to each setback with a consolidation of the Maastricht Plan and a redoubling of their efforts to achieve it. In this way, they were able to convince both their own electorates and international capital markets that EMU would come about.

By 1998 the leaders of Europe were able to reap the harvest of this determination. In March, eleven member states qualified for EMU. In

April/May, two-thirds of the populace in the participating countries declared their support for the project—including, for the first time, a majority of Germans, Austrians, Portuguese, and Finns.[19] Finally, during the summer months, Europe emerged as an island of currency stability in a world rocked by financial crises in Asia, Russia, and Latin America. Even before the official launch of Europe's monetary union, EMU not only appeared credible, it appeared to work. Moreover, the success of the project began to exert its attraction even on those countries determined not to join, such as Denmark, Sweden, and the United Kingdom.

A FRAMEWORK FOR ANALYSIS

Having concluded this short history on a high note should not be taken to imply that Europe's monetary union was an immediate and overwhelming success. Indeed, EMU was beset with problems almost as soon as it officially started in January 1999. Not only did the euro lose value rapidly against the dollar, but also Italy showed signs of difficulty in keeping up with its fiscal commitments, and a number of analysts began to speculate about the long-term viability of the single currency as a monetary regime. However before we can begin to evaluate the seriousness of these challenges, it is necessary to move beyond the basic conceptual lessons derived from Europe's history of monetary integration and into a more systematic analysis of the politics of EMU as it operates in Europe today.

This analysis builds on rationalist foundations and specifically on the belief that the political issues surrounding the creation of a single European currency should be understood in terms of the distribution of costs and benefits: What matters is who wins and who loses from the change in monetary regimes. Chapter 1 makes this argument in general terms, looking at the role of money and monetary policy in theory and practice. The central claim is that the distribution of costs and benefits from monetary policy changes is hard to identify before the fact. Therefore, in political terms, the real question concerns the rule used for setting monetary policy and not the direct manipulation of policy instruments. Whether the rule is that monetary policy will be determined by political actors on a case-by-case basis, or whether monetary policy will be the same under all circumstances, it is the choice of the rule that is politically significant.

The monetary rule was not the only rule adopted as part of EMU. Therefore, chapter 2 broadens the theoretical analysis of the first chapter to encompass the institutional design of Europe's economic and monetary union. As a starting point, it acknowledges that once again the distribution of costs and benefits from policy changes is hard to identify before the fact. As a result, the adoption of rules is more important than the specific manipulation of policy instruments. The objective of the chapter is to examine the implementation of economic and monetary policy rules and their enforcement. The chapter also analyzes the interaction between policy areas. The contrast it strikes is between the dynamic interaction between the effects of following the various policy rules and the relative isolation of the institutional arrangements for implementing the rules. EMU is a complicated arrangement, yet the institutional framework for EMU contains no overarching political authority to manage the trade-off between monetary goals and other economic objectives. Indeed, the establishment of a politically independent central bank makes such overarching authority difficult if not impossible to establish.

The absence of an overarching political authority to govern the trade-offs between different aspects of the European Union's EMU is potentially problematic for European democracy. How can Europe's heads of state and government avoid the charge that they have ring-fenced a core set of economic responsibilities beyond the reach of democratic accountability? Chapter 3 examines this question through the lens of distributive preferences. Building on the recognition that the distributive outcomes of policy changes may be difficult to identify before the fact, the chapter questions whether it really matters that some policy rules are beyond the operational control of the electorate. It argues that so long as the process of adopting the rules was democratically legitimate, then there is no need for further detailed accountability. European electorates may demand such accountability, but so far they have not, and they do not need to do so.

The legitimacy analyzed in chapter 3 is a categorical concept: Institutional arrangements either are or are not legitimate. Because it is absolute, however, such categorization tells us very little about whether or how well institutional arrangements will function. Therefore, chapter 4 examines Europe's EMU not as a constraint on European democracy but as a potential subject for European political and economic debate. The question it asks is whether EMU will be able to accommodate the conflicting political pressures that could arise from the winners and losers of monetary integration. The argument it makes is that the assignment of costs and benefits either from EMU or within EMU will be as hard to predict as the distributive consequences of policy changes outlined in chapters 1 and 2. Therefore, the likelihood that groups within Europe will either recognize EMU as the source of their economic difficulties or will mobilize against EMU as a first-best means of political redress is very small. EMU is likely to prove stable precisely because the interaction between policy areas is so complicated.

The stability of EMU is not the only concern to address. Its utility is important as well. Given that we find it hard to identify the winners and losers from EMU, whether initially or over time, it is necessary to ask why the heads of state and government were so determined to see the project through to implementation. It is also necessary to consider how a single set of policy rules can satisfy a diverse array of political constituencies. Chapter 5 analyses these issues within the context of claims that capital market integration and monetary union work together to constrain national policy autonomy. Using both aggregate data and national case studies, the chapter argues that—contrary to conventional wisdom— EMU helps to increase the range of policy combinations that are available to member state governments. In this way, the function of EMU is not simply to insulate Europe's economies, but also to enhance the flexibility or range of options available for European macroeconomic policies. Moreover, this increased diversity is reflected both in the function of EMU as an exchange rate regime and in the design of EMU as a set of policy rules.

The functionalist account of EMU provided in chapter 5 leaves open the explicit objectives of the policymakers who set up Europe's economic and monetary union. Therefore chapter 6 looks at a broader range of stated objectives for EMU in order to consider what are the constraints on one set of institutions as a means to achieve multiple outcomes. The argument in the chapter is that internal objectives have priority over external objectives—the single currency is better at providing for macroeconomic stability than it is at countering the international presence of the dollar. By extension, Europe's EMU remains under the influence of the euro-dollar exchange rate. Moreover, that influence has increased as the dollar-value of the euro has declined.

The external weakness of the euro is not the only source of vulnerability for EMU. The strained relations between France and Germany are problematic as well. Given the central role of the Franco-German couple in the construction of EMU, it is necessary to consider whether Europe's economic and monetary union can survive a foundering of that relationship. More fundamentally, what if EMU is actually a source of Franco-German discord? Chapter 7 analyzes the Franco-German relationship within the context of EMU. It argues that the basis of the Franco-German relationship has changed, but the central importance of economic issues remains the same. Moreover, the dynamics of the relationship have adapted to suit (and to influence) the new institutional environment in Europe. The Franco-German couple constituted EMU, and now EMU shapes the Franco-German relationship.

EMU has a constitutive effect on the other member states as well, both rational and irrational. The rules and functioning of Europe's economic and monetary union clearly have an impact on the interests of European countries, whether or not they participate in the single currency or in the European Union. EMU also has an impact on the politics of European countries. And, while it is often useful to assume that interests and politics are co-determined, it is frequently dangerous to do so. Therefore, chapter 8 examines the role of EMU as a symbol in contemporary political debates. Drawing upon the preceding chapters, it argues that the symbolic content of EMU is characteristically different from that of existing national currencies and also that the use of EMU as a symbol differs from one country to the next. In this way, the normative dimension of the single currency is every bit as varied and idiosyncratic as its distributive implications. Analysts are right not to ignore EMU as a symbol, but they would be wrong to be too hasty in making generalizations about it as well.

THE POLITICS OF EMU

The book concludes with an analysis of the politics of EMU as they bear on the continued stability of the monetary union. Here I return to the claim that Europe's bilateral exchange rates are likely to remain "irrevocably fixed" for the simple reason that it is possible to address great political variety within the context of that single choice. By extension, I suggest that the greatest threat to EMU is not that one country or another might be disadvantaged or might even attempt to secede. Rather it is that EMU will become the focus for conflict between cleavages which cut across the monetary union, be it north and south or labor and capital or some other set of opposing coalitions. Whether the basis for such conflict is real or imagined may be less important than the symbolism of EMU as a crystallizing force. Such a conflict would bring order to the politics of EMU. However, it might also spell the collapse of EMU itself.[20]

NOTES

1. By other accounts, EMU began in December 1998 when eleven of Europe's central banks coordinated a change in interest rates as their first expression of the common monetary policy.

2. These cross rates are published in Council of Ministers (1998).

3. For example, Tomaso Padoa-Schioppa (1994, 4, italics in original) argues forcefully that "a monetary union is *not* an exchange rate regime" and therefore that decisions should be supported with analysis from "the theory of monetary systems and institutions, rather than the theory of exchange rate regimes."

4. Magnifico (1973) provides an early and authoritative analysis of the Werner Plan as well as a strong plea that Europe's EMU project should culminate in the creation of a single currency, rather than the perpetuation of national currencies under conditions of irrevocably fixed bilateral exchange rates.

5. This group of wise men was chaired by French economist Robert Marjolin and published as CEC (1975). For detailed analysis of the European snake system, see Tsoukalis (1977) and Thygesen (1979).

6. This point is made strongly in the Marjolin Report (CEC 1975) and echoed in Padoa-Schioppa (1994).

7. This comparative political economy of the 1960s and 1970s is gleaned from Zysman (1983), Hall (1986), Kennedy (1991), and Jones (forthcoming).

8. The classic description of this debate is found in Tsoukalis (1977).

9. This contrast between Belgian and Dutch performance runs against the grain of the conventional wisdom that the Netherlands had a strong currency and Belgium a weaker one. The difference between my interpretation and the conventional one derives simply from a change in the time frame for analysis. Over the longer period, it is true that the Belgian franc depreciated more against the Deutschemark than did the Dutch guilder. However, on a month-to-month basis the Belgian franc was actually more stable against the Deutschemark than the guilder. See Jones (forthcoming).

10. The most widely cited analysis of the EMS negotiations is Ludlow (1982). Another interesting treatment in the same publication series is Kruse (1980).

11. Much of this early history of the EMS is described in greater detail in Gros and Thygesen (1998).

12. For a careful analysis of the Franco-German relationship during this period see McCarthy (1990 and 1993).

13. This point is contentious and the debates surrounding it are handled in chapter 7.

14. The security aspect of the Franco-German relationship is analyzed in Gordon (1995). The argument about "commitment" is loosely derived from Andrew Moravcsik's (1993) claims about how European integration strengthens the core executive and Giavazzi and Pagano's (1988) classic analysis of "the advantages of tying one's hands" via the EMS.

15. The Delors Plan is published by the European Commission (CEC 1989) and was supported by an impressive array of background studies (Emerson et al. 1992).

16. The definitive account of the Maastricht negotiations is Dyson and Featherstone (1999). See also Dyson (1994) and Italianer (1993).

17. The Philip Morris Institute issued a paper that captured the popular sentiment in asking "Is Monetary Union Dead?" (PMI 1994).

18. The argument about self-fulfilling speculative attacks is taken from Eichengreen and Wyplosz (1993).

19. These polling results were published in September 1998 by Eurobarometer (1998: 46).

20. Indeed, this is the starting point for Dyson's (2000) analysis of *The Politics of the Euro-Zone*.

1

✛

Technology:
Theory and Practice

Money is a very basic form of economic technology. It is also a vitally useful one. In his *Inquiry into the Wealth of Nations*, Adam Smith explains how money is necessary to generalize the process of exchange across the division of labor.[1] The argument he makes runs something like this: each person produces some things in excess of their needs, while wanting for other things. The difficulty lies in matching precisely those persons who have excesses with others who have wants. Moreover, this difficulty is compounded by the fact that some of the things produced tend to perish, such as fresh vegetables, while others must be traded whole or at a loss, such as racehorses. Thus any solution to the problem of exchange across the division of labor must take into account when things are available for trade, and how much is offered in relation to what is demanded.

That solution, Smith argues, is money—preferably metallic currency. Such currency can provide a means of exchange because everyone can use it; a store of value because metal deteriorates only very slowly; and a unit of account, because metallic currency loses nothing when broken down into change. Thus it is hardly surprising, Smith notes, that every civilized society at one point or another came up with the notion of money. Currency, it would seem, lies at the basis of the modern economy. It also lies at the foundation of modern economics. Using his simple discussion of money as a foundation, Smith constructs a wide ranging argument about the market economy, the labor theory of value, and the difference between nominal (or money) prices and real (or barter) prices.

Of course the trouble with money is getting everyone to use the same metal of the same quality and in relatively standardized weights or

measures. It is here, Smith suggests, that the state has an important role
to play. The state can determine which metal will form the basis of its
currency, it can establish a uniform quality for assay, and it can denominate standard weights and measures. Moreover, once the state sets
the basis for the currency, it can then promote its use either through
written promissory notes that are redeemable in set quantities of the
relevant metal or, more simply, by minting the metal into coins.

This argument from the *Wealth of Nations* is useful in understanding
monetary integration if only because it is so fundamental. The point is
that—as a form of economic technology—money is as necessary to commerce as paper is to writing. Money is also as replaceable as paper, at least
in the physical sense. Following this line of argument, electronic banking
is a more sophisticated technological solution to the problem of generalizing exchanges across the division of labor than the metallic currencies
Smith described in his *Wealth of Nations*. It offers all of the advantages of
currency without the inconveniences of metal. Even more amazing, electronic banking makes it possible to access "local" accounts from anywhere across North America, Europe, and most places on the globe in order to trade currencies and get hold of liquidity. Hidden behind the paper
and coins lies a virtual currency of bits and bytes capable of generalizing
exchanges across the marketplace.

Electronic banking pushes us beyond Smith's world of minted metal
and into the incorporeal currencies of telephone banks and automated
teller machines. In doing so, electronic banking suggests an important
question. Why do different countries continue to possess different currencies in the first place? If peoples and nations can agree on the utility of
electronic banking, why do they continue to differ on how the bits and
bytes are called? Put another way, why did the major technological ad-
vance delivered by the harmonization of electronic banking practices
across Europe in the late 1980s and early 1990s raise so little fuss in comparison with the proposal to create a single currency? It is as if no-one in
Europe noticed the crushing domination of the IBM standard for personal
computers, yet everyone cried out against the threat that American letter-
sized paper posed to European A-4.

The reason that people accepted electronic banking and yet disputed
the merits of a single currency is the same as the reason that different national currencies continue to exist. The technology involved is not the issue, or at least not in its own right. The power to control the creation of
money is. The purpose of this chapter is to explain why. The argument is
that who benefits or suffers from state control over currency creation is
more important than the precise technology for generalizing exchange
across the division of labor. However, the nature of the currency—which
is to say, the particular technology involved—may influence the assign-

ment of winners and losers. Moreover, some currency technologies are more viable than others—particularly in a context where other forms of economic technology are changing rapidly. Therefore, the technology of a currency is important, but it is not the central issue of concern.

This argument is made in five stages. The first looks at the relationship between politics and money. The second examines the difficulty of imagining a world where money operates without concern for politics. The third analyzes the costs and benefits of moving from a world of political money to a world where money and politics are more separate. The fourth reflects this theoretical discussion against the specific backdrop of European monetary integration. The fifth section concludes with a comparison of EMU and the alternatives.

MONEY AND POLITICS

The link between money and politics is twofold in nature.[2] The first—and least tangible—is symbolic. The minted coins and paper notes produced by a government "symbolize" the importance of the sovereign and the cultural identity of the nation and therefore are essentially political. However, the importance of this symbolism is difficult to estimate. In the United Kingdom, for example, the government allows the issuance of eight different series of notes—one by the Bank of England, three by banks in Scotland, and four by banks in Northern Ireland. Although tempting, it would be difficult to argue that the difference between the English and Scottish currencies explains (rather than simply reflects) the differences between England and Scotland. It would be even more difficult to claim that the multiple currencies in Northern Ireland explain (or even reflect) the fractious political situation in that part of the country. Moreover, while the Scots would surely object to the replacement of their Scottish pound with an English one, they seem less averse to (and even enthusiastic about) the replacement of the pound with the euro. The symbolic politics of money may be important, but it is likely to prove too idiosyncratic for coherent analysis.[3]

The second link between money and politics emerges out of Smith's notion that currencies exist to generalize the process of exchange across the division of labor. Specifically, money and politics intertwine in the gap between what people believe to be the value of their needs and contributions and the prices for goods and services set in the market. Each person's perspective on the value of what they need or contribute is subjective, and reflects a variety of psychological and material factors that may be unique to a particular individual or set of circumstances.[4] The market prices for goods and services, however, derive from the interaction between aggregate supply and demand and are (at least in theory) uniform for all participants in the marketplace. Given the different factors that go into their construction, the subjective values are unlikely to match up coherently with the market prices for all participants. It is the gratification or disappointment that arises from the difference between subjective and market values that provides the stimulus for the political interest in money.

It is easy to understand how frustrated ambitions can lead to political action. People are apt to find justice in market values that work in their favor and injustice in market values that work against them. Corporate executives justify their own salaries as a function of the "hard work" they perform or the value-added they contribute while they mark down the salaries of migrant workers as a consequence of inexorable market forces. For their own part, migrant workers decry the exploitation of their wage-labor as well as the injustice of a system that often places the value of one individual at more than 100 times that of another even when both work in the same firm. In such a context, we should expect corporate executives to strive politically to preserve the market system and migrant workers to reform it.

What is more difficult to anticipate is how the politics emerging out of the gap between subjective and market values can focus on state control over the creation of money. While it is easy to see that the rich and the poor hold differing opinions about the justice of the marketplace, it is more difficult to find any correlation between particular social or economic groups, on the one hand, and the direction of monetary policy, on the other hand. The focus for politics around monetary matters lies in the basic functions of the currency—means of exchange, store of value, unit of account. And the question is whether these basic functions can be manipulated to alter subjective and market values.

This explanation is a complex one and probably deserves the fuller treatment found in a textbook on monetary economics. However, in the most simple terms, the link between money and politics can be explained with reference to three policy instruments—the money supply, the interest rate, and the exchange rate. The money supply relates to the currency as a means of exchange, the interest rate touches on the currency as a store of value, and the exchange rate translates the currency as a unit of account from one market to the next. Changes in the money supply affect those who hold currency and those who do not. Changes in the interest rate affect lenders and borrowers. And changes in the exchange rate alter the unit values of domestic goods abroad and foreign goods at home.

In a world where each of these levers works in isolation—the money supply, interest rates, and exchange rates—it would be possible to imagine political cleavages emerging around any of the three. In each case, the cleavage forms around how the instruments can best be manipulated in order to alter subjective or market values. For example, those who have regular access to money would differ over the appropriate money supply from those who suffer periodic liquidity shortages—not necessarily because an increase in the supply of money would make people who lack liquidity better off, but because it would make them feel better off by making it easier for them to participate in the marketplace. More directly, those with money to lend would differ over the interest rate from those needing to borrow because the interest rate reflects the time-value of money (in other words, the price of money over time). Finally, those who buy or sell in foreign markets would differ over the appropriate exchange rate from those who participate only in the domestic market because of the manner in which the exchange rate translates unit prices between foreign and domestic markets. The politics of money, therefore, derives from the balance of forces within and across each of these cleavages— liquid/illiquid, lender/borrower, traded/non-traded.

In reality, however, the politics of money is complicated by two factors. The first of these is that the three policy variables interact with one another through their effect on prices. For example, an increase in the money supply may lead to an increase in prices that would lower the real (or price adjusted) interest rate while at the same time raising the real (or, again, price adjusted) exchange rate.[5] In this way, a change in the money supply to suit one group—those with periodic liquidity problems— would have a knock-on effect across the cleavages between lenders and borrowers and between traded and non-traded sectors of the economy. A similar point can be made for changes in the interest rate or in the exchange rate. Put another way, the policy instruments are interdependent and cannot operate in isolation.

Interdependence is not a problem in and of itself. The economic mechanisms that link the three monetary variables—meaning the money supply, interest rates, and exchange rates—are largely predictable in a formulaic manner. Although not all economists agree on the precise formulas for describing the monetary economy, most do agree on the contention that formulaic modeling is the appropriate technique for analysis as well as on the broad principles for choosing between models. The problem is that the interdependence between policy instruments blurs the simple rules of thumb regarding where groups will or should stand with respect to any particular policy change. Even if we can predict what impact a policy change will have on the monetary economy, that does not mean we can predict whether a given political constituency will support the policy beforehand or benefit from it afterward.

The second complication is that political and economic groups do not organize coherently along the logic of monetary cleavages—liquid/illiquid, lender/borrower, traded/non-traded. Both lenders and borrowers can suffer from liquidity problems and participate in foreign markets; both traded and non-traded goods producers or service providers can engage in lending or borrowing; and so on. For this reason, the political implications of the interdependence between monetary policy variables are less predictable than the economic mechanisms at work. For example, it may be possible to argue that an increase in the money supply will raise inflation, thereby lowering real interest rates and sparking an appreciation of the real exchange rate. What is more difficult is to decide how economic actors will respond to these developments *in political terms*. Will they encourage or oppose the government in its actions? Will they reward or punish the government once the policy takes effect?

Any answer to such questions depends on structure and timing. In structural terms, support for the government's action will rely upon the overlap between the various cleavages—on the extent to which the same people who encouraged the government to increase the money supply are likely to benefit or suffer from the impact of rising prices on interest rates and exchange rates. The point is not whether the political left is more concerned with unemployment than with inflation while the political right is more concerned with inflation than unemployment. Rather what is important is how inflation affects different groups on the left and right—including whether the policies leading to inflation actually reduce unemployment, and for whom. This broader notion of structure encompasses not only the Anglo-Saxon market economies (where the left-right distinction held for a time), but also the countries of north-central Europe (where the left and right share an aversion to inflation).[6]

The timing part of the explanation derives from the fact that most political activity is only periodic—and culminates in elections—while the economic effects of any policy changes are developmental. Thus a policy designed to reap political support in one time frame can result in economic hardship at some later point. The classic example here is an increase in the money supply to benefit the illiquid—say, for example, farmers who earn money only at harvest time but spend money all year round. The policy works initially as the farmers suffering from liquidity problems between harvests benefit from the greater availability of money. However, as these farmers begin to participate in the marketplace they push up the demand for goods and services which in turn raises prices. The rise in prices lowers the real value of any single unit of currency and thereby eliminates the benefits of the initial increase in the money supply.

The inconsistency of the benefits from manipulating monetary policy instruments over time is not limited simply to erasing the gains of one group or another. The farmers who called for the increase in the money supply may not have anticipated or planned for the price rise that followed the policy action. Therefore, to the extent to which their perceptions of prosperity encouraged them to overspend, they are also worse off.[7] Nevertheless, a government that cleverly planned the increase in the money supply to have an effect at election time will also have succeeded in garnering the farm vote—despite the fact that the ultimate impact of the policy was to hurt farm interests. Such cynical manipulation of monetary instruments may be good politics, but it is certainly bad policy.

The interface between politics and money is difficult to predict and—where prediction is possible—it is open to manipulation. Moreover, given the interdependence between monetary instruments, the complex structure of monetary interests, and the differing effects of policy actions across time, there is no guarantee that a given policy change will enjoy consistent political support from beginning to end. Indeed, the most likely outcome of any policy movement is to trigger another policy change as different groups coalesce in response to effects that are once, twice, or even three times removed from the original action. A sudden expansion of the money supply to benefit farmers may encourage the banking industry to call for interest rate hikes while stimulating the export sector to call for an exchange rate devaluation. Unfortunately for policymakers, the interest-rate and exchange-rate policy reactions threaten to work against each other, and either is likely to hurt the farm sector. Money is a simple and yet vital form of economic technology with complex and potentially destabilizing political implications.

MONEY WITHOUT POLITICS

Politics is essentially about choice. Therefore, if money is to operate without danger of political manipulation it must also operate outside the boundaries of political choice. The key to imagining a world of money without politics is to establish a set of general (a priori) rules for the use of policy instruments such as the money supply, the interest rate, and the exchange rate. Of course such rules could never alleviate the symbolic importance of the currency as a reflection of sovereignty and culture. It may always be necessary to leave the design of notes and coins (or the name of bits and bytes) open to political expression. However, designing the currency and controlling its creation are two different things. While the one may be essentially political, the other need not.

For economists, the notion of placing monetary policy outside the reach of politicians is particularly attractive. In an ideal world, economists believe that a clear set of general rules for the management of policy instruments would enable them to ignore the complex structure of monetary interests as well as the possibility of political manipulation in their analysis.

In this way, the rules would free economic policymakers to focus on managing the interdependence between policy variables, thereby improving the technical functions of the currency.

Stripping the politics out of money is a concern shared by virtually all economists—including Keynesians as well as monetarists. Where they disagree is over when rules are necessary for the management of economic policy instruments and what constitutes the best set of a priori rules for adoption. For example, Keynesians argue that government deficit spending can be used to stimulate economic activity, while monetarists express concern that such deficits will only result in greater inflation. On the surface, this disagreement is both analytical and empirical— it concerns the assumptions underwriting the models used for understanding the economy and fit between various models and the historical data. That said, no matter what assumptions are built into a model or how well the model performs in a particular circumstance, the complex relationship between politics and money is both a burden for analysis and a possibility for abuse. Thus while economists may not agree on what exactly should be done, almost all accept that some set of a priori rules should be adopted.

Beneath this superficial disagreement between different groups of economists, the problem with adopting any a priori rules is twofold. To begin with, the establishment of such rules is (inherently) a political act. Depending upon the circumstances, a given set of rules could favor borrowers over lenders, traded goods producers and services providers over the non-traded sectors, and so forth. As a consequence, the choice of rules is at least as political as a choice of policy. Indeed, given that rules last longer than any specific policy action, the choice of rules is likely to be even more political than the policy choice.

The political act of selecting the rules for economic policy is a problem because the selection process necessarily remains open to contestation on technical as well as political grounds. Put another way, the differences between schools of economic thought may not be so much analytical and empirical as they are political. In their advocacy of different sets of rules, economists become politicized—either directly through their participation in a particular group, or indirectly through the co-option of their ideas. Thus the political strength of one side over another plays a role not only in selecting the appropriate rules for the management of policy instruments but also in assessing their "technical" merit. As a result, the adoption of a set of a priori rules does not so much remove the politics from money as lock in a particular political coalition of monetary interests.[8]

The second problem with adopting a priori economic policy rules is that economic circumstances might change in a manner that undermines the cohesion of the coalition responsible for promoting the rules in the first place. Relevant changes here could come from any of a variety of sources including taste, technology, institutions, weather, and war. The important point is not how the change originates but how the resulting distribution of costs alters the balance of political forces across and between different monetary cleavages. If the rules for managing policy instruments can be forged by one coalition of interests, they can also be broken by another.

This notion of change and adjustment is straightforward. To find examples it may be useful to think of the re-branding of Japanese "quality" cars, the introduction of electronic payment facilities and interest-bearing current accounts, the liberalization of international capital markets, the El Niño weather patterns, and the oil price fluctuations that periodically accompany conflict in the Middle East. Each of these changes has had economic effects that have forced specific actors to adjust through a reallocation of resources—new investment in advertising or production facilities; increasing reliance on more expensive liabilities and the narrowing of margins for financial intermediation (or the growth of asset risk); increased hedging against exposure to foreign exchange markets; greater spending on energy and investment in more energy-efficient equipment. In turn, these adjustments ripple across the economy as different economic agents attempt to shrug off the costs of making the adjustment onto workers (redundancies or wage cuts), consumers (price rises), investors (default), firms (wage raises or tax increases), or the government (moral hazard).

The essential point is that each of these economic changes may have a political consequence. And this political consequence may be relevant to the coalition surrounding a particular set of policy rules. Returning to the three policy instruments used as illustration—the money supply, the interest rate, and the exchange rate—does the economic change increase or decrease the political importance of liquidity, indebtedness, or international exposure? If the answer to this question is "yes" in any regard, then the economic change and consequent adjustment may bring into question the continuing political viability of the policy rules.

The emphasis on political rather than economic effects of an adjustment process is important. The issue is not which set of rules makes the most sense speaking in general terms. Rather, the issue is for whom the rules make sense at a particular point in time. Moreover, just because the cost of adjusting to an economic change is small does not mean that it is politically irrelevant. On the contrary, small costs concentrated on a limited group of firms or other economic agents can have dramatic political significance while large costs that are diffused over an equally large and diverse group of actors can have little or no political impact.[9]

The challenge of ensuring the stability of a given set of a priori rules is not only to anticipate that economic circumstances might change, but also to estimate the political impact of such changes. Moreover, the range of factors to consider in determining how different groups will react to a change in circumstances under a given set of rules is just as broad as those used in deciding how different groups will react to a change in policy as circumstances remain the same. The notion of money without politics may be something for economists to aspire to, but it is hard to imagine and even harder to bring about.

TAKING THE POLITICS OUT OF MONEY

Limiting the influence of politics on money is difficult, but not impossible. Two conclusions emerge out of the discussion of a priori rules for the management of policy instruments. First, any policy rules will have to be difficult to change in order to be effective in the face of adjustment to unforeseen developments. Second, the stability of any set of a priori rules can be increased if they are supported by an additional set of rules concerning the distribution of adjustment costs.

The reason for making a priori rules difficult to change is to shield them from the fallout of minor fluctuations in the marketplace. The harder it is to change the rules, the greater the level of adjustment will have to be to make changing the rules worthwhile for any particular group. The "difficulty" suggested here can be institutional, but it can also be symbolic. Governments can introduce complicated procedures for changing the rules or they can attach public importance to the achievement of highly visible targets. It is one thing to promise to fight inflation and another to pass legislation entrusting responsibility for meeting inflation targets to an independent central bank. Similarly, attempting to shadow the inflation performance of another country is less restrictive than announcing a fixed exchange rate target against that country's currency. The political cost of revoking central bank independence or devaluing the exchange rate will be high, and so the political motives for doing so will have to be weighty.

Politicians and policy analysts have long recognized the importance of both institutional and symbolic commitments. The recent emphasis on central bank independence is a good example. Although many economists note that independent central banks are not politically neutral, they emphasize that the cost of overturning central bank independence is high—and in many cases out of proportion with any conceivable benefit from bringing monetary policy under more political control. Thus while the bank's policies may tend to serve one group at the expense of another, the advantages of having a consistent rule-based monetary policy are enjoyed by the society as a whole.[10] The symbolic commitment of an exchange rate target plays a similar role, though with more clearly biased effects. Governments are often reluctant to devalue the currency even though the damage of a high exchange rate for manufacturing competitiveness is clear for all to see. Indeed, this has been particularly true of left-wing governments who sought to retain the advantages of policy continuity despite the impact of an overvalued exchange rate on their own constituencies in the manufacturing trade unions.[11]

The logic behind setting up additional rules for the distribution of adjustment costs is to cut through the complexity of anticipating a change in circumstances and of estimating its political significance. The politics of adapting to economic change could be worked out beforehand through a considered debate over the formula for distributing adjustment costs arising from any unforeseen circumstances. The mechanisms for setting a distributive formula could include any of a number of factors from marginal tax rates to means-testing on benefits and from redundancy payments to insolvency and receivership. The monies flowing through taxes and benefits tend to stabilize income performance across minor fluctuations in economic conditions.[12] Similarly, redundancy payments encourage firms to retain workers while insolvency and receivership provisions make it possible for investors to hold onto firms.

Once the distribution of adjustment costs is agreed, different actors in the economy can take the necessary measures to limit their exposure to risk. Instruments ranging from unemployment insurance to personal pensions to complex currency hedges are all available to workers, employers, and investors who know that they are likely to be forced to accept the cost of adjusting to any unforeseen change in economic circumstances. This way, the change in circumstances under a given set of policy rules should not pose a political problem for the maintenance of the rules themselves.

That said, the distributive formulas represented by tax and transfer systems or market institutions do not exist wholly (or even principally) to support rules for monetary policy. Issues concerning tax rates, benefits payout, labor market protection, and the rights of investors are all likely to be settled according to the broader political objectives of those in power when the institutions are put into place or the payment levels are set and amended. In this sense, fiscal and market rules are just as political as monetary rules, if not more so. What is important is that monetary policy rules benefit from the certainty arising out of the existence of specific distributive formulas. So long as different economic actors feel insulated from any adverse effects arising out of the conduct of monetary policy, the actual levels of benefit are irrelevant. All that matters is that the groups promoting a set of a priori policy monetary rules can rest assured that they will not be adversely affected by economic developments and so will have no reason to change the rules.[13]

The monetary coalition and the distributive coalition are closely intertwined. Many of the most important advantages deriving from the promotion of a priori monetary policy rules result from the greater certainty such rules offer for the resolution of distributive questions—between employers and workers, taxpayers and benefits recipients, and so forth. Here it is perhaps sufficient to note that accurate economic forecasting is important to wage bargaining as well as investment decisions, the management of social security as well as the promotion of growth and profits. Thus, to the extent to which rules facilitate economic analysis, they also facilitate the efficient operation of the mixed economy. The certainty of stable monetary conditions helps to set the basis for the resolution of distributive conflicts and therefore for the promotion of distributive "justice" no matter how that may be defined in a particular context.

A priori policy rules should be difficult to change and they should be insulated from political reactions to developments in the wider economy. Taken together, these conclusions help to focus attention on the initial choice of policy rules and on the coalition of political forces behind that choice. These conclusions also reflect the extent to which monetary policy rules may be embedded in other economic policy rules at the heart of the mixed economy. The constitution of monetary institutions benefits from and benefits the functioning of fiscal and market institutions. By implication, the act of separating money from politics reaches beyond the monetary sphere and into the structures of the welfare state.

PROSPECTS FOR THE
DE-POLITICIZATION OF EUROPE'S MONEY

The formation of an economic and monetary union (EMU) in Europe is part and parcel of a wide ranging attempt to de-politicize Europe's money. The technical advantages offered by the project are important but not compelling. EMU promises to improve the efficiency of money at the European level, enhance the accuracy of European economic analysis, provide greater certainty for Europe's economic actors, and improve the functioning of Europe's markets. Estimates of the direct financial benefits from the project range between 0.4 and 1 percent of European gross domestic product on a one-off basis. More indirect benefits are likely to be far greater, however, as the improved technical environment stimulates investment, employment, and commerce. EMU's great strength is not as a technical innovation but as a rule capable of introducing greater clarity and certainty for the management of (and participation in) the economy.[14]

The indirect benefits of EMU underscore the importance of the fact that monetary integration is not solely a technical venture. Throughout the process of monetary integration, Europe's policymakers must face three questions of immediate political significance. Will any particular group or groups be permanently disadvantaged by any set of a priori rules for the stabilization of monetary conditions at the European level? Can Europe's member states agree on a *single* set of a priori rules? Can the European Union be entrusted with a set of institutions and symbols of sufficient complexity and importance to consolidate agreement on monetary policy rules for the foreseeable future? The first question concerns whether Europe should attempt to form a monetary union at all. The second asks what type of monetary union is possible. The third draws attention to the constraints that monetary integration will pose for national economic policymaking.

Economists and policymakers have attempted to address the first question through the theory of "optimum currency areas." This theory starts from the assumption that monetary policy can be depoliticized and then works backward to describe those structures and institutions that work best within a common monetary framework. The notion of "best" is closely akin to the notion of optimality, and translates into the maximization of welfare for the monetary union as a whole. Thus, for example, an optimum currency area would encompass a well diversified industrial structure, would conduct only a small proportion of its commerce with other monetary areas, and would be supported by a common set of fiscal institutions and market rules.[15]

Once having established those structures and institutions that work best under a common monetary framework, economists and policymakers work backward to claim that these features are criteria for the successful construction of a monetary union. Diversified industrial structures together with a low dependence on foreign markets mitigate the possibility that a sudden change in economic circumstances will have an important impact on aggregate welfare. Meanwhile, common fiscal institutions and market rules facilitate the process of adjustment and the distribution of adjustment costs. Therefore the appropriate tests for whether Europe should form a monetary union focus on the diversity of European industrial structures, the nature and frequency of external shocks to the European economy, and the functioning of European fiscal and market rules in comparison with those of existing monetary unions.

Examination of Europe's fit with the optimum currency area criteria is mixed, but on balance favors the creation of EMU. Unfortunately, however, such analysis loses sight of the role of particular groups in the economy to focus almost exclusively on the functioning of the monetary union as a whole. Indeed, much of the analysis of optimum currency areas assumes

away the potential political importance of particular groups through estimates of the symmetry or asymmetry of shocks to Europe's economy. If all
groups are affected in the same way, so the reasoning goes, then no one
group can make a claim for particular political attention.

The possibility that a particular group might be disadvantaged by any
attempt to harmonize monetary conditions at the European level cannot
be dismissed. Nevertheless, it can be folded into the question about what
monetary union Europe's member states can agree to form. This second
question confronting Europe's policymakers is rooted more deeply in politics than in economics. In agreeing to a particular form of monetary
union, Europe's heads of state and government necessarily take into consideration the political effects this will have within their own constituencies. Such effects will require redress whether they would take place no
matter what type of monetary union is adopted or they derive from a specific type of union. In a sense, then, the choice of monetary union at the
European level is dependent upon the possibilities for accommodating
those groups who will be adversely affected at the national level.

The selection of rules for a monetary union can be summarized in terms
of two approaches. One is to form a new set of rules appropriate to all
would-be participants. The other is to accept only those participants who
are willing to support a pre-existing set of rules. Either way, the decision
reflects not only the relative bargaining strength of particular member
states but also their capacity to make the necessary domestic adjustments
to a new monetary arrangement—which includes planning for the possibility of adjustment to changing economic circumstances within that new
monetary arrangement. Just as at the domestic level, the construction of a
de-politicized European monetary regime involves a prior consideration
of the distribution of adjustment costs both to the regime and within it.

Because it touches on distributive concerns, EMU has become entangled in the construction and reform of Europe's welfare states as well as
in the contrast between different welfare state traditions. Domestic distributive coalitions necessarily take an interest in European policy
arrangements. At the same time, European monetary arrangements assume a greater importance in domestic notions of economic justice and in
the operation of the mixed economy. This interdependence between domestic and European policy rules raises the possibility that member
states' attitudes toward monetary union could change for political reasons unrelated to economic performance per se—and instead deriving
from changes in the welfare state and its capacity to promote broader social and economic objectives.

Consideration of the appropriate institutions and symbols for Europe's
monetary constitution must address the possibility of unforeseen changes
to political—as well as economic—circumstances. EMU must be suffi-

ciently complex and important to be insulated from minor fluctuations in surrounding conditions and to ensure that necessary distributive issues are considered beforehand. Somehow in the constitution of EMU, the complex distributive politics must be worked out so that any agreement reached can be sure to last. Indeed, the essence of constituting a monetary union is the notion that exchange rates between participating countries are irrevocably fixed.

FROM THE TECHNOLOGY OF
MONEY TO THE TRIUMPH OF POLITICS

The irrevocable nature of EMU *is* the a priori monetary policy rule. Its permanence represents the difference between Europe's member states sharing a currency in the technical sense and their participating in a monetary union. If EMU can be revoked, then it never existed in the first place. In this sense, EMU is more about politics than about money. The advantages it promises may be technical, but the means through which those advantages are actually achieved are not.

The alternatives to EMU are political as well. If Europe's member states did not agree to fix their exchange rates irrevocably, they would have chosen some other a priori rule for that aspect of monetary policy. Moreover, they would have chosen the rule most likely to garner the same advantages afforded by EMU. If exchange rates cannot be irrevocably fixed, then they should be made fixed but adjustable. In an age of electronic banking, there is no compelling technical reason for different countries to call the bits and bytes by different names and there are a number of reasons for countries to use the same unit of account, store of value, and means of exchange. A second best alternative is to announce that different sets of bits and bytes are equivalent, but subject to change.

The difficulty with subjecting fixed exchange rates to the possibility of change is that it invites a political assessment of when it is necessary to alter the value of one currency relative to another. In doing so, the a priori rule that exchange rates are fixed *but adjustable* inadvertently emphasizes the distributive consequences of exchange rate levels and adjustments across different economic circumstances. The more volatile the economic circumstances, the greater will be the political attention given to a fixed but adjustable exchange rate. Moreover, with each movement in the exchange rate, the certainty and clarity afforded by the fixed but adjustable rule decreases. This means not only that the value of the rule diminishes, but also that the rule itself becomes subject both to closer political scrutiny and to a lower threshold for changes in economic circumstances necessary to trigger mobilization around an exchange rate adjustment. Far from facilitating the de-politicization of money in the face of changing economic circumstances, a fixed but adjustable exchange rate encourages it.

The comparison of EMU with its closest alternative underscores that even a minor change in the technology of money can make a difference between the success or failure of a policy rule. It also reinforces the centrality of politics to monetary integration. What is significant is not the name of the currency but the power to create it. This power is important because it touches upon politically sensitive distributive issues both as they relate to adjustment to unforeseen changes in economic circumstances and as they reflect conceptions of economic justice. Therefore the issue is not really between one currency or several, but rather between a fixed conception of equitable distribution and a more flexible one and between common conceptions of economic justice and more disparate ones. Money is a simple and yet vitally useful form of economic technology that lies at the very heart of state-society relations. Therefore, any change in the technology of money that transfers control over its creation away from the state or from society is first and foremost a matter of political concern. In theory, EMU is apolitical. In practice, it implies a political system in its own right.

NOTES

1. Smith's argument can be found in Book One of the *Wealth of Nations*, and principally in chapters IV–V, VII, and XI. The edition I have relied on is Smith (1983).

2. This argument is suggested by Dyson (1994) who claims that the complexity of monetary integration can be explained—at least in part—by the dual nature of money as a political symbol and as a form of economic technology.

3. This dismissal of the symbolic importance of money is too hasty in that it avoids the complex relationship between monetary creation and state-building. In U.S. history, for example, the promotion of a common currency was closely identified with the consolidation of the Union after the Civil War (Sheridan 1996). More recently, former colonies have attached tremendous importance to the construction of a stable national monetary regime. This point will reemerge in chapters 4 and 8.

4. This is not to suggest that subjective values are determined by whimsy. Because the values associated with particular objects are relative and (by assumption) transitive, subjectivity largely reflects either a real-world utility or, following Simmel (1978, 62–63), a psychological reality.

5. The strong assumption here is that both interest rates and exchange rates are determined by policy and not by market forces. Under this assumption, a relative increase in the rate of inflation in one country will cause that country's currency to appreciate in real terms across a fixed exchange rate. However, if exchange rates are floating—with the level determined by market forces as opposed to by gov-

ernment policy—then a relative increase in the rate of inflation of one country will cause that country's currency to depreciate in nominal terms, leaving the real exchange rate constant over the long term.

6. There have been a number of econometric studies done to determine whether the left- right presumption actually plays out in terms of policy—looking for a correlation between left-wing governance and higher inflation as well as between right-wing governance and higher unemployment. The results of these studies have ranged from yes to no to inconclusive, and have varied considerably from one country to the next. See, for example, Alesina (1989).

7. This point is made forcefully—and repeatedly—by Milton Friedman (1969).

8. Any double entendre here is unintentional. My point is not that the community of professional economists is directly politicized around schools of thought, but more simply that economists are made party to national political discussions about the appropriate constitution of monetary institutions.

9. This argument alludes to the classic analysis of Mancur Olson (1971, 1982).

10. See Bernhard (1998). The logic of the argument can also be reversed to say that an independent central bank needs a strong coalition to support it (Posen, 1993).

11. Left-wing governments have often postponed devaluations to their own detriment. Two classic examples are Leon Blum's 1936–1937 popular front government in France, and Harold Wilson's 1966–1970 Labour government in the United Kingdom.

12. This point was first suggested by Kenen (1969), but has been a recurrent theme in discussions of monetary union (Masson and Taylor, 1993).

13. The debates among economists over the correct estimate for fiscal stabilization in the United States overlooks this crucial point in the chain of causality. What is important is not how much stabilization is afforded by the U.S. federal fiscal system, but rather that economic agents in the United States are satisfied that the monetary policy rules in effect in the United States are neutral in distributive terms.

14. These estimates can be found in a range of sources, however the European Commission has among the best. See Emerson et al. (1992) and European Commission (1998).

15. The classic discussion of optimum currency areas is also the most accessible. See Mundell (1961), McKinnon (1963), Kenen (1969), and Corden (1972).

2

✛

Design: Interdependence and Accountability

The creation of an economic and monetary union (EMU) in Europe constitutes a policy rule for national currencies. Come what may, exchange rates between participating countries will be irrevocably fixed. That said, Europe's EMU is more than just a type of exchange rate regime and more than just a monetary union. It is an economic and monetary union of a particular type. At the same time Europe's policymakers opted to fix their exchange rates, they also adopted a range of other policy rules. Specifically, they chose:

- to assign monetary policy to the promotion of absolute price stability;
- to consolidate and monitor fiscal policies; and (somewhat later),
- to use active measures for employment creation and welfare state reform.

These choices were not inevitable given the desire to move to a monetary union as a form of exchange rate regime. Yet they are complementary: Adoption of any one rule makes it easier to choose the others as well. Stable prices across the monetary union support the maintenance of fixed exchange rates between participating countries. Fiscal consolidation through the reduction in public debts and deficits helps to underpin price stability. Active labor market policies and welfare state reform facilitate fiscal consolidation. And, as will be explained in later chapters, monetary union, price stability, and fiscal consolidation all play roles in the process of reforming labor markets and welfare states. In instrumental terms, the four policy rules—irrevocably fixed exchange rates, absolute price stability, fiscal consolidation and monitoring, labor market and welfare state reform—are interdependent. The pattern of interdependence between policy rules is formidably complicated. Not only does it engage a wide range of actors and mechanisms, but it also gives rise to complex (and institutionally contingent) distributive outcomes. Virtually every level of government has a role to play in the process across the European Union, both in those countries that participate in EMU and in those that do not. Non-governmental actors, including employers, trade unions, investors, manufacturers, financial services, retailers, and consumers all have roles to play as well. This multiplicity of actors and institutional dynamics parallels the distributive complexity surrounding monetary policy changes analyzed in chapter 1. Once again, the difficulty is that the vested interests of political actors with respect to particular policy movements cannot be predicted.

The interdependence between the sets of rules is both a weakness and a strength. It is a weakness because it complicates the achievement of the objectives for any particular cluster of rules. It is a strength because the overlap between the rules functions to defuse political conflict over the maintenance of irrevocably fixed exchange rates across what are surely to be changing economic conditions.

Despite the significance of the interdependence between policy areas, the architects of Europe's economic and monetary union treated the policy rules as constitutionally discrete. The Treaty Establishing the European Community (TEC) clusters the rules into three separate institutional arrangements—for monetary, economic (read fiscal), and employment-related policies.[1] Each of these institutional arrangements is distinct, whether in terms of the constituencies it engages, the organization and hierarchy of its constituents, or both: Monetary rules center on the European System of Central Banks (ESCB), the Council of Ministers, the European Parliament, and financial actors; economic rules focus on the Council of Ministers and the member states; and the rules related to employment encompass both the member states and the social partners, meaning industry and labor. As a result, the politics of the system is fragmented along institutionally specific (or administrative) lines rather than broader economic, social, or political cleavages. It makes less sense to talk about EMU in terms of left and right than to talk about it in terms of monetary, fiscal, and market preferences. And, within this fragmented political system, the mechanisms for accountability are functionally specific. Each cluster of rules is subject to clear direction and oversight. The system as a whole is not.

The purpose of this chapter is to analyze the design of Europe's economic and monetary union. The argument is that while systemic interdependence is strong, systemic accountability is weak. The argument is made in four sections. The first section surveys EMU as three separate clusters of institutionalized policy rules: monetary, economic, and employment-related. The second describes the mechanisms for holding policymakers to account in all three areas. The third examines the problem of interdependence. The fourth section concludes.

THREE SETS OF POLICY RULES

The construction of EMU is a drawn out, messy, and uneven affair. It is also incomplete, at least in the sense that the institutions that constitute Europe's economic and monetary union continue to evolve on all fronts even after the exchange rates between national currencies in Europe became irrevocably fixed. Therefore any attempt to describe the economic constitution of the European Union in great detail is doomed to failure. Institutions and procedures change, their names change, and their membership (or adherence) changes, all at a pace that renders detailed description almost immediately obsolete.[2]

This seemingly perpetual evolution of Europe's economic and monetary union should not be surprising. The myth about policy change is one of sudden coherence. Policymakers recognize what they are doing wrong or what they could be doing better, so they shift from one type of activity to another, fundamentally transforming the rules of the game. The reality behind this myth is more hesitant, more tentative, more incremental. For example, the shift from classical economics to Keynesian demand management—while revolutionary—was a drawn out, messy, and uneven affair as well (Hall 1989). The point to note with EMU (as with Keynesianism) is that the broad outlines of the policy rules and their constitutional arrangements have been fairly stable over time. Within such a context, the focus for analysis is not on what changes, but rather on what remains the same.

Monetary Rules

The constant features of the single currency are the irrevocably fixed internal exchange rates, the assignment of monetary policy to the promotion of absolute price stability, and the political insulation of monetary policymakers. These policy rules are set down explicitly and repeatedly in the TEC: The objectives of the European Community "shall include the irrevocable fixing of exchange rates leading to the introduction of a single currency . . . and the definition and conduct of a single monetary policy and exchange rate policy the primary objective of both of which shall be to maintain price stability" (TEC, Article 4, Paragraph 2).[3] Moreover in allocating primary responsibility for the achievement of these objectives to the ESCB and to the European Central Bank (ECB), the TEC stipulates that both policymakers and politicians share the obligation to insulate the conduct of monetary policy from political influence:

> When exercising the powers and carrying out the tasks and duties conferred upon them by this Treaty and the Statute of the ESCB, neither the ECB, nor a national central bank, nor any member of their decisionmaking bodies shall seek or take instructions from Community institutions and bodies, from any government of a Member State or from any other body. The Community institutions and bodies and the governments of the Member States undertake to respect this principle and not to seek to influence the members of the decisionmaking bodies of the ECB or of the national central banks in the performance of this task (TEC, Article 108).

The institutional arrangements set down in the TEC and in the "Protocol on the Statute of the ESCB and the ECB," which is attached to the treaty, juxtapose the three policy rules at the heart of the single currency in a reinforcing manner. The institutional framework makes explicit links between exchange rates, price stability, and political independence. And, while the basic documents appear to provide some exceptions to the general framework, the leeway such exceptions provide is tightly circumscribed by the overlap between policy rules. Hence, while the TEC instructs the ESCB to "support the general economic policies in the Community" the language is explicit that such support should not "prejudice the objective of price stability" (TEC, Article 105, Paragraph 1). The member states retain some influence through the Council of Ministers over the broad guidelines for the conduct of exchange rate policy in relation to third parties. However here, too, such "general orientations shall be without prejudice to the primary objective of the ESCB to maintain price stability" (TEC, Article 111, Paragraph 2). Finally, "each Member State shall treat its exchange-rate policy as a matter of common interest" until it joins the single currency, regardless as to whether it has any intention to become a member (TEC, Article 124).[4]

In its most powerful form, the overlap between policy rules emerges as an institutional tautology. Monetary authorities not only bear responsibility for using their policy instruments to achieve domestic price stability, they also must determine how both they will measure "price stability" and how they will ascertain whether it is secure or at risk. Finally, they must make their determination without influence from other political actors. As a result, the juxtaposition of irrevocably fixed exchange rates, absolute price stability, and politically independent monetary authority forms a defining feature of the European economic policy landscape. Small wonder, then, that some would argue that EMU is essentially an asymmetric or ECB-centric system (Verdun 1996; Dyson 2000).

Economic Rules

Too much emphasis on the monetary framework, however, risks obscuring the significance of the economic side of EMU. The monetary policy rules constitute only the most clearly defined features of the system. By themselves, however, they are not all-encompassing. The rules that govern the conduct of economic policy within the member states have a powerful role to play as well. And, importantly, these economic policy rules are not purely derivative of the requirements for the stability of European exchange rates or prices, or for the political independence of European monetary authority. The economic and monetary aspects of EMU are separable if not completely separate.

The TEC establishes three basic principles for the conduct of economic policy within the member states:

- "Member States shall conduct their economic policies with a view to contributing to the achievement of the objectives of the Community"—ranging from "balanced and sustainable development" to "a high level of employment and of social protection" to "a high degree of competitiveness and convergence" to "economic and social cohesion and solidarity among the Member States" (TEC, Article 2).[5]
- "Member States shall regard their economic policies as a matter of common concern and shall coordinate them within the Council" (TEC, Article 99, Paragraph 1).
- And, member states shall not "risk jeopardizing the proper functioning of economic and monetary union" (TEC, Article 99, Paragraph 4).

The first of these principles establishes the wide range of objectives for the conduct of economic policy in contrast to the singular objective of absolute price stability that is the focus for monetary policy. The second principle is horizontal in that the economic policies of one member state should not be allowed to disrupt the economic activities of other member states. The third principle is vertical in that the economic policies of one member state shall not be allowed to disrupt the economic activities of the Union as a whole. Taken together, these principles not only define a coherent framework for the broad conduct of economic policy, but they also extend this framework to all member states whether or not they participate in the single currency.

The primary exception to the encompassing nature of the TEC framework for economic policymaking concerns the elaboration of rules governing "excessive government deficits." Such rules specify both a broad norm for fiscal behavior and a particular context within which the economic policies of member states might disrupt the proper functioning of EMU. The United Kingdom objected to the close linkage between the fiscal rule and EMU—and consequently obtained an exemption from the excessive deficit procedure during the European Council negotiations at

Maastricht in 1992. In spite of this exemption, however, the government of the United Kingdom has consistently accepted the general principle that governments should strive to avoid excessive deficits. And, when that principle was revisited by the 1997 European Council at Amsterdam in the context of the "Stability and Growth Pact," the United Kingdom joined the rest of the European Union's member states in making the commitment "to respect the medium-term budgetary objective of close to balance or in surplus."[6]

This commitment to budgetary balance constitutes a fourth policy rule which underwrites the general framework for economic policymaking with an absolute norm for fiscal behavior. In summary form, economic policy should be directed across a wide range of objectives, it should be consistent across member states and with EMU, and it should rest on balanced fiscal foundations. This framework is neither as precise nor as absolute as that constituted by the monetary rules described above. Economic policy has multiple objectives and—with the exception of the commitment to balanced budgets—only vague constraints. That said, the comparison between economic and fiscal policy is hardly like-with-like.

Within a single currency, monetary institutions are necessarily connected across member states. Economic institutions and particularly fiscal flows need not be. Therefore, the relevant comparison in Europe's EMU is not between economic policy and monetary policy. Rather it is between how much economic policy is constrained in Europe and the degree of constraint or flexibility that is necessary or possible within an economic and monetary union. Viewed within that context, the economic policy rules established by the European Union are remarkably encompassing and well-articulated.

Employment-Related Rules

The employment-related rules that underwrite the creation of EMU are in many ways as encompassing and well-articulated as the economic rules—at least in principle. Not only do such rules engage all member states, whether or not they participate in the single currency, but also they offer a relatively narrow range of prescriptions across a relatively diverse institutional background. Moreover, the similarity between the structure of economic rules and market rules is intentional. Borrowing from the conclusions of the 1997 Luxembourg European Council summit on employment: "The idea is, while respecting the differences between the two areas and between the situations of individual Member States, to create for employment, as for economic policy, the same resolve to converge towards jointly set, verifiable, regularly updated targets" (European Council 1997a).

Nevertheless, the differences between economic policy and employ-ment policy are considerable. Where economic policy tends to center around fiscal measures, employment policy tends to expand across every-thing from patterns of state intervention in labor and product markets to the structure of specific labor and product market institutions. The neces-sary range of actors is broader as well. Economic policy is an activity of the state, while employment-related policy includes both the state and the social partners.

Given these differences, the rules adopted for employment-related pol-icy pay greater attention to the process of policymaking than to the policy outcome. For example, the emphasis is not on specific targets for job cre-ation, but rather on the fact that there should be targets as well as some sort of action toward their achievement. These rules developed across a series of European Council summits: Luxembourg (November 1997), Cardiff (June 1998), and Cologne (June 1999). In the jargon of the Euro-pean Union, the innovation provided at each summit constitutes a "process" rather than a rule per se. Borrowing from the language of the Cologne European Council summit, these processes are:

- further development and better implementation of the coordinated employment strategy to improve the efficiency of the labor markets by improving employability, entrepreneurship, adaptability of busi-nesses and their employees, and equal opportunities for men and women in finding gainful employment (Luxembourg process);
- comprehensive structural reform and modernization to improve the innovative capacity and efficiency of the labor market and the mar-kets in goods, services and capital (Cardiff process);
- coordination of economic policy and improvement of mutually sup-portive interaction between wage developments and monetary, budgetary, and fiscal policy through macroeconomic dialog aimed at preserving a non-inflationary growth dynamic (Cologne process) (European Commission 1999b: paragraph 7).[7]

The overriding objective of these employment-related policy rules is progressive and yet still vaguely worded. Both the Treaty on European Union (TEU) and the TEC maintain that the goal is to promote "a high level of employment" whether in the context of "economic and social progress" (TEU) or "a high level . . . of social protection" (TEC).[8] Neither the Treaties nor subsequent European Councils have clarified exactly how high is "high," although they have gone some way in identifying which actors and which activities should be involved in the promotion of em-ployment. In this way, the employment-related rules do not benefit from the tautological certainty of the price stability rule and neither can they

Table 2.1. Three Clusters of Policy Rules behind EMU

Policy Area	Policy Rules
Monetary	• irrevocably fixed internal exchange rates • absolute domestic price stability • political insulation of monetary policy authority
Economic	• achievement of Community objectives • coordinated across member states • consistent with proper functioning of EMU • fiscal balance or surplus over the medium term
Employment-related	• coordinated measures to increase employment • complementary efforts at market structural reform • active consultation and dialogue with social partners

draw upon the transparency of the balanced fiscal accounts rule. However, the three processes do constitute a significant departure from the incoherence of European approaches to employment-related policy in the past and, correspondingly, have a significant potential for the reconstitution of employment policy at the European level in the future.

EMU as a Collection of Rules

The rules adopted in relation to monetary, economic, and employment-related policy represent the difference between EMU as an exchange rate regime and the EMU implemented by the European Union. For convenience, these rules are summarized in Table 2.1 as three sets of clusters. Looking across the table as a whole, no single rule is indispensable to the functioning of the system as an economic and monetary union. Equally, no two clusters of rules are characteristically the same. The monetary rules are more precise than the economic or employment-related rules; the economic rules are more broadly targeted; and the employment-related rules are more process-oriented.

The point to note, however, is that Europe's economic and monetary union is a collection of rules.[9] More important, it is a collection of rules founded on political choice as opposed to mechanical necessity. As a result, it is not enough to consider how the rules work. It is also necessary to consider how the collection as a whole functions in relation to the expectations of those who chose to adopt the rules in the first place.

THREE MECHANISMS FOR HOLDING TO ACCOUNT

The first problem with respect to all three policy areas—monetary, economic, and employment-related—is to ensure that the rules are obeyed to desirable effect. This problem is more complicated than it may seem at first glance. And this complexity is evident not only in any analysis of the policy areas, but also, and more importantly, in the constitution of mechanisms for policy-oversight at the European level.

To begin with, at least three different categories of political actors lie implicit within the phrasing of the problem of holding policymakers to account: one category of actors to follow the rules, one to assess whether the rules have been followed, and one to evaluate the desirability of the effect. Social scientists tend to cluster these categories into two groups, agents and principals.[10] The agents follow the rules and the principals assess both the performance of the agents and the desirability of the outcome. This analytic convention derives from an analogy with delegation by private contract, where principals delegate responsibility to agents and then must themselves enforce the terms of the contract (or delegation).

The convenience of carving up the problem of accountability between agents and principals is that it emphasizes the distinction between performance and evaluation. The agents act, and the principals hold the agents to account. The weakness is that analogy with private contract blurs the distinction between following the rules and having a desirable effect. Indeed, much of the literature assumes that only the results of the policy can be observed and not the actions of the agent itself.[11] This leaves open the possibility that agents might do as they are told and yet without achieving the desired effect. By extension, it also creates the possibility that different groups of principals will evaluate the performance of the agent differently depending upon whether they place greater emphasis on rules or outcomes. Given that EMU is a rule-based system, the potential for confusion is considerable.

Monetary Evaluation: Reporting

No fewer than three different groups lay claim to the right to evaluate the performance of the ESCB as the agent of European monetary policy: the Council of Ministers, the European Parliament, and financial actors. Moreover, all three groups claim to be able to evaluate not only the performance of the ESCB but also the desirability of the effects of monetary policy and monetary policy changes. The difficulty is that they do not strike the same balance in their understanding of what is important: the rule-following behavior of the ESCB or the overall desirability of monetary policy outcomes. At the extremes, financial actors have expressed greater concern for the predictability of monetary policy decisions (that is, rule-following behavior) and the European Parliament has tended to emphasize the importance of achieving a desirable outcome. For its part, the Council of Ministers has expressed the range of opinions depending upon which member state holds the presidency (or the microphone).

The strategy of the ECB has been to report directly to all three groups both through publications and through institutionalized interaction. The ECB produces a range of publications on its general activities from press releases to monthly bulletins to annual reports. It also produces working documents, research reports, and conference proceedings, all of which relate both to how ECB economists understand economic policymaking and how ESCB policymakers understand their role within the larger framework of European macroeconomic performance. These publications are freely available for downloading from the ECB Website (www.ecb.int) and they are widely disseminated within the institutions of the European Union.

The pattern of institutionalized interaction encompasses both cross-participation in meetings and oral presentations for cross examination and debate. For example, both the presidency of the Council of Ministers and a representative of the European Commission have the right to sit on the decisionmaking bodies of the ESCB (TEC, Article 113, Paragraph 1). From the standpoint of the central bankers themselves, however, the pattern of institutional interaction is somewhat at odds with the institutional design of EMU. Constitutionally, the ESCB is a highly decentralized network. Both the Governing Council—which both manages the ESCB and decides the direction of monetary policy—and the General Council—which manages the enlargement of the EMU—include more representatives of national central banks than officials from the ECB. Indeed, only the president of the ECB Executive has voting rights on both councils. The vice president and the four ordinary members of the ECB Executive have voting rights only with reference to monetary policy (Governing Council) and not with reference to the enlargement of EMU (General Council).

Nevertheless, it is the ECB Executive and particularly its president that is responsible for most of the inter-institutional dialog at the European level. Specifically, the president of the ECB:

- shall be invited to participate in Council [of Ministers] meetings when the Council [of Ministers] is discussing matters relating to the objectives and tasks of the ESCB;
- shall present [an annual report on the activities of the ESCB and on the monetary policy of both the previous and the current year] to the Council [of Ministers] and to the European Parliament;
- may [together with the other members of the Executive Board], at the request of the European Parliament or on their own initiative, be heard by the competent committees of the European Parliament (TEC, Article 113, Paragraphs 2 and 3).

This dialog is not as voluntary as the language used by the Treaty may suggest. Neither the invitations of the Parliament nor those of the Council may be refused easily. Indeed, when the president of the ECB did decline to attend an informal meeting of the Council of Economics and Finance Ministers (ECOFIN) in September 2000 because that meeting conflicted with a prior engagement, he was roundly criticized by politicians and the media.[12]

The pattern of interaction between the ESCB and financial actors is also relatively centralized. For example, the president and vice president of the ECB hold a monthly press conference to explain the decisions taken in the Governing Council. In addition, the ECB publishes not only the prepared remarks of its representatives, but also a transcript of the question-and-answer with financial journalists. Finally, all six members of the ECB Executive Board maintain an active speaking schedule—usually to financial or business groups—both across Europe and around the world (Harrison 2001). In fact, the prior engagement that forced the ECB president to miss the September 2000 ECOFIN informal meeting was a Canadian financial conference that promised to include top policymakers from the United States as well as Canada. Given the profound weakness of the European currency against the U.S. dollar at that time, it is hardly surprising that the ECB president would be eager to put his case to the North American financial community.

The contrast between decentralized authority and centralized reporting creates considerable scope for contradiction. National central bank presidents or junior members of the ECB have a disconcerting tendency to voice their opinions or observations even when these may be at odds with the message that the ECB president is trying to convey to one group or another (Mayes 2000). At times, such indiscretions threaten to undermine the reporting strategy altogether. For example, on one occasion, a financial journalist overheard a national central bank president discussing a monetary policy decision even before it was announced by the ECB president in the press conference.[13]

The problems of consolidating the reporting strategy are problems of implementation and not design. Members of the ESCB and the ECB can learn to do better in their official communications and they can adapt their procedures accordingly without dispensing with the strategy of reporting altogether. More problematic is what the different groups (or principals) do with the information that is reported. Given the constitutional design of the ECB and the ESCB, there are few formal sanctions available to any party should the behavior of European monetary authorities be found wanting. ECB members cannot be dismissed except for gross misconduct, they do not seek re-appointment, and they have protected financial resources upon which to draw. National central bank officials are similarly protected by virtue of the legislation that guarantees their political independence.[14] Here it is important to note, however, that the facility for changing national legislation is much greater than that for amending the TEC or the ESCB Statute. In this sense, the political independence rule protects the ESCB much more than it protects the national central banks, and arguably more than any central bank has ever been protected in a national state.[15] By extension, it would seem, there is very little that any group can do with the information reported to it by the ECB.

Such appearances are somewhat misleading. The ability of the Council of Ministers, the European Parliament, and financial actors to act on their evaluations of the performance of European monetary policy authorities is highly varied and broadly informal, but it is effective nonetheless. Not only have the Council of Ministers and the financial press succeeded in challenging the monetary policy decisions of the ECB's Governing Council, they have also provided the ECB executive with a harsh lesson in the importance of managing a coherent and transparent communications policy. For its part, the European Parliament has forced the ECB to provide it with ever more—and more specific—information about the factors upon which monetary policy decisions are based. Such success has relied more on the Parliament's powers of moral suasion than on the threat (or possibility) of institutional sanction. The point is that the pressure worked, at least partially. The ECB continues to refuse to publish a record of the meetings of the General Council or of the voting on particular monetary policy decisions even in the face of repeated calls for this information by Members of European Parliament (MEPs). Yet the ECB now publishes not only its own inflation forecasts but also the econometric models that it uses for forecasting—largely as a result of parliamentary pressure. What is clear is not only that the putative principals to the ECB as agent are satisfied with the reporting strategy, but also that they would prefer the strategy be improved rather than replaced.

The problem with the reporting strategy is twofold. First, the strategy cannot embrace the rule that monetary policy authorities should be insulated from political influence. Not only is there no clear mechanism for reporting political independence, but also—as mentioned above—the obligation to insulate monetary authorities applies with equal force to political actors on both sides of existing reporting procedures. The ECB is not only one of several agents responsible for carrying out this mandate, but it is also one of the principals responsible for its enforcement. Second, the three groups that lay claim to the right to evaluate the performance of the ESCB represent different (if overlapping) constituencies. The member states represent their national electorates, the Parliament represents the European people, and financial actors represent themselves.[16]

The two problems—political independence and multiple principals—are reinforcing. Any assertion of the political independence of the ESCB and the ECB threatens to obviate the performance evaluations made by the Council, the Parliament, or financial actors. By the same token, any attempt by one group to assert the authoritativeness of its views over the others risks drawing the accusation of violating the political independence of the ESCB. While Europe's monetary authorities have the sole right to define and implement the price stability rule, virtually all interested parties have the obligation to uphold the political independence rule and so all of them would assert the right to define it as well.

This conundrum is not unique to Europe's monetary constitution. Virtually any politically independent monetary authority confronts the same accountability dilemma. Moreover, the joint problem of political insulation and multiple principals is also not a function of the reporting strategy per se. Rather the difficulty lies in the identification of an authoritative principal to evaluate the performance of the ESCB coupled with an objective standard for establishing the political independence of monetary policy authority. How this can be done is the subject of chapter 3. For the moment, suffice it to say that in the absence of this conundrum, the ECB's strategy of reporting is appropriate to the evaluation of the price stability rule—albeit, as implemented, there is considerable scope for improvement.[17]

Economic Evaluation: Auditing[18]

Direct reporting is less appropriate to economic policy than to monetary policy. The problem is that the agents and principals with respect to the rules overlap. The member states are individually responsible for ensuring the consistency of their economic policies with Community objectives, with each other, and with EMU. They are also individually responsible for achieving something close to fiscal balance or surplus over the medium term. However, the member states are collectively responsible in the Council of Ministers for policing each other's conformance with these economic policy rules.

This juxtaposition of individual and collective responsibilities creates a conflict of interest for the member states. One the one hand they have little incentive to provide information that can be used against them. On the other hand, they need access to information both to judge the performance of individual member states and—more important—to establish a common frame of reference for policy coordination.

The common frame of reference is crucial given the wide range of objectives that are meant to be served through economic policy. Therefore, the TEC asserts that the Council of Ministers should establish "the broad guidelines of the economic policies of the Member States and of the Community" even before attempting to assess the economic policies of specific countries (TEC, Article 99, Paragraph 2). Once the broad economic policy guidelines (BEPGs) are established, the Council can then begin the process of assessing the coordination of member state economic policies.

The Council's assessment of member state performance relies on two intermediaries, the European Commission and the Economic and Financial Committee (EFC). The Commission receives the economic reports of the member states, monitors member state performance, provides consistent data for analysis, and makes recommendations and proposals to the Council. In essence, the Commission shoulders the primary responsibility for auditing member state compliance with the economic policy rules.[19]

By contrast, the EFC plays a more intermediary and political role. The primary task of the EFC is to liaise between the member states, the Commission, and the European Central Bank in order to prepare the agenda for decisions in the Council. Like the Commission, the EFC monitors, analyzes, and comments on the performance of the member states. Unlike the Commission, the EFC has no independent sources of statistical information and its deliberations are confidential.[20] In addition, the membership of the EFC is heavily weighted in favor of the member states—with each country providing two committee members as compared to only two members each for the Commission and the ECB.[21] Finally, when the Committee considers matters that will be decided upon by the Council, only the representatives of the member states have the right to vote.[22]

The basic model for oversight on economic policy is that the Council establishes the terms of reference, the member states provide the basic information, the Commission and the EFC audit and analyze that information in order to prepare recommendations for the Council, then, finally, the Council decides as to whether the member states have lived up to their obligations and commitments. If the Council determines that a particular member state is not in compliance, it will instruct the member state to reform its policies and, if necessary, it will apply relevant sanctions. This model for oversight is the same for both of the major procedures set out in the TEC—the "multilateral surveillance" procedure and the "excessive deficit" procedure. These procedures are summarized in Table 2.2.

The major differences between the two procedures lie in the focus for oversight and in the range of sanctions available to the Council. The multilateral surveillance procedure has a broad focus and a limited range of sanctions. The excessive deficits procedure has a narrow focus and a broad range of sanctions. In theory, the combination of narrow focus and broad sanctions makes the excessive deficit procedure more limiting on the freedom of the member states.[23] In practice, however, the multilateral surveillance procedure is likely to prove more problematic. Given the broader remit of the procedure, it is more difficult for member states to avoid a negative audit. And, despite the narrower range of sanctions, it is unlikely that a member state will ever face worse than a public humiliation by the Council in any event.

Table 2.2. Economic Accountability Procedures

Procedure (Location)	Auditor	Subject of Evaluation	Result/Sanction
multilateral surveillance (Article 99-TEC)	Commission EFC	• compliance with Board Economic Policy Guidelines • consistency with EMU	• recommendations to member state • publicize recommendations
excessive deficit (Article 104-TEC)	Commission EFC	• budgetary situation • government debt	• recommendations to member state • publicize recommendations • notice of non-compliance • additional information before borrowing • review lending of European Investment Bank • non-interest-bearing deposit • "fines of an appropriate size"

The Irish reprimand of February 2001 is instructive in this regard. Although running a substantial fiscal surplus, the Irish government also confronted relatively high rates of domestic inflation. As a result, the Council recommended that Ireland "be ready . . . to use budgetary policy to ensure economic stability given the extent of overheating in the economy [and] gear the budget for 2001 to this objective" as part of the broad economic policy guidelines for 2000 (Council of Ministers 2000, 57). By the winter of 2000–2001, however, it was clear that Ireland's fiscal stance—while still significantly in surplus—was not in line with the guidelines. Indeed, the Irish government had voted to reduce taxes and raise expenditure in a manner likely to reduce the surplus from 4.7 percent of gross domestic product (GDP) to around 4.3 percent of GDP. As a result, the ECOFIN Council voted on 12 February 2001 to reprimand the Irish government for its "expansionary and pro-cyclical" fiscal policy and to instruct the Irish government to rescind its tax and spending proposals.[24] This reprimand not only forced the Irish government to explain its fiscal position in Brussels, but also to justify the nature (if not the content) of the Council's intervention back in Ireland. And, while it is true that the Irish government refused to back down, it is also likely that the government will not ignore the possibility of such public humiliation in the future.

That the Council would reprimand Ireland for running too small a fiscal surplus is testament to the seriousness with which the Council regards the commitment of the member states to the process of policy coordination—at least superficially. At a deeper level, it is unclear whether the ECOFIN Council would have been as direct in reprimanding a larger member state. The strategy of relying on the Commission and the EFC can eliminate only some—and yet not all—of the conflict of interest between the member states as agents responsible for implementing the economic policy rules of the Union and the Council of Ministers as the principal responsible for the oversight and enforcement of such rules. Indeed, given the controversy that surrounded the qualification of France and Germany for EMU membership in 1998, there is strong reason to believe in the weakness of the system with respect to the larger member states (Pierson, Forster, and Jones 1999). Still, such criticism should not be taken to mean that the strategy of auditing is somehow inherently flawed. Like the reporting strategy deployed by the ECB, it can be improved and yet it remains appropriate.

Employment-Related Evaluation: Benchmarking

The strategy for enforcement of the rules regarding employment-related policy is altogether different. Because the employment-related rules are process-centered, compliance has more to do with participation than with the outcomes of participation per se. Moreover this distinction is explicit in the strategy for accountability. Throughout the European Council summits from Amsterdam (1997) onward, the presidency conclusions have been careful to admit that the employment problems confronting the member states are characteristically different from one country to the next—whether in terms of possibilities for state intervention, market structures, or the organization of labor and industry. What the member states share in common is the fact that they all confront problems, and not that they confront the same problems.

The employment-related rules more closely approximate a form of self-help than a form of delegation by contract: The member states are both the agents and the principals. By contrast, the institutions of the European Union are primarily just concerned intermediaries. The focus for supranational activity is support and not supervision. Thus, while the Commission fulfills many of the same analytic functions on the employment side as it undertakes with respect to economic policy, such functions do not channel into specific sanctions per se. The Commission can be brutal in its criticism of member state performance in relation to employment policy (call it tough love, perhaps), but it cannot be punitive.

A similar point applies to the Economic Policy Committee (EPC), which serves an analogous function in terms of employment-related policy to that served by the EFC in terms of economic policy. The EPC contributes to the process of establishing the broad guidelines for economic policies as these relate to a range of objectives including market efficiency, productivity, employment, and competitiveness. Yet it does not play a direct role in either the multilateral surveillance procedure or the excessive deficits procedure except insofar as it contributes to establishing the general framework for evaluation. Moreover, where the EFC is required to maintain confidentiality, the EPC has both the option to disclose its deliberations and the obligation to publicize its reports or opinions.[25] The centerpiece for the European Union's strategy to ensure accountability in employment-related policy is a strategy to help the member states help themselves tackle the problems of unemployment and structural reform. This strategy was adopted at the Lisbon European Council summit of March 2000 and is called the "open method of coordination." In the words of the Lisbon presidency conclusions:

This method, which is designed to help Member States to progressively develop their own policies involves:

- fixing guidelines for the Union combined with specific timetables for achieving the goals which they set in the short, medium, and long terms;

- establishing, where appropriate, quantitative and qualitative indicators and benchmarks against the best in the world and tailored to the needs of different Member States and sectors as a means of comparing best practice;
- translating these European guidelines into national and regional policies by setting specific targets and adopting measures taking into account national and regional differences;
- periodic monitoring, evaluation and peer review organized as mutual learning processes (European Council 2000, section 37).

Of the four features, the use of benchmarking constitutes the most significant departure in terms of accountability. The member states of the European Union are not meant merely to live up to their obligations. They should strive to emulate best practice. There is no punishment for failure. However, the member states are expected to learn from their mistakes.

EMU as a Collection of Accountability Structures

If EMU is a collection of rules it is also a collection of mechanisms for ensuring the accountability of the political actors involved. Moreover, the structure of accountability differs depending upon the underlying rules. Hence it is not surprising that the European Union would have treated the three policy areas—monetary, economic, and employment related—as constitutionally discrete. The monetary rules have one agent and many principals, and are implicated as deeply in the process of rule-following behavior as in the outcomes. The economic rules have overlapping agents and principals and, in many respects, the outcome is the process. As in the Irish case, policy coordination and consistency is really only known after the fact. The same is not true for employment-related rules. There, not only are the principals also the agents, but the process is also the outcome. What matters is that the member states are involved. What results from their involvement can only be assumed.

The accountability structures deployed by the European Union run the gamut from reporting, to auditing, to benchmarking. Each of these strategies is appropriate to its particular context. None of these strategies would be appropriate across the board. Thus while the broad economic policy guidelines play a role in all three areas of activity, that role is characteristically different from one area to the next. Monetary policy provides a basis for the guidelines and not the other way around. And, where the guideline can determine economic policy, they can only suggest policy in relation to employment or structural reform. In this sense, EMU is a collection of accountability structures that are linked but that are not integrated. Each of the policy rules is subject to enforcement. The interaction between them is not.

THE PROBLEM AND PROMISE OF INTERDEPENDENCE

The difficulty for Europe's EMU is that the interaction between policy areas has a strong influence on the outcomes that result from following the rules within policy areas. EMU is a rule-based system. It is not, however, a deterministic system. Following the rules will not always result in desirable outcomes either within the specific policy areas or from one policy area to the next.

This problem is most pronounced in the policy area where the rules are clear but the mechanism linking policy and outcomes is contentious: monetary policy. The TEC is explicit in setting out the requirement to direct monetary policy toward the achievement of some absolute level of price stability. In turn, that mandate is underwritten by the belief that stable prices contribute to a macroeconomic framework which is conducive to growth and employment (Jones 1998). However, while there is broad agreement that stable prices have a desirable impact on economic performance over the long run, this does not translate into a consensus on the impact of monetary policy on economic performance at any given period of time.

The problem manifests in conflicts over the explanation for poor economic performance. While the member states or MEPs contend that the monetary stance of the ECB is inappropriate in a given context, the ECB argues that any economic weakness is due either to the need for greater fiscal consolidation or to the slow progress for structural reform.[26] This contrast in views emerged most strikingly during the first months of EMU in the form of a personalized conflict between the German finance minister, Oskar Lafontaine, and the president of the ECB, Wim Duisenberg. The conflicting interpretations have continued to flare up despite Lafontaine's peremptory resignation from public office.[27]

Monetary policy is not the only point of contention. Economic policy is also subject to conflicting interpretations. However, the contrast is that while the rules are relatively vague, the mechanisms linking policy to outcome are more clear cut. This contrast will strengthen once the member states succeed in consolidating their public debts and so have less difficulty in maintaining fiscal balance or surplus over the medium term. Returning to the Irish case, the Council was correct in its assertion that any decrease in the fiscal surplus would represent an increase in domestic demand—by definition. Given the monetary stance of the ECB and the contrast between the relatively high rates of inflation in Ireland and the relatively low rates of inflation elsewhere in EMU, the case against adding further stimulus to the Irish economy was relatively straightforward. What made the reprimand seem so unreasonable (and therefore controversial) is the fact that Ireland was already running a substantial surplus in order to pay down its outstanding public debt. Once that debt is repaid, the need for such huge surpluses will diminish, as will the surpluses themselves, and as will the potential for controversy surrounding Irish fiscal policy.

The problem of rules and outcomes is least evident in the area of employment, where the rules are procedural rather than prescriptive and where the outcomes are highly contingent upon environmental factors. For example, even those who are most critical of the monetary stance of the ECB are happy to admit that the member states should make greater efforts at structural reform. In political terms, the argument for structural reform is uncontroversial. The argument for a reform of specific structures is a different matter. Hence while the March 2000 Lisbon European Council summit succeeded in establishing the open method of coordination, it was considerably less successful in its objective "to speed up liberalization in areas such as gas, electricity, postal services and transport" (European Council 2000, section 17).

The promise of interdependence lies in the decreasing political salience of the "problem" from one issue to the next: the monetary rules are potentially controversial, the economic rules less so, the employment-related rules least of all. Viewed as a system, the three sets of rules work to bleed political controversy away from the monetary arena and into the fiscal and structural arenas. Moreover, as the focus for political attention moves away from monetary policy, the possibilities for policy variation to meet the needs of different distributive coalitions increases. Economic policy must be balanced over the medium term but that says little about either the constitution of revenues and expenditures or about the ratio of public spending to gross domestic activity. Employment-related policy must strive to emulate best-practice, but how policymakers achieve this and at what pace are points for flexibility and negotiation. Following the analysis posited in chapter 1, this arrangement is consistent with the need for different political groups to extract different benefits from the same set of monetary policy rules despite changing economic conditions.

ECONOMIC AND MONETARY
UNION WITHOUT POLITICAL UNION

What the European Union lacks is some singular authoritative body capable of accounting not only for when the rules are being followed but also for whether the outcome is desirable. This absence is most apparent in the conduct of monetary policy and least apparent in the conduct of employment policy. Still, it is a consistent feature in all areas of EMU. It is also an essential element of the constitutional arrangement for removing monetary politics from the political arena.

The three pillars of Europe's economic and monetary union are tightly interdependent—at least in mechanical terms. Yet each of the pillars has separate institutional arrangements. This combination of factors is not the result of incompetence or conspiracy on the part of EMU's architects. Rather it is a function of the types of rules applied in different areas and the actors implicated in their implementation and enforcement. It is also a function of the strategy to depoliticize the monetary union.

That said, however, no obvious institutional solution presents itself. For example, those EU member states that participate in EMU have attempted to coordinate their policy positions through informal meetings of their economics and finance ministers prior to full meetings of the ECOFIN Council. This collection of EMU ministers—called the Eurogroup—has no decisionmaking authority. Yet it does constitute an authoritative collection of member state representatives. Moreover, the Eurogroup has won the grudging respect of the ECB. Even so, however, there is little chance that such an organization can resolve the lack of systemic accountability in Europe without there first being a change in the structure of the policy rules—particularly with regards to the political independence of the ESCB. ECB President Duisenberg explained his institution's position while speaking before the European Parliament in June 2000:

> Any move . . . to create an institutionalized political body, if it enhances the cooperation and coordination amongst the Ministers of Finance in fields other than monetary policy, can only be applauded. If it is meant to exert influence on the European Central Bank, it will not succeed.[28]

Duisenberg's statement reflects the underlying reality that the fragmentation of accountability structures is political as well as institutional. Not only does it arise from the policy rules and their implementation, it also derives from the overwhelming complexity of the distributive politics underlying the choice for multiple and interdependent policy rules. There is no obvious distributive coalition behind the constitution of all three sets of rules (Frieden and Jones 1998). Indeed, there was frequent opposition between the proponents of any one set of rules and the proponents of the others (Jones 1998; Pierson, Forster, and Jones 1998). By the same token, it is questionable whether a coherent coalition of political actors can be identified with respect to any one cluster of rules across the different member states.

Of course such complexity holds in purely national economic and monetary unions as well, and particularly in those with federal arrangements or well established sub-national political arenas. The difference is that where national politics largely preceded the constitution of national policy rules, the choices constituting Europe's EMU have largely preceded the development of a truly European politics.[29] The question to consider is what this implies for the state of European democracy. And, given the central significance of Europe's monetary rules both as an institutional feature and as a point of contention, the democratic implications of EMU are particularly relevant to the establishment of a single currency bolstered by a politically independent central bank that is committed to a goal of absolute price stability.

NOTES

1. The policy area omitted from consideration by the TEC is the management of exchange rates between the single currency and the outside world. As will be noted below, the treaty makes provision only for the Council of Ministers to establish broad guidelines under the stipulation that these not contradict the monetary framework. The tension this creates between policy areas in EMU is the focus for analysis in chapter 4.

2. Two recent examples of this sudden obsolescence of description can be found in the otherwise excellent volumes by Dyson (2000) and by Levitt and Lord (2000).

3. The references to the TEC and the TEU shall use the Amsterdam numbering conventions throughout this chapter.

4. Note that even the United Kingdom has accepted to be bound by the terms of this article. See Paragraph 6 of the "Protocol on Certain Provisions Relating to the United Kingdom of Great Britain and Northern Ireland" as appended to the Maastricht version of the Treaty on European Union.

5. The list of objectives is not exhaustive. The injunction to direct economic policy toward the achievement of those objectives is taken from Article 98 of the TEC.

6. Note that Sweden never secured an opt-out from EMU and Denmark's opt-out from EMU did not encompass the excessive deficits procedure. The UK opt-out from the excessive deficit procedure can be found in the "Protocol on Certain Provisions Relating to the United Kingdom of Great Britain and Northern Ireland" as appended to the Maastricht version of the Treaty on European Union. In that opt-out, the UK rejected the injunction that "Member States shall avoid excessive government deficits" and yet accepted that "Member States shall *endeavor* to avoid excessive deficits" (emphasis added). Clearly this language is superceded by the commitment announced in the Stability and Growth Pact. See European Commission (1997a).

7. In the original document, the Cologne process is presented first rather than last. I have reversed the ordering to follow their chronological development.

8. The citations are taken from Article 2 of both treaties.

9. This point is a recurrent theme in Dyson (2000).

10. The principal-agent literature is vast. For an early introduction, see Moe (1984).

11. See, for example, Arrow (1985) and Bergman and Lane (1990).

12. For a sample of the criticism, see the opening question at the ECB press conference of September 14, 2000—the full text of which is available from the ECB Website.

13. See the ECB press conference of 6 May 1999.

14. The relevant provisions are outlined in both the TEC and the Statute of the ESCB and the ECB. For an analysis of these provisions as they related to central bank independence, see De Haan (1997).

15. Such concern has been expressed by, inter alia, De Haan (1997), Elgie (1998), and Verdun (1998).

16. This problem of multiple principals is suggested in CEPS (1999: 9–13).

17. This is not to say that the content of the strategy is comprehensive. A number of analysts argue that the ESCB could give more information both about its decisions and about its decisionmaking procedures. The argument I make in Chapter 3 is that whatever the merits of these claims, the basic standards for accountability have been met.

18. This section has benefitted greatly from Hallerberg (2001).

19. These Commission responsibilities are outlined in Articles 99 and 104 of the TEC.

20. The statutes of the EFC are set out in the *Official Journal of the European Communities* L 5 (January 9, 1999) 71–73.

21. The membership of the EFC is set out in the *Official Journal of the European Communities* L 358 (December 31, 1998) 109–110.

22. This provision on voting is set out in Article 4 of the statutes of the EFC.

23. See, for example, Eichengreen and Wyplosz (1998), who draw particular attention to the constraints implied by the excessive deficits procedure in the aftermath of the stability pact.

24. For the text of the decision, see Council of Ministers (2001).

25. The statutes of the Economic Policy Community are set out in the *Official Journal of the European Communities* L 257 (October 11, 2000) 28–31. The instructions relating to confidentiality are given in Article 15.

26. For example, consider the testimony of ECB Vice President Christian Noyer before the Economic and Monetary Affairs Committee of the European Parliament on September 27, 1999.

27. This conflict is described in greater detail in chapter 7. See also Jones (2000).

28. This citation is drawn from a transcript of Duisenberg's testimony before the Economic and Monetary Affairs Committee of the European Parliament on 20 June 2000.

29. The difference here may be important for the development of political society. As Thorlakson (2000, 133) has argued, the top-down imposition of decentralized institutional structures can lead to the fragmentation of national politics and national political identity. By contrast, however, the centralization of institutional structures on already fragmented politics only very rarely leads to the centralization of politics and political identity.

3

+

Legitimacy: Delegation and Distributive Preferences

In theory, Europe's economic and monetary union (EMU) is apolitical. In practice, it is a political system in its own right. Moreover, it is a political system where interdependence is strong but accountability is weak. The question, therefore, is whether EMU necessarily poses a problem for European democracy. Specifically, the European Central Bank (ECB) is the most politically independent institution of its kind in Europe. Both its strong constitutional position outlined in the Treaty on European Union and the difficult requirements for amending the treaty make it unlikely that the ECB will be overturned.[1] Moreover, the lack of an elected counterpart equal in continental scope suggests that the ECB is unlikely to face a united and powerful political counterweight. Not all member states represented in the Council of Ministers may benefit from the day-to-day management of monetary policy, but it is difficult to imagine that they will all suffer from the ECB's actions at the same time or that they would all gain from exerting influence over the bank. Divisions within the European Parliament will be even more extreme, and so the prospect of a united political front forming in opposition to the ECB is remote. Thus, in many respects, the management of Europe's economic and monetary union appears to operate beyond the reach of democratic control.

Given the very public support of the European Union (EU) for liberal democratic values, the apolitical management of EMU suggests an important contradiction. If democracy is about process and not outcome, why should EMU be exempt from electoral oversight? If the focus is on outcome and not process, then how indispensable are democratic values? The answers to such questions are not one-sided. Put another way, the case against the political independence of EMU—and in favor of a more democratic arrangement—is strong. First, following Berman and McNamara (1999), democracy is more about process than outcome. Therefore, any marginal improvement in economic performance may not outweigh the cost in terms of the perceived legitimacy of the European system of governance. Second, the role of an independent central bank in producing favorable economic outcomes is dependent on other institutional conditions such as fiscal or wage-bargaining regimes. To the extent to which such conditions do not exist at the European level, a politically independent EMU may actually produce worse economic outcomes than no EMU at all (Hall and Franzese 1998). Finally, what really matters for economic performance is a "culture of price stability"—or a powerful vested interest in stable prices (Posen 1993)—and not an institutional formula per se. Such factors are decisively political and so should be mediated through political institutions rather than insulated from political influence.

Nevertheless, much of the strength of the argument against the political independence of the ECB rests on a crucial assumption. Critics of the democratic legitimacy of central bank independence assume that macroeconomic outcomes, and particularly inflation and unemployment, are the subject of direct and relative political preferences within the democratic electorate. Voters want to trade off inflation against unemployment or unemployment and inflation against other factors directly, and therefore require that monetary policymakers be directly accountable to their wishes. Any attempt to delegate monetary policy authority beyond the oversight of national electorates will necessarily violate the most basic requirements for the democratic representation of popular preferences.[2]

Under different assumptions, the arguments against the democratic accountability of central bank independence become less compelling if not irrelevant. For example, voters may have preferences concerning macroeconomic outcomes that are direct and absolute rather than direct and relative. Under this assumption, voters do not want to trade off inflation and unemployment against anything. Rather, they prefer to have consistently low inflation and consistently low unemployment in all circumstances. The empirical possibility that voters can only have one (such as low inflation) at the expense of the other (such as low unemployment) should not be taken to negate the fact that voters would prefer to have both.

Under the assumption that voters have direct and absolute preferences regarding macroeconomic outcomes, the focus for political accountability would rest on establishing mechanisms to work toward the achievement of those absolute objectives. If such mechanisms involve the delegation of monetary policy authority to some extra-national agency, then so be it. Moreover, not all possibilities have to be made available. Even if there is an empirical basis for believing that the manipulation of monetary policy instruments can either facilitate or limit the achievement of direct and absolute macroeconomic objectives, that is no reason to thrust monetary policy into the public domain. Capital expropriation and forced labor also work to hold down prices and unemployment, and yet few would regard the prohibition of such practices as undemocratic. In the extreme case where monetary policy is the *only* possible means for achieving macroeconomic objectives, democracy still does not necessitate discretionary control. The requirements for popular representation or procedural accountability are limited to identifying the objectives for policymakers. The form of this identification is open, and can fall anywhere on a continuum from direct intervention to a permanent rule. Hence, there can be no categorical objection to central bank independence on the basis of democratic principles.

Alternatively, it is conceivable that macroeconomic outcomes like unemployment and inflation concern members of the electorate only through their effects on the distribution of economic resources. Under this assumption, voters have direct preferences about, for example, the return to capital and labor. However, they have only indirect or instrumental preferences about the movement of macroeconomic variables. Inflation and unemployment can be good or bad depending on how they influence the income and wealth of workers and capitalists. If voters are principally interested in distributive outcomes, then there is no a priori reason for specific macroeconomic instruments—like monetary policy instruments—to be subject to political manipulation. What matters is that the electorate have some control over macroeconomic outcomes or over the influence of macroeconomic outcomes on the distribution of resources. By implication, fiscal regimes, wage bargaining institutions, or any number of other arrangements can repair the absence of a politically accountable central bank. Once again, there can be no categorical objection to central bank independence.

The argument in this chapter is twofold. To begin with, critics of the democratic legitimacy of central bank independence are mistaken. Independent central banks may or may not provide for superior macroeconomic performance, but that is beside the point. The assumption that macroeconomic outcomes are the subject of direct and relative preferences within the democratic electorate is simply incorrect. Voters do not seek to trade off inflation and unemployment either against each-other or against other macroeconomic outcomes. To the extent to which direct preferences concerning macroeconomic outcomes do exist within the electorate, they are absolute. The voters want inflation and unemployment to be as low as possible given the circumstances. An independent central bank can satisfy such preferences as easily as a dependent one. Moreover, to the extent to which an independent bank provides the appearance that such absolute objectives are not to be sacrificed on the altar of short-term political gain an independent central bank may even be more appealing.

The second argument has more fundamental importance for how we understand the politics of EMU. Essentially, what voters are concerned with is the distribution of economic resources and not the movement of macroeconomic variables per se. If movements in macroeconomic variables influence this distribution of resources, voters will adopt instrumental preferences to their own benefit. However, the structure of these preferences will be determined not just by the direction in which the macro-economy moves, but by a variety of institutional arrangements as well. By implication, the success of Europe's economic and monetary union will not lie with the ECB alone, or even with the central bank and some other *crucial* institutional arrangement. Rather, it will lie in the complexity of distributive outcomes as mediated by a variety of institutions across the European Union and its member states. To the extent to which that welter of institutions confuses the distributive impact of monetary policy changes, coherent political cleavages may never form around the operation of the ECB. A European "culture of price stability" could be the result.

The chapter has four sections. The first explains the emergence of assumptions about the direct and relative macroeconomic preferences of voters in the economic arguments for central bank independence. The second argues for replacing the direct and relative macroeconomic preferences with a combination of direct and absolute preferences and instrumental (or distributive) preferences. The third demonstrates that a combination of direct and absolute macroeconomic preferences and distributive preferences fits better with the empirical record than the direct and relative preferences used in the initial discussion of central bank independence. The fourth extends the argument to the European level to examine how assumptions about distributive preferences can influence our understanding of European (monetary) integration as well as the democratic legitimacy of EMU.

MACROECONOMIC PREFERENCES

The notion that voters hold direct and relative preferences concerning macroeconomic outcomes derives from a series of facilitating assumptions used in economics. For example, economists routinely assume that politicians and voters recognize a trade-off between inflation and unemployment (the Philips curve). Alternatively, they might assume that voters and politicians regard inflation as a legitimate source of government revenue (the inflation tax). Such assumptions can be backed by empirically plausible mechanisms. A rise (fall) in unemployment can place downward (upward) pressure on wages and so lower (raise) the incentive for firms to raise prices. Alternatively, a rise in the rate of inflation can erode the value of outstanding cash balances and so decrease government liabilities. Importantly, however, there is no direct empirical support for hypotheses that voters and policymakers attempt to trade off inflation against unemployment or inflation against other forms of revenue. Thus while the mechanisms remain plausible, their use in the real world is unproven.

Plausibility is all that is required. Hypotheses concerning the trade-off between inflation and unemployment or between inflation and other sources of government revenue can operate as assumptions. In turn, these assumptions can allow economists to investigate other hypothetical relationships between political action and economic performance—such as political business cycles or macroeconomic credibility. Assuming that voters and politicians confront an "exploitable" Philips curve or strive for the "optimal" inflation tax or would want to manipulate some other plausible economic mechanism, what can we predict about the interaction between politics and economics?

The structure of the question is important. Sometime during the 1970s, economists came around to the realization that political behavior may have a systematic and powerful influence on the functioning of the economy.[3] The challenge for positive economic analysis, therefore, is to develop tools for formulating and testing hypotheses about this influence (Friedman 1977, 459–460). Assumptions about the exploitable Philips curve or the optimal inflation tax were originally intended to bridge the gap between theoretical analysis and empirical data. If we believe that politicians are using macroeconomic policy to further their own interests, and we can measure the movement of macroeconomic variables, then it is necessary to connect the theory of manipulation and the data on outcomes.

The problem is one of motivation. Following Downs (1957), economists can start with prior assumptions that politicians want to be re-elected and voters want to be better off. However such assumptions only bridge part of the gap between theories of policy manipulation and data on macroeconomic outcomes. The rest of the distance is covered via assumptions about policies and outcomes. Politicians manipulate the macro-economy and voters assess their well-being on the basis of government policies. Crucially, voters do not have to base their assessments on the movement of macroeconomic variables per se. All that matters is that they make the connection between government action and personal well-being.[4] In this way, assumptions about the macroeconomic policies pursued by governments do not have to make sense at face value. No politician should be expected to run on the pro-inflation platform. What matters is that assumptions about macroeconomic preferences should be reasonable given appropriate qualifications about mechanism, etc. Politicians could run on a platform of higher wages or lower taxes with higher inflation being the result. This is a reasonable assumption with the qualification that politicians benefit from raising wages or lowering taxes and that higher wages or lower taxes would result in inflation. At the end of the story, economists can correlate inflation performance with indicators of political success in order to test hypotheses about the political-economic relationship.

Through continued use, however, assumptions about the preferences surrounding policy trade-offs such as the exploitable Philips curve and the optimal inflation tax have developed into shorthand assumptions about macroeconomic preferences. The utility curves of politicians and voters are described as a function of macroeconomic outcomes. At the same time, these shorthand assumptions have also acquired such an acceptance in the economic literature as to be attributed with quasi-empirical status. Economists no longer need to describe the chain of reasoning behind their assumptions about preferences because the arguments are already well-rehearsed in the literature (much of which dates back to the 1950s). Moreover, continuous repetition of qualifications distracts from the object of the analysis, which is to test some new hypothesis concerning the relationship between political action and economic performance and not to analyze political preferences per se. This is not to suggest that economic analysis is somehow inherently wrong, sloppy, or irrelevant. Rather my point is that the qualifications surrounding such facilitating assumptions as the exploitable Philips curve or the optimal inflation tax have tended to get lost through repetition.

Consider the exploitable Philips curve. The assumption is that politicians trade-off inflation against unemployment in order to gain some political benefit. In the Downsian sense, the benefit could be to win re-election as an incumbent. Here an example is Nordhaus's (1975) electoral business cycle. Incumbent politicians encourage economic growth just before the election to raise employment and so increase their chances of winning. After the election, politicians confront the rising inflation that results from the pre-electoral boom and so rein in on the economy even at the cost of rising unemployment. The assumption is that voters experience the growth and connect it with the government when they go to cast their votes: more growth, happier voters, reelection. Once the election is over, the government has to slow down growth again—and presumably alienates voters in the process—but retains the capacity to engineer another boom in time for the next election.

The manipulation of the economy does not have to follow the cycle set out by Nordhaus, although his mechanism is plausible. With a slight change of assumptions, the pattern of interaction could be altogether different. For example, the benefit to politicians could be to compete for the support of different groups in society—some of whom dislike unemployment more than they dislike inflation, while others dislike inflation more than they dislike unemployment. The exemplar here is Hibbs's (1977) partisan business cycle, where center-right governments manage the economy with lower inflation but higher unemployment while center-left governments provide for higher inflation but lower unemployment. Of course, at the basis of all this politicians still want to get elected and voters still want to be better off. All that has changed from Nordhaus to Hibbs are the assumptions about preferences that bring the two groups—politicians and voters—together.

Both hypotheses—Nordhaus's electoral business cycles and Hibbs's partisan business cycle—rely on untested facilitating assumptions about political preferences surrounding the trade-off between inflation and unemployment. For Nordhaus (1975, 181–182), the assumption is that voters prefer employment in the present even at the expense of inflation in the near future, a government retrenchment, and a return of unemployment. This assumption cannot be tested directly, and so is verified indirectly through the success of the model as a whole. Moreover, as Nordhaus admits, if this assumption of voter preferences is empirically unfounded, then his hypothesis of the electoral business cycle cannot be true.

For Hibbs (1977, 1468–1470), the assumption is that wage and salary earners fear unemployment more than inflation while groups relying on profit-based income fear inflation more than unemployment. This assumption is a weak one in that it can be (and has been) tested empirically, at least in part. Hibbs discusses survey data about macroeconomic concerns by income class from Great Britain and the United States but without going into great detail about the stability of preferences over time or the link between macroeconomic preferences and partisan allegiance. Even with fully specified panel data over an extended period of time, however, it would be difficult to distinguish the direct and relative preferences of voters for specific macroeconomic outcomes from the instrumental preferences of voters for the distributive implications of these outcomes. Therefore, Hibbs necessarily qualifies his analysis with an explanation of the distributive reasons for partisan macroeconomic preferences. Presumably, if the distributive consequences of inflation and unemployment were to change, then the partisan business cycle would change as well. If the consequences were to be the same for wage and salary earners on the one hand, and profit-income groups on the other hand, then the partisan business cycle would vanish.

Assumptions about the optimal inflation tax could be used to connect political behavior with economic outcomes in ways that are similar to those described by Nordhaus and Hibbs. Politicians could spend their way into reelection and then inflate away the debt afterward. Alternatively, politicians could alternate between using inflation to tax creditors (or the holders of cash balances) and other instruments to tax debtors (or

those who do not hold cash) depending upon which group was more important in winning the next election. The mechanisms have changed, but
the qualifications remain the same. Voters have to be short-sighted for the
electoral cycle to function, and they would have to be divided across distributive outcomes for the partisan cycle to function.

Hypotheses such as those put forward by Nordhaus and Hibbs are particularly attractive because they can be tested so easily using macroeconomic and electoral data. Time series for inflation, unemployment, and
electoral outcomes are widely available and can be made readily subject
to regression analysis. The pattern of testing is the same whether the focus is on the exploitable Philips curve or the optimal inflation tax. In either case, the test of competing hypotheses is still deduced from the
model as a whole—which is to say, from the extent to which macroeconomic outcomes correlate with indicators for political success. Moreover,
the existence of two different sets of hypotheses—electoral cycle and partisan cycle—provides the basis for a credible research program. Given two
different hypotheses, both equally plausible, which is better and under
what conditions?

This pattern of argument lies at the heart of economic support for central bank independence: If political behavior creates inefficiencies in the
functioning of the economy, then perhaps it is necessary to remove
macroeconomic policymaking from direct political influence. The difference is that while the plausible mechanisms in these arguments become
ever more sophisticated, the macroeconomic preferences become ever
more straightforward. Thus, Kydland and Prescott (1977) make their argument for "the [time-] inconsistency of optimal plans" around the assumption that voters will anticipate attempts by policymakers to exploit
the trade-off between inflation and unemployment. Barro and Gordon
(1983) focus on how politicians respond to the economic expectations of
voters about government incentives to resort to an inflation tax as well as
to changes in those expectations. Backus and Driffill (1985) work from
the assumption that the public may not be aware of the government's
true preferences regarding inflation and unemployment. And Rogoff
(1985) argues that the government's macroeconomic preferences should
be systematically different from that of the electorate. In each case—albeit for different reasons and under different conditions—one solution to
the problem of politically-induced macroeconomic inefficiency is the appointment of an independent central bank.[5]

The assumptions about macroeconomic preferences are not only
straightforward, they are also largely untestable—at least outside of the
hypothetico-deductive analysis of the models as a whole. It is one thing to
look for correlations between political success or institutional design and
macroeconomic performance, and yet it is harder to map the macroeco-

nomic preferences of the electorate, harder still to distinguish between different types of preference, and hardest of all to assess how strongly such preferences feature in the actions of voters and politicians. Thus the empirical debate about central bank independence focuses on large macro-correlations and not on verifying each intermediate step in the analysis. Whether the voters are ignorant of political manipulation or government preferences, and whether governments seek to deceive the electorate or to appease it, is judged indirectly through the correlation of political institutions or successes and macroeconomic outcomes.

The use of correlations to verify whole models for political-economic interaction is so deeply ingrained in the literature that the possibility that politicians and voters would not perceive a trade-off between inflation and unemployment or between inflation and other forms of taxation—or that the distributional consequences of macroeconomic outcomes may no longer divide across partisan lines—virtually never receives consideration. In journal articles, there simply is not the space—and so, for example, Alesina (1987) starts off by assuming the existence of two parties with different macroeconomic preferences. Even in book-length analyses, however, the focus for empirical examination remains at the macro level. Alesina, Roubini, and Cohen (1997) review a wealth of data for correlations between political indicators and macroeconomic outcomes, but do no more than reiterate evidence from Hibbs (updated to 1987) about the partisan-distributive consequences of unemployment and inflation in the United States. Their reason: "most people (excluding some political scientists) would agree that different parties have different political goals" (45).

This line of analysis is not intended as a criticism of the research program centered upon the hypothetico-deductive verification of macromodels for political-economic interaction. Both types of political business cycle—Nordhaus's electoral model and Hibbs's partisan model—have a strong intuitive appeal, and it is reasonable to attempt to see which accords better with the empirical record. By the same token, more complicated game-theoretic analysis of the interaction between policymakers and voters promises to shed important light on the problems of policy implementation—particularly when anticipation by the marketplace can produce perverse outcomes. Given the prior assumption—as in Friedman (1977)—that political-economic interaction may be the principal cause for systematically poor macroeconomic performance, plausible speculation as to the form of such interaction is welcome. Any estimation of the relative plausibility of different lines of analysis is more welcome still. Finally, to the extent to which combinations of political business cycles and game-theoretic approaches help to focus attention on institutional solutions for systematically poor economic performance, that is most welcome of all (Lohmann 1992). Small wonder, then, that the argument for central bank independence has acquired such broad acceptance. The criticism is not with the research itself. Rather it is with how the facilitating assumptions of the research program are used and (in the weak and unintentional sense of the term) abused.

EXCHANGE AND DISTRIBUTION

Once outside the context of macro-models for political-economic interaction, however, the case for making assumptions about the direct and relative macroeconomic preferences of voters and politicians loses force. Whether weak or strong, such assumptions exist to bridge the gap between theoretical interaction and directly observable data. Therefore the standard for assessing the merits of these assumptions is a combination of plausibility and utility.[6] Do such assumptions really make sense and how much do they help to provide for a meaningful test of the hypothesis? If there is no hypothesis for explicit testing, consideration of utility ceases to have meaning. The question, then, is whether the assumption that voters and politicians have direct and relative macroeconomic preferences makes sense at face value. The answer, in short, is that it does not.

To begin with, it is necessary to clarify that the only important macroeconomic preferences are those held by the voters. This point is most easily established in the political business cycle literature, where politicians care about macroeconomic outcomes only insofar as these influence electoral fortunes—the Downsian assumption. If the voters do not care about macroeconomic performance, then the politicians do not care either. The status of elite preferences in the game-theoretic literature about policy credibility is only slightly more problematic. Politicians and monetary policymakers may hold macroeconomic preferences that—particularly in the case of central bankers—are independent of electoral outcomes and therefore popular preferences. Nevertheless, politicians and policymakers receive their preferences in much the same way that everyone else does. Elite preferences are no more than elevated popular preferences mediated through institutions. Therefore, most analysts assume that any systematic differences between elite preferences and popular preference are institutionally determined in some predictable manner—as a result of binding policy rules, bureaucratic incentives, epistemic communities, and the like. All non-systematic differences between elite preferences and popular preferences—which is to say, any uncertainty about elite preferences that cannot be explained away as some function of their institutional environment—are not somehow inherent to elites as such but rather derive from the location of particular elites within the distribution of popular preferences. As a result, popular preferences and institutional design are all that matter in the final analysis.

But where do popular preferences come from? The connection between policy action and macroeconomic outcome is hardly a direct cause and effect relationship. From a mechanistic standpoint, politicians cannot simply "lower" unemployment and then wait for prices to rise, or announce a tax cut and then expect markets to hold on to depreciating cash balances or government obligations. By the same token, voters cannot stop working in the hopes of seeing prices fall, or pay premiums for goods and services in the expectation of receiving a job, or withhold some of their income tax with the promise to keep the money in cash. Even those who believe in the existence of an exploitable Philips curve or an optimal inflation tax have to admit that some intermediate process must come into play between government policy and macroeconomic outcomes.

More fundamentally, some intermediate process must come into play between perception, evaluation, accreditation, and action. Voters have to perceive the change in macroeconomic conditions, they have to translate it into some kind of personally meaningful framework, they have to accredit the change to government policy, and they have to formulate an appropriate response. This type of mechanism is at least as complicated as the economic mechanics that relate prices to employment. It is also less intuitive—as least from the standpoint of direct and relative preferences.

The problem is that macroeconomic outcomes and policy instruments are non-fungible. At a personal level, inflation and unemployment cannot be freely exchanged, and neither can inflation and other forms of taxation. Thus the trade-offs implied by the Philips curve and the inflation tax have no meaning without the introduction of an intervening value—something voters can perceive in common to both inflation and unemployment or inflation and other sources of government revenue. Downs (1957), for example, relies on the notion of utility in order to translate policy outcomes into comparable units of personal welfare. Once the existence of utility as a sort of universal currency is assumed, however, it is possible to denominate all objects and outcomes in terms of a third currency—which, for convenience, may as well be actual currency (money) rather than notional currency (utility). All that is required is a constraining assumption that the utility value of money is independent of the utility value of other objects. Everything has its price apart from money itself.[7]

The introduction of money as an intermediate and universal value solves the first two steps in the mechanics of popular preferences. Macroeconomic change is perceived and interpreted in terms of changes in personal money—which is to say, income or wealth. As the function of money is to facilitate exchange between otherwise non-fungible goods, this impact relates to command over goods and services in the economy (real income) and not to the units of money per se (nominal income). Moreover, even if macroeconomic developments do not affect all the people all the

time, we could recast the argument in probabilistic terms as expected
changes without affecting the logic of the claim. Finally, the accreditation
of macroeconomic change to government action can be assumed as a natural outgrowth of the political process—incumbents will always try to lay
claim to what is good, while aspirants will highlight what is not. From this
basis, it is easier to understand why Hibbs (1977) focuses a good part of his
analysis on explaining the income effects of macroeconomic changes and
Alesina et al. (1997) reiterate Hibbs's approach.

Intermediate monetary values also suggest the existence of direct and
absolute macroeconomic preferences. Voters will dislike unemployment
to the extent to which it reduces or threatens to reduce income. They will
like growth, to the extent to which it adds to the amount of goods and
services available for consumption or to the extent to which it represents
an increase in personal income. And they will dislike inflation to the extent to which price changes undermine the value of money or alter the relative rates of exchange between goods or services. These preferences are
direct in that they attach to specific macroeconomic developments and
they are absolute in that each development has a consistent effect on real
income—positive for growth and employment, negative for unemployment and inflation.

Beyond these direct and absolute preferences, however, two issues remain to be addressed. The first is left over from the mechanics of popular
preferences—even if we can identify how voters perceive, value, and accredit macroeconomic changes, we still must consider how they will respond. For example, to what extent will the political response of different
groups vary with the intensity of the personal wealth and income effects
and to what extent will it vary with the expected costs and benefits of the
response itself? The second is new, and derives from the existence of an
intermediate and universal value. If, at the base of the matter, popular
preferences revolve principally around (expected) changes to personal income and wealth, it makes no sense to assume that politicians are concerned with macroeconomic manipulation. Again, if voters are not inherently interested in macroeconomic outcomes, then politicians are not
either. Following Downs (1957), the assumption should be that politicians
will strive to manipulate whichever policy instrument is available and is
most likely to secure reelection. Put another way, politicians will do whatever they can to generate a beneficial response.

These issues can only be addressed within the context of real-world
constraints. To begin with, the volume of available income or wealth is
limited. The economy can produce only so much—both in static terms,
and in terms of real growth. Second, political action—whether directly at
the polling booth, or indirectly through lobbying or campaigning—has a
cost. For the electorate, this implies that the expected gain from acting

should exceed the cost of doing so.[8] For politicians, the combination of these two constraints suggests the need to target their efforts. Simply, distribution matters. If politicians hope to create substantial income effects for a particular group in the electorate, they can only do so either by concentrating the effects of growth or by taking wealth from one group to give to another. In turn, this strategy of concentration raises a third constraint on political action. It is always going to be more efficient for politicians to target distribution first-hand, rather than to effect some macroeconomic change in the anticipation of second-order distributive outcomes. Targeted mechanisms not only promise to raise the income or wealth of those concerned, but they also underscore the chain of perception, valuation, and, most important, accreditation.

The notion of targeted redistribution is at least as intuitive as the notion of a political business cycle. Moreover, the two views are not mutually exclusive. They are, however, prioritized. Within the distributive context, macroeconomic manipulation is a residual. Politicians resort to macroeconomic policy only when more efficient distributive mechanisms are either unavailable or too costly to use. Following this hierarchy, the question is not whether politicians attempt to manipulate macroeconomic variables in their own interests, but why. The focus is not on motivation but on constraint. In this way, what started as a question of popular preferences can thus be reduced to a set of basic assumptions about motivation and a set of more complicated institutional factors affecting the relative cost or availability of direct distributive mechanisms.

Economists have long recognized the importance of distributive outcomes to popular evaluations of policy performance. For example, Bailey (1956, 93, 110) pioneered the analysis of the "optimal inflation tax" as a means to look beyond "the redistributive and disruptive aspects of inflation." Nevertheless, he concluded by emphasizing the overwhelming significance of distributive effects. If governments are attempting to raise revenue via inflation, he suggests, it must "be that the costs are at first largely hidden, whereas the costs of other forms of taxation—the costs of administration and compliance—are obvious." Building on this position, Gordon (1975) suggested that if governments are generating inflation around elections, it is not because they want inflation per se, but rather because they have no other means to meet the distributive demands of the electorate. And, along similar lines, Stigler (1973, 166–167) argued that macroeconomic performance—whether measured in terms of inflation, unemployment, or even per capita income—is unrelated either to incumbency or to party programs. "One should not infer that economic questions are unimportant to the policies of parties or to the various groups in the population who systematically support one of the parties . . . . [Nevertheless] the economic bases for party affiliation must be sought in this area of income distribution."

The problem for economists in the 1970s was to build a research program around the political-economic dynamics of distributive outcomes. While the chain of reasoning is robust, the manifestation is more likely to be idiosyncratic. Politicians confronting diverse constituencies within the electorate are forced to make a judgment call about whose support to encourage based on the prevailing circumstances at the time. The choice may well be rational in the manner described by, for example, Dahl and Lindblom (1976), however it will be difficult to model in any detail before the fact. The logic of this claim follows directly from the analysis of money as technology provided in chapter 1. However, for the present discussion, the implications are potent. In commenting on Gordon's argument, Brunner (1975, 853–854) stressed the overwhelming political significance of targeted distributive mechanisms only to admit that:

> This analysis suggests . . . the fundamental irrelevance of most chapters in the theory of economic macro-policy and implies that systematic and deliberate macro-policies are somewhat improbable. The prevailing pattern of macro-policy results from a political process of detailed allocative struggle covered by a rhetoric occasionally borrowed from textbooks on macro-policies.

Commenting on Stigler, McCracken (1973, 171) offers a less cynical and yet still telling synopsis:

> What all this seems to suggest is that, within reasonable tolerances, changes in political sentiment are more apt to reflect the myriad of other factors that bear on voter sentiment. If the swing is outside these tolerances, or if the event is sufficiently visible or discrete, economic developments can exert a substantial effect on citizen support of the incumbent. If, therefore, the economic indicators start to waver, the economist may sleep well at night, knowing that in all probability it means little, but the politician may for very good reasons remain awake, wondering if this will be one of those cases that transforms him into a statesman.

Even without a forward-looking research program, however, it is possible to consolidate the argument by way of a couple of observations. To begin with, the critique of central bank independence as undemocratic lacks analytic basis. Given that voters do not have (at least inherently) direct and relative preferences for macroeconomic outcomes, there is no a priori reason to make macroeconomic policymakers subject to democratic accountability. Obviously if democratic electorates demand procedures to oversee the delegation of monetary policy authority to the ECB, then such demands must be addressed. Nevertheless, the point is that ensuring the accountability of monetary policymakers may or may not be something that the voters or that politicians choose, but they do not have to do so, and neither do they have to consider the option. Second, some justification for central bank independence remains, although it is perhaps different from the traditional arguments developed by Kydland and Prescott, Barro and Gordon, Rogoff, and the like. Within this distribution-oriented political economy, having an independent central bank may help to prevent distributive conflict from undermining monetary conditions. Following Brunner (1975, 854): "The role of monetary rules appears in this context in a new light. They define a constraint on the political process and are intended to move some portions of macro-policy beyond the allocative process of the 'political market.'"

COMPETING EXPLANATIONS

The argument that voters are more interested in distributive outcomes than in macroeconomic performance is compelling—at least on analytic grounds. Politicians want to be reelected, and voters want to be better off. Politicians face resource constraints, and voters demand incentives to act. Therefore politicians make choices, target voters and reward them by redistributing either existing wealth or the benefits of economic growth. Such actions may have macroeconomic implications and, in moments of political desperation, may even manifest as macroeconomic policy changes. However, macroeconomic manipulation is not a usual means for politicians to seek reelection and it is not what the voters want (or are likely to respond to) in any event. This is a convincing interpretation—or at least a highly plausible one—but can it really tell us anything beyond the obvious? Recalling that the twin test for any framework of assumptions is utility as well as plausibility, what research program can a distributive focus for political-economic interactions offer?

At this point it is important to concede that much of the existing economic analysis behind the argument for central bank independence is consistent with the distributive interpretation of political-economic interactions. For example, the political business cycle literature can be accommodated as a plausible description of the indirect effects of distributive policies (Gordon 1975; McCracken 1973), with the qualification that politicians only resort directly to macro-economic manipulation *in extremis* (Brunner 1975). Such a modification would require that analysts of political business cycles pay more attention to the distributive basis for electoral and partisan support (Okun 1973, 177). However, it would not vitiate their models per se.

The game-theoretic analysis about policy credibility is only slightly more difficult to accommodate within a distribution framework of preferences.

Where the literature focuses on direct preferences for macroeconomic out-comes, a revised interpretation would focus on direct preferences for distributive outcomes with indirect macroeconomic effects. Such a change would not require rewriting any of the equations, but would imply a different notion of "credibility"—one focusing more broadly on the consistency of government policies with the maintenance of price stability, rather than deriving from a narrow focus on personal or institutional commitment to a price stability rule. Within this context, politicians might lack credibility because they try to satisfy too large a constituency or too many different elements within the electorate, rather than because they (are expected to) attempt to exploit a short-run Philips curve trade-off or create a surprise inflation.

The argument for central bank independence is strengthened in both cases. From the political business cycle standpoint, the principal advantage of an independent central bank is to mitigate the influence of distributive conflict on monetary conditions and, *in extremis*, to shield politicians from the temptation to resort to destructive macroeconomic manipulation (Bailey 1956). Similar advantages also operate in the realm of policy credibility. On the one hand, an independent central bank—unbeholden to any specific distributive outcome—will be consistent with a broader range of other government policies than a central bank that is assigned to satisfy a particular constituency. On the other hand, the cost of conflict between the government and the central bank will increase the likelihood that some other policy will give way rather than monetary policy in the event of a broader inconsistency in the government's distributive programs. Such arguments already exist in the literature on central bank independence, and yet they receive renewed importance within a distributive framework.

The distributive framework also helps to integrate other arguments about central bank independence and the political determinants of macroeconomic outcomes into the mainstream of the literature. Specifically, the distributive framework helps establish a common causal mechanism (distributive conflict) as the link between institutional arrangements and macroeconomic outcomes. Thus, following Bernhard (1998), it should be possible to explain the incidence of central bank independence as a function of the (potential) importance of distributive conflict within and between political parties. Alternatively, following Calmfors and Driffill (1988), it should be possible to identify other institutional correlates of favorable macroeconomic outcomes. In turn, such institutions may complement or substitute for central bank independence (Hall and Franzese 1998; Bleaney 1996).

Focus on distributive conflict also helps to account for some of the empirical anomalies in the existing literature. Thus, for example, the revised argument for policy credibility is consistent with Beck's (1987) findings that inflation tends to accelerate during election quarters in the United States despite the political independence of the Federal Reserve. As Beck notes, such inflation does not result from the manipulation of monetary instruments but rather from the monetary accommodation of increased government outlays. The Fed's governors are not bowing to political pressure, however, neither are they pushing against the wind. The revised credibility argument is also consistent with Lohmann's (1998) claim that the behavioral independence of the German Bundesbank is an inverse function of the ease with which the sitting government could cobble together a coalition in support of reforming the bank's statutes.

However, being consistent with too many arguments is not necessarily a virtue. The claim that adoption of a distributive framework would allow us to retain the status quo is hardly a ringing endorsement—particularly as it is far from clear that adherence to a distributive framework over the past two decades would have fostered anything beyond the nihilism suggested by Brunner (1975). Even clarifying positions within the existing literature is not enough. To warrant adoption, a distributive framework has to account for something that the assumption of direct and relative macroeconomic preferences cannot. And it does.

Within the context of distributive preferences it is possible to dispense with ad hoc cultural explanations for comparative macroeconomic performance. Recall that popular preferences no longer attach to macroeconomic outcomes, but rather to distributive outcomes. As a result, the institutional intermediation of political pressures and distributive outcomes is all that necessarily differs from one country to the next. Thus, for example, the favorable record of German inflation derives not from some vague "culture of price stability" but instead results from a complex and overlapping network of institutions for resolving distributive conflict without jeopardizing monetary stability (McNamara and Jones 1996). The strength of German direct and absolute preferences for price stability may be unique—and Loedel (1999, 26–38) makes a strong case that they are in the context of Germany's own history. However, to the extent to which all populations share direct and absolute preferences about macroeconomic outcomes, with the implication that poor performance is always an unintended consequence, the relative strength of German preferences is more relevant to understanding institutional design than performance per se (which is essentially Bernhard's [1999] claim).

A focus on distributive preferences also makes it possible to encompass changes in the pattern of macroeconomic performance across relatively consistent institutional conditions without having to invoke an *ex ante* change in direct and relative preferences for macroeconomic outcomes. This argument is made in general terms by Rowthorne (1992), who finds that the influence of centralized wage bargaining on macroeconomic outcomes can be moderated through the introduction of a notional variable for "cooperative behavior." The more willing economic groups are to cooperate with one another, the better the macroeconomic outcomes within a constant institutional environment. The reverse is also true, and an increase in conflictive behavior results in a worsening of macroeconomic performance. Moreover, for Rowthorne as for Gordon (1975), the motivation for conflict and cooperation is distributive.

The hypothesis that macroeconomic outcomes are affected by a change in the intensity of distributive conflict can be made subject to empirical research more easily than the alternative hypothesis concerning a change in direct and relative macroeconomic preferences or a change in cultural economic attributes. Thus, for example, it is easier to find evidence of the distributive coalition behind recent Dutch improvements in unemployment than it is to explain how the Dutch were suffused with a spirit of cooperation at the start of the 1980s (Jones 1999). In this way, the research program supported by the distributive framework is richer than that traditionally used to drive research into political business cycles and policy credibility. At stake is not only the appropriate institutional context or the necessary balance between rules and discretion, but also an understanding of the conditions under which distributive conflict is most likely to increase and to decrease.

EMU AND THE DEMOCRATIC DEFICIT

Within the context of this argument, EMU is irrelevant to European democracy because democratic principles need operate only at the level of the member states. In turn, the member states delegate responsibility for monetary policy to the ECB and are held accountable by their electorates for the performance of that delegation. From this perspective, European integration is driven by and controlled by the actions of democratically constituted member states. Importantly, this state-centrism is true by definition and not in empirical terms. It derives directly from the dual assumptions that all values can be made fungible and that politics is only about winners and losers. However, clearly such assumptions do not reflect the whole reality that is European integration (Dyson and Featherstone 1999). Therefore at this stage in the analysis it is appropriate to accept that analytic reliance on distributive preferences may suffer from many of the same shortcomings as the analytic reliance on macroeconomic preferences that it replaces—it is a heuristic convention rather than a true reflection of the world as it is.

Nevertheless, by working back to distributive preferences rather than macroeconomic preferences we can sharpen our understanding of monetary integration even if we cannot elucidate the process in its entirety. Specifically, focusing on distributive preferences reduces the discussion of EMU and Europe's democratic deficit to three questions: Was EMU underwritten by a Europe-wide distributive coalition? Does the existence of EMU somehow constrain the member states or their citizenry in their desire to undertake redistribution either at the European level or at the national level? Will the operation of Europe's monetary union likely heighten the intensity of distributive conflict within and between Europe's member states? If the answer to all of these questions is negative, then the construction of EMU has no negative impact on the democratic character of Europe's constitution. There has been no conspiracy, there are no limitations on the fulfillment of popular aspirations, and there is unlikely to be any concerted backlash against EMU, against the European Union, or against the member states themselves.

Indeed, the preponderance of evidence suggests that EMU is democratically a non-event. To begin with, and elaborating on arguments made in chapters 1 and 2, it is almost impossible to find evidence of any coherent transnational coalition of interests underwriting the project to their own benefit.[9] A few authors have found a distributive basis for *national* support for EMU, however none has been able to establish coherent linkages between these distributive groups across Europe as a whole.[10] Indeed, the pattern of European monetary integration appears best explained by the combination of ideational conformity and distributive idiosyncrasy.[11]

Second, and drawing again on the analysis in chapter 2, EMU places no constraint on the redistribution of income at either the European or national levels. While the member states have agreed to limit their debts and deficits, they have neither accepted nor imposed any constraint on the size of government spending as a percentage of total output or on the size of distributive policies as a percentage of total government spending. Moreover, the creation of Europe's monetary union has—if anything—increased pressure for the construction of a Europe-wide tax and transfer system. Such pressure has been resoundingly rejected by the member states. And, along similar lines, voters in the member states have made clear their resistance to any change in the status of their national net contributions to EU coffers (Jones 1998). Finally, to the extent to which EMU does constrain national politicians from redistributing large amounts of income across time by running up deficits and debts, this constraint more closely reflects a growing awareness of the limits of social democracy in globalized financial markets than any requirements of monetary integration per se.

Once these first two questions are answered, the argument that EMU is somehow inherently undemocratic lacks analytic basis. Thus while it may be the case that the Maastricht Treaty fails to provide adequate means through which national and European politicians can supervise their delegation of monetary authority to the ECB—and the adequacy of the ECB's reporting strategy as outlined in chapter 2 is a subject about which reasonable people can disagree—such failings need not hinder the functioning of European democracy.

Indeed, if anything, the adaptation of Europe's member states to EMU may yield a positive impact of monetary union on the practice of democratic accountability. Where before, national politicians may have relied on macroeconomic manipulation to absorb the externalities generated by their attempts to reward too many groups within the electorate at the same time, EMU promises to internalize the costs of excess. Moreover, thanks to the stability pact and to the independence of Europe's central bank, politicians must conduct their redistribution through fiscal means instruments that are not only more efficient but also more transparent. Echoing Bailey (1956), politicians may have resorted to excessive inflation for the simple reason that the costs were hidden from the voters. Now that is no longer the case. In this sense, at least, EMU does not threaten democracy but rather strengthens it.

With reference to the third question—concerning whether EMU will somehow increase distributive conflict within Europe—the evidence is mixed. Despite a wealth of economic analysis about the possibility for asymmetries in macroeconomic performance that are exacerbated by the operation of Europe's common monetary policy, evidence of heightened distributive tensions is little apparent. Indeed, Europe's member states already seem to have made considerable progress in adapting their national distributive formulas to the constraints and possibilities of monetary integration. Moreover, as with the distributive groups in support of EMU, such adaption is more clearly idiosyncratic than trans-European in nature.

NOTES

1. The point is made in greater detail by Verdun (1998) and Elgie (1998).

2. Commentators on earlier drafts of this chapter have questioned the underlying notion of democracy. For purposes of this argument, however, a precise definition is unnecessary. All that is required is that democracies necessarily involve some representation of popular interests either in the exercise of sovereign authority or in the delegation of such authority. The debate here is whether monetary policy inherently requires direct representation or whether it can legitimately be delegated elsewhere. My argument is that such delegation cannot be ruled out a priori.

3. For the microeconomic perspective, see Krueger (1990).

4. This point is stressed by Downs (1957, 38) who emphasizes that "only benefits which voters become conscious of by election day can influence their voting decisions; otherwise their behavior would be irrational."

5. For an excellent survey of this literature, see Forder (1998).

6. The emphasis on utility and the prior allusion to research programs are not intended to highlight detailed Lakatosian presuppositions so much as to suggest the existence of different criteria for selecting foundational assumptions of which "fruitfulness" ranks among the most important. See, for example, Miller (1987, 197–199).

7. This is the reverse of the point made in chapter 1 about the distinction between market values and subjective values.

8. Obviously, a more sophisticated version of this same point would have to account for externalities as well as the organizational problems of collective action.

9. The same claim may not apply to epistemic communities, where some evidence does exist that central bankers and monetary economists had a disproportionate influence over the design of EMU (Verdun 1998). Crucially, however, such influence reflects epistemological and not distributive considerations and so does not factor into the present analysis per se. The claim that having like-minded individuals control the process of institutional organizations beyond the influence of popular preferences is somehow inherently undemocratic may have currency, but it is outside the scope of this argument.

10. See, for example, Frieden (1996) and Oatley (1997).

11. For ideational conformity, see McNamara (1998). For distributive idiosyncrasy, see Frieden and Jones (1998) and Frieden (1998).

4

+

Symmetry:
Mobilization and Adjustment

Whether Europe's economic and monetary union (EMU) necessarily poses a problem for European democracy is only the smaller part of the problem. Whether EMU can retain the support of Europe's democratic electorates is the larger part. Simply, EMU did not get off to an auspicious start. Although launched with much fanfare in January 1999, the single European currency (the euro) soon collapsed in value relative to the U.S. dollar. Worse, concern arose that the monetary union would fall apart even before Europe's national currencies could be replaced in 2002. A prominent German banker complained about the euro's "weakness." The newly appointed president of the European Commission, Romano Prodi, suggested that Italy would be unable to meet the obligations of membership. And a group of economists working in the research division of the International Monetary Fund (IMF) argued that Europe's currencies are still vulnerable to speculative attack (Berthold et al. 1999).[1] Meanwhile, European unemployment remained above 10 percent of the workforce and Europe's center-left policymakers appeared unable to agree on how best to respond (Dyson 1999a). Given the potential for lasting disagreement over how to manage the monetary union, the prospects for EMU's immediate future look grim. At the extreme, as Martin Feldstein (1997a) has argued, Europe's member states may even go to war!

Still, looks can be deceiving and the future is usually less exciting than we would imagine. The problem is that, despite the debate that has surrounded Europe's EMU project, we still know very little about how the introduction of a single currency will affect how Europeans respond to economic change. The bulk of existing analysis focuses on the costs and benefits of the project—including the implications of differing institutional regimes—as well as the political motivation behind it. What it does not cover is the extent to which EMU will affect how different groups monitor developments in the economy, how they protect themselves from economic misfortune, and how they react to the necessity of changing either what they produce or where and how they produce it. Rather, most of the existing work on EMU *assumes*, and does not analyze, the political economy of adjustment.

This distinction between assumption and analysis is important. On close examination, the assumptions made about the political economy of adjustment in Europe are open to question. For example, when Rolf Breuer, chairman of Deutschebank, claimed that the rapid drop of the euro against the dollar undermined the currency's credibility he went on to point out that the change in relative values would actually be good for European exports during a period of otherwise slow growth. His assumption, then, is that Europeans care about the external value of the currency even when that value is unrelated (or inversely related) to European economic performance. Such a claim may be plausible in empirical terms no matter how illogical it appears. The history of the member states provides numerous examples of unpopular but necessary devaluations. Nevertheless, such an illogical assumption is a strange basis for asserting that the euro's depreciation during its first six months is an "embarrassment." Moreover, Breuer's belief that Europeans attach symbolic importance to the external value of the euro contradicts one of the foundations of the theoretical literature on monetary integration, which is that popular concern about exchange rates should decrease as the size of the monetary union increases (Mundell 1961, 662–663).

The economists at the IMF also rely on questionable assumptions. In their analysis, they doubt that "further rises in unemployment in EMU member countries are politically sustainable" and therefore suggest that national politicians may choose to leave EMU "as the costs of staying inside . . . become too large to bear" (Berthold et al. 1999, 23). The assumption here is not that EMU causes unemployment—a claim that they make great efforts to justify in their analysis—but rather that any political mobilization resulting from a rise in unemployment will focus on participation in EMU rather than on any one of the numerous other factors that contribute to the jobs crisis. Even if we accept the claim that EMU contributes to Europe's unemployment problem that is no reason to believe that membership is the only or even the most important factor behind any rise in the number of people affected. Of course it is conceivable that opposition parties or other groups representing the interests of the unemployed will attempt to use EMU membership as a rallying point. However, Eurobarometer public opinion polling reveals substantial commitment to EMU in all of the participating countries, and such commitment usually crosses traditional party divides (Eurobarometer 1999). Moreover, even if EMU does cause unemployment that does not mean exiting from EMU will create jobs. Therefore, the belief that political mobilization in response to unemployment will center on EMU membership can only be regarded as a weak basis upon which to conclude that "large asymmetric shocks during the transition phase might constitute a serious challenge to the viability of EMU" (Berthold et al. 1999, 24).

Martin Feldstein's assumptions are almost purely speculative. Where the IMF economists suggested that political mobilization in reaction to a rise in unemployment would organize around membership in EMU, Feldstein (1997a, 60–62) assumes a cumulative four-step chain of causality. First, EMU would encourage deeper integration among participating countries. Second, "there would be important disagreements among the EMU member countries about the goals and methods of monetary policy." Third, such disagreements could underscore "incompatible expectations about the sharing of power." And fourth, disagreement over methods and expectations could escalate into armed conflict within the monetary union, between EMU members and non-members, and between Europe and the outside world. Drawing upon the experience of the American Civil War, Feldstein cautions that "a formal union is no guarantee against an intra-European war." Therefore, he concludes that the prospect of war "is too real a possibility to ignore."

Feldstein's reality exists by assumption. Indeed, the same criticism could be applied (though perhaps with weaker force) to the claims made by the IMF economists and by the German banker. Under different assumptions, EMU's launch could be a success as easily as a failure. Following Cowles and Smith (2000, 4), we could conclude that the euro's performance so far demonstrates "that [the euro is] behaving as a 'normal' internationally traded currency"—all of which depreciate relative to other currencies from time to time, and few of which have ever sparked either a limited secession or a full-scale war.[2] However, such contrasting assessments of Europe's performance become a test of wills between EMU supporters and detractors—much like the debates underway between the pro- and anti-Europe wings of the UK Conservative Party and arguably just as unenlightening.

The problem is that argument by competing assumption can provide only limited insight on how EMU is likely to develop in the near or distant future. A more robust framework for analysis is required, one that explains both how Europeans are adjusting to EMU and how EMU is changing the pattern of European adjustment. The purpose of this chapter is to examine how the creation of EMU has resulted in a new political economy of adjustment in Europe. The central claim is that European adaptation to

EMU is changing how Europeans adjust to other economic developments as well. In turn, these changes in the pattern of European adjustment will affect the stability of EMU. Some of these changes were anticipated by the economists and policymakers who designed Europe's monetary union, and others were not. Therefore, some reconsideration of the project may be warranted. However, such reconsideration can only take place on the basis of analysis and not assumption.

The chapter is divided into five sections. The first argues that while existing analysis of EMU has paid considerable attention to the problem of economic adjustment, it has assumed (or ignored) the political and economic mechanisms that make adjustment relevant to the sustainability of EMU. The second examines how processes of adjustment differ across institutional environments. The third analyzes how the introduction of the single currency is affecting national patterns of adjustment. The fourth expands the analysis to encompass transnational processes of adaptation. The fifth concludes with an assessment of the risks this new political economy of adjustment poses for Europe.

EMU AND ADJUSTMENT

Existing analysis of Europe's economic and monetary union incorporates strong assumptions about the political economy of adjustment because it centers on the member states. For example, economists view EMU as a problem of macroeconomics—whether and how the member states should sacrifice control over their national currencies and therefore also over domestic monetary policy. Such an approach has the advantage of providing a single framework for member states to use in making the choice about participation, referred to as the theory of optimum currency areas. The idea is that politicians and their economic advisers can rely on a theoretical notion of the "optimum" currency area as a benchmark in determining whether their national currency is too small or, presumably, too large. Using this theory and its accompanying criteria, economists can also make broad estimates of the relative costs and benefits of a given country or group of countries adopting fixed or flexible exchange rates (Kawai 1992; Tavlas 1993). From the member-state perspective, economists support EMU when the cost of sacrificing policy autonomy is less than the benefits of irrevocably fixing exchange rates.

Political scientists view EMU as a problem of international relations—whether and how the member states can make a binding or "irrevocable" commitment to fix the value of their currencies relative to one another (and therefore also perhaps commit to other modes of behavior). Here the advantage lies not in evaluating the participation of a single member state, but rather in making assessments about the sustainability of the system as a whole. Political scientists support EMU when the institutions or agents responsible for maintaining the commitment to irrevocably fixed exchange rates are stronger than the incentive for member states to defect from the monetary union (Cohen 1994). In both cases, the member states provide the basic (and irreducible) unit for analysis.

Thus, while economists and political scientists refer to actors or processes within the member states—such as sub-national regions or economic sectors—they do so for one of three reasons:

- a vertical comparison across levels of aggregation (EMU is like a member state);
- a horizontal comparison across the member states (some member states are more suitable for participation than others); or,
- a reductio ad absurdum (Mundell's [1961, 660] famous dictum that "the optimum currency area is the region").[3]

Meanwhile, the member states are assumed to be subject to a common rationality—the relative cost of irrevocably fixing exchange rates is the incentive for countries to defect from the monetary union. The assumption is that when the relative cost of participation in EMU is high enough, Europe's member states will stay out of the monetary union in order to maintain, or will leave the monetary union in order to regain, their policy autonomy.[4] When this assumption does not hold, both economists and political scientists are wont to decry the influence of a "politics" beyond rationality and to regard the situation as either whimsically temporary or practically unsustainable. No matter how fervent the desire to create EMU at a particular point in time, the inexorable logic of costs and benefits must eventually take hold.[5]

This synthesis of economic and political science perspectives on EMU begs two questions: First, what are the "costs" of sacrificing policy autonomy by irrevocably fixing exchange rates? Second, how and to what extent are states motivated by such costs? The answer to the first of these questions is relatively straightforward. According to the theory of optimum currency areas, the cost of sacrificing policy autonomy derives from the difficulty of economic adjustment. Because prices and wages do not move downward easily in the marketplace, firms cannot respond efficiently to changes in demand for their output. As a result, when the demand for exports falls in foreign markets, the government of the exporting country is faced with a trade-off: Either it can try to stimulate demand at home to compensate for the shortfall (and run the risk of accelerating inflation) or it can accept an increase in unemployment. Alternatively, the government can allow its currency to depreciate relative to its foreign markets and so avoid (much of) the inflation-unemployment trade-off. The cost of EMU, therefore, is the lack of exchange-rate depreciation as a policy alternative as well as whatever inflation or unemployment that results from the country's adjustment to the shortfall in foreign demand. This cost is higher the more often a country suffers from shocks (or sudden changes) to its exports and the more important the shocks.[6]

The usefulness of exchange rates in obviating or facilitating economic adjustment is disputed. In theoretical terms, the cost of giving up the exchange rate as a policy instrument rests on the assumption that changes in the exchange rate can influence developments in the real economy—which is to say output and jobs. In empirical terms, it rests on the belief that policymakers can manage exchange rates and that they will do so to facilitate adjustment problems (Wyplosz 1997). Even accepting the theoretical condition, the empirical questions remain in contention. Few if any currency areas can be explained on the basis of an economic rationality (Goodhart 1995, 449). Moreover, while there is some evidence that countries (and currency markets) engage in exchange rate intervention in response to economic shocks (Bayoumi and Eichengreen 1998), there is little evidence that movements in the exchange rate are useful in stabilizing employment—or, surprisingly, that countries suffer from a significant shock-adjustment problem in terms of unemployment (Belke and Gros 1999). Thus, even if governments can use exchange rates to facilitate adjustment problems they may not want to do so and it may not be necessary.

The synthesis of economic and political science perspectives on EMU, then, rests on the question of state motivations. To reiterate, how and to what extent are states actually motivated by the costs of foregoing the exchange rate as an adjustment mechanism? It is in answer to this question that the strong assumption about the political economy of adjustment implicit in the member-state centered approach is most apparent. Simply, the process through which any shock-adjustment problem is translated into a demand for state autonomy over exchange rates is a black box, with economic shocks on one side and political action on the other. When firms experience a shock to their exports they will pressure national politicians to exit from the monetary union.

Opening the box is difficult. Any attempt to establish the micromechanisms behind member state preferences for or against participation in EMU threatens both the generalizability and the parsimony that are the principal advantages of existing economic and political science approaches to monetary union.[7] Moreover, without such microfoundations, large statistical comparisons of member state attitudes toward EMU based on structural factors such as trade integration or left-right coalition ideology are incapable of replacing the black box with an endogenous model of "rational maximizing behavior."[8] Not

only do such studies derive their testable hypotheses from a macro—
rather than a microeconomic analysis of self-interest (and so reiterate
strong assumptions about individual or group rationality), but they
also rely on assumptions about the effectiveness of lobbying in influ-
encing policy outcomes. Therefore, while broad statistical comparisons
can facilitate the understanding of monetary integration as a process—
which, in fairness, is usually their objective—they shed little additional
light on the political economy of adjustment. Indeed, the results of such
studies are sometimes counterintuitive. For example, recent (and still
preliminary) analysis by Jeffry Frieden (1998) suggests that while particular interests may be able to influence exchange rate policy, that influence does not reflect (or correlate with) a country's suitability for
participation in EMU. Taken to its logical extreme, this finding suggests
that the sustainability of Europe's monetary union may be unrelated to
the political economy of adjustment altogether.

THE ROLE OF INSTITUTIONS

Nevertheless, it stands to reason that adjustment is an important issue
and therefore also a potential political problem. A sudden and unexpected
drop in income, whether to a firm or to an individual, is sure to provoke
some sort of reaction—in the marketplace, in the political arena, or on
both fronts at the same time. Empirical evidence that trade shocks do not
correlate with changes in the level of unemployment only serves to rule
out or mitigate one type of response (Belke and Gros 1999). Such evidence
cannot be interpreted to suggest that shocks are somehow irrelevant.
Therefore, in order to question the standard assumption about the political economy of adjustment—which is that firms will respond to economic
shocks by forcing governments to reconsider participation in EMU—it is
necessary to provide some alternative explanation for how reactions to
economic shocks play out.

Where the standard assumption is that the political response to an economic shock will be to call for a change in the exchange rate regime, the alternative is simply for firms and individuals to work through those institutions—patterns of behavior structured by rules, norms, conventions—that
already exist. Thus firms could respond to a sudden shortfall in foreign demand through a reduction in dividends, delayed investment, access to
credit facilities, or an internal reallocation of productive resources. Firms
could also call upon pre-existing government support mechanisms or they
could lobby for exceptional subsidies to be made available. If the shocks are
frequent enough, firms could engage in some type of insurance activity beforehand, whether directly through contracting arrangements and futures

markets, or indirectly through negotiations over flexible working-time and profit sharing with their employees. For their own part, the employees could protect their income by negotiating multi-period contracts, severance bonuses, or even private redundancy insurance. In short, the range of responses to shocks—and therefore also to uncertainty—is as varied as the activities of states and markets.

Two examples are sufficient to illustrate the point: Finland and Ireland. Both are member states located at the periphery of Europe's monetary union and both are widely regarded as likely to suffer a substantial shock-adjustment problem within EMU. Yet neither country seems ready to abandon membership. On the contrary, concern about the danger of economic shocks has been directed at domestic institutions and not at participation in EMU. The Irish chapter of the European Anti-Poverty Network has called for "effective labor market and industrial support policies" to redistribute the costs of adjustment at the national level (EAPN Ireland 1999). Meanwhile, Finnish representatives of industry and labor have agreed to make additional social insurance contributions in order to create a financial buffer for use in the event of an adverse shock (EIRO 1997).

Of course economists and political scientists are aware of the variety of responses to shocks that are available to firms and individuals. However, such variety is cumbersome to analyze and difficult to rely upon in predicting outcomes. For example, it is easier to identify a correlation between the size of the trading sector and the size of the government than to anticipate what form government intervention will take (Rodrick 1998). Worse, many of the mechanisms used by firms and individuals to respond to shocks work at cross purposes, being helpful under one set of circumstances or to a particular group, and harmful under different circumstances or to another group. The institutions used in anticipating or responding to sudden shocks to income are potentially inefficient, and they have important re-distributive properties. Thus, as Blanchard and Wolfers (1999) argue, economic shocks by themselves cannot explain Europe's unemployment but the interaction between economic shocks and domestic institutions can.

A good example of the good and bad sides of institutionalized adjustment is multi-period wage contracting. Multi-period contracts protect employees from sudden shocks to their income. As a result, such contracts also explain to a large extent the downward price and wage stickiness in the marketplace. Firms may need to lower wages in response to an economic shock but—because of multi-period contracting—cannot. In turn, this stickiness lies at the heart of the unemployment-inflation trade-off that governments would manipulate the exchange rate to avoid in the first place. If it were not for wage rigidity (that is, if employees would accept a change in their wages from one day to the next), then countries would not need to maintain control over the exchange rate.

The bulk of empirical evidence suggests that firms and individuals respond to shocks through institutional mechanisms rather than relying on exchange rate autonomy. Such evidence includes not only Belke and Gros's (1999, 21–23) finding that changes in the exchange rate do not correlate with changes in unemployment, but also Frieden's (1998) observation that economic "suitability" for monetary union is unrelated with the choice of exchange rate regime. Firms are generally more interested in how much their products cost in foreign markets than in the institution through which domestic prices are translated into foreign currency. Indeed, case studies of how the member states prepared for EMU demonstrate that national approaches depended more heavily on the structure of domestic markets and state institutions than on any of the criteria economists use to define an optimal currency area (Frieden and Jones 1998).[9] More fundamentally, the central importance of institutionalized responses to shocks is evident in the fact that virtually no existing currency area is optimal—and many are clearly sub-optimal—from an economic perspective.

This point can be overstated. The argument is not that adjustment is irrelevant to EMU but rather that Europe's monetary union encompasses a variety of national institutional environments where many mechanisms for adjusting to or avoiding shocks are already provided. Within this context, EMU can be interpreted as a mechanism for adjustment—or for obviating adjustment—in its own right. Such an interpretation is evident in the broad claims made by the European Commission that EMU is necessary for the completion of the internal market (Emerson et al. 1992). It is also apparent in the attitudes of European business leaders. From the perspective of the firm, exchange rate volatility is a shock with effects that are often more important than other shocks to foreign trade (Gros 1998). The irrevocable fixing of exchange rates between European countries represents an institutional response to the threat of exchange rate volatility.[10] Exchange rate stability will not necessarily increase trade, but it will decrease the uncertainty that surrounds it (Bacchetta and van Wincoop 1998; Sekkat 1998). As a result, monetary union is popular among large enterprises even in countries where general opposition is strong.[11]

The advantage of viewing EMU as one institution among many is that it shifts the focus from optimality per se. The irrevocable fixing of exchange rates and the constitution of a single monetary policy are no more "optimal" than any other set of institutions in the economy (or in the polity). Like other institutions for responding to the problem of economic uncertainty, EMU should be expected to work better under some conditions and to offer advantages to some groups, but to work less well under different conditions and to present disadvantages to other groups. EMU should be expected to be inefficient and to have important re-distributive properties. From this standpoint, the link between the theory of optimum currency areas and the debate between fixed and flexible exchange rates is clear: Should governments intervene or should they let the markets decide? If all institutions are sub-optimal, then perhaps the absence of institutions is better. Moreover, the assumption that sudden shocks to exports would result in pressure to recapture exchange-rate autonomy is wishful thinking from the proponents for flexible exchange rates *qua* market forces: Better a change in the exchange rate regime than an inefficient institutional arrangement.

The institutional approach to EMU also directs attention to the question of institutional interaction and away from the structural characteristics—size of the trading sector, diversity of exports, and so forth—embedded in the theory of optimum currency areas. The economics literature has long recognized the intermediary role of institutions in support of sub-optimal currency areas or inefficient monetary unions. Robert Mundell (1961) introduced the notion of the optimum currency area as that space within which adjustment already took place through efficient factor markets, meaning markets for capital and labor. Later, Peter Kenen (1969, 47) suggested that national (read monetary union-wide) fiscal institutions might play a vital role in facilitating the adjustment process. Union-wide fiscal systems redistribute financial resources across regions as well as across individuals and so could absorb any shocks to income and thus facilitate adjustment.

In the optimum currency area literature, the focus is on maximizing the efficiency of adjustment and therefore on general welfare effects. For the present argument, however, the role of domestic institutions is not to render the process of adjustment more efficient. Two or more inefficient institutional arrangements do not add up to an efficient system and neither should they be expected to do so. Rather the effect of compounding institutional arrangements is to redistribute the cost of anticipating or responding to economic shocks in a manner that is or can be—at least in broad terms—politically predetermined. The shock adjustment problem is a problem of redistribution and not efficiency. Therefore the institutional solution should be expected to have distributive outcomes as well.

The link between domestic adjustment mechanisms and distributive outcomes is well established in the literature on comparative political economy (see, for example, Gourevitch 1986). In broad terms, groups in power design institutions that will redistribute the costs of the shock-adjustment problem onto others who have less political influence. In this context, the implications of EMU for exchange-rate policy autonomy are only of secondary or derivative concern. The principal political focus of economic actors centers on the design of domestic fiscal and market institutions far more than on responding to a particular shock or shocks. This proposition explains the central dilemma concerning the attitudes of Europe's heads of state and government toward EMU: Although economists have consistently argued that the shock-adjustment problem should be addressed at the European level either through the adoption of a union-wide tax and transfer system or through the facilitation of union-wide labor mobility, the heads of state and government have consistently refused even to open the discussion. The member states would be hard-pressed to design a union-wide system for facilitating adjustment without generating undesired distributive effects and do not perceive the political support for any institutionalized and union-wide redistribution (von Hagen and Hammond 1998; Jones 1998).

DOMESTIC ADJUSTMENT

The problem of member state adjustment within EMU is not whether economic shocks will occur but how the costs will be redistributed. To what extent does participation in EMU affect the ability of groups in power to predetermine the distribution of costs arising from adjustment to economic shocks? This is the question that has moved to the center of concerns about EMU in the participating countries and the answer is as yet unclear.

Recall from the start of this chapter that the political economy of adjustment encompasses how different groups monitor developments in the economy, how they protect themselves from economic misfortune, and how they react to the necessity of changing either what they produce, or where and how they produce it. Participation in EMU has an impact on all three aspects of this process—by changing the information content of prices, by altering the hierarchy of risks, and by facilitating the movement of capital, goods, and services. In turn, these changes have obscured the distribution of adjustment costs under existing national institutions. Thus while public opinion within the EMU member states is generally supportive of monetary union, respondents to public opinion polls are concerned about how much monetary integration will cost them in particular. Moreover, their attention is directed not at the possibility of an unforeseen shock necessitating adjustment under EMU, but rather at the imminent adjustment to the single currency itself.

To illustrate this point it is useful to look at the rank-ordering of concerns expressed about the euro in 1998 public opinion polls (European Commission 1999a). Across the fifteen EU member states, 58 percent of respondents feared losing money when exchanging their national currencies into euros, 55 percent worried about bank charges for converting their accounts, and 52 percent expressed concerns about how retailers would changeover prices. Meanwhile, only 43 percent of respondents foresaw difficulties in "getting used" to the euro, 42 percent worried about mixing up national and European currencies, and 38 percent feared they would not be able to understand euro prices. Although clearly there are some psychological hurdles to overcome, the adjustment to the single currency was not so much the problem as who pays for it. Moreover, perceptions of inequity resulting from Europe's new single currency can persist even under ideal circumstances, and can have real impact through the cancellation of contracts or other disruptions to economic activity (Servet et al. 1998, 14–15).[12] Small wonder, then, that Europeans were overwhelmingly in favor of prolonging the introduction of the single currency for so long a period of time as possible (Eurobarometer 1999, 69). As it turned out, the speed of the changeover exceeded even the most optimistic estimates.

The process of converting denominations is only the most obvious impact of introducing the single currency. Less obvious, though still important, is the elimination of currency risk as a factor in making investment decisions. With the irrevocable fixing of exchange rates and the consequent reduction in transaction costs, Europe's marketplace is no longer subdivided into geographic regions with more and less stable domestic currencies. In other words, EMU eliminates two of the most important sources of geographic division in Europe with the effect being to create a more homogenous and competitive environment for business. Inadvertently, however, EMU also increases the relative importance of investment risks associated with differing national institutional environments. Any institutional difference across countries resulting in relatively higher production costs—or any fiscal policy change resulting in a rise in relative wages—can now exercise greater influence over the pattern of investment both within and across national boundaries (Barrell and Pain 1998). By implication, geographic risk remains a factor under EMU, but the assignment of good and bad places for investment has changed.[13]

A final challenge for domestic adjustment strategies arises from the operation of Europe's single monetary policy. Over the long run, the European Central Bank should provide for low inflation and low interest rates, thereby lowering the cost of capital for European firms. The introduction of the single currency should deepen European financial markets and thereby lower the cost of capital even further. These two factors together—stable financial conditions and greater liquidity—represent strong advantages that will accrue to all participants in Europe's monetary union. That is not to say that all member states will benefit equally. Countries with long histories of financial instability or with relatively limited capital markets will benefit more than those—such as Germany—with long histories of stability and already substantially liquid markets. Nevertheless, all participants will benefit. In terms of lowering the cost of capital, EMU is a win-win proposition.

The cost of maintaining Europe's stable and liquid financial markets is not so easily distributed. Changes in Europe's monetary policy will likely have different effects in different parts of the monetary union - and specifically across systematic differences in the borrowing practices of consumers or firms (Ramaswamy and Sløk 1998). Whether households rely on fixed or flexible mortgages, and firms rely on bank, bond, or equity financing can all influence the real effects of monetary policy changes within a particular member state. Moreover, econometric evidence from the United States reveals that monetary policy changes can impact more strongly across some types of industry than others (Carlino and DeFina 1998a). Member states which concentrate their economic activity in interest rate-sensitive areas such as manufacturing or construction will experience stronger real effects from changes in monetary policy than other member states. On both counts, therefore, it is possible to identify member states that will consistently suffer more than others from changes in the European monetary policy stance and for structural reasons (Carlino and DeFina 1998b; Ramaswamy and Sløk 1998).[14] These countries will face an additional set of adjustments under EMU—and it would be wishful thinking to conclude that they will abandon their institutional differences altogether.

In addition to these structural differences, the monetary stance taken by the ECB will not always be appropriate to macro-economic conditions in each and every member state. This is the concern most often raised in Britain about joining EMU, and it has received considerable attention in the economics literature. Nevertheless, the universal appropriateness of European monetary policy is likely to be less important to EMU's future than the differential impact of monetary policy changes. To begin with, the possibility that Europe's monetary stance will not suit domestic macroeconomic conditions is one that faces each of the member states—rather than those with peculiar credit markets or industrial structures. Second any such discrepancy between European monetary policy and domestic macroeconomic conditions can be mediated through changes in national fiscal policy—even while adhering to the terms of the broad agreement between the member states to limit fluctuations in their fiscal positions (Gros and Jones 1997). A union-wide fiscal system may be more efficient, but it is unnecessary (Bayoumi and Masson 1998). Finally, the emergence and strengthening of a "European business cycle" should mitigate the macroeconomic differences between countries.[15] As the member states of EMU move into a common pattern of slower and faster growth, the monetary stance of the ECB will become more generally appropriate even if member state reactions to monetary policy changes continue to differ.

Whatever the case, the adaptation of national adjustment processes remains national in scope. Thus while it is unclear how the costs of adjusting to EMU will be distributed, it is clear that the formula for distributing these costs will differ (characteristically) from one participating country to another. The flurry of activity within the member states indicates an important process of institutional adaptation but few signs of institutional convergence. This is particularly the case in the area of labor markets, where the member states are developing action plans for employment under European supervision but along explicitly national lines (Pierson, Forster, and Jones 1999). However, the claim also applies to national financial markets and product markets. Although there is considerable industrial restructuring underway (European Central Bank 1999b), the emergence of a European business cycle and the completion of the internal market have not resulted in a homogenization of national institutions.[16]

EUROPEAN ADJUSTMENT

A recurrent theme in this volume is that the institutional differences from one member state to the next make it difficult to identify stable coalitions of interests across countries. This problem was particularly evident at the European Commission, where officials in the information directorate often complained about the difficulty of consolidating the campaign in support of EMU. The process of winning the public over to monetary union was largely a piecemeal affair, with each member state taking a slightly different approach (Frieden and Jones 1998). Nevertheless, the creation of a monetary union is a European as well as a national event. Therefore, it is necessary to ask the extent to which EMU will affect how groups monitor developments in the economy, protect themselves from uncertainty, and respond to the need for change at the European level. Has EMU affected some fundamental shift in how Europe adjusts? The preliminary analysis is mixed both in terms of what is happening and whether it is good or bad.

To begin with, there is little indication that groups are organizing across national boundaries either for EMU or against. Moreover, and, as mentioned earlier, there is little support for the construction of Europe-wide institutions for facilitating adjustment in support of EMU: The heads of state and government have not agreed to the construction of a union-wide tax and transfer system and they are unlikely to encourage any wide-scale labor mobility across national boundaries. In this sense, EMU is in many ways more an economic and monetary union of European member states than a European monetary union.

That said, EMU has generated some important and Europe-wide effects. The most troubling of these is in the area of wage bargaining. And, the trouble is that while the mechanisms at work are ambiguous, the potential consequences are important—particularly in distributive terms (Calmfors 1998). According to some analysis, Europe's labor markets will become more competitive and its workforce necessarily more flexible, with the consequence that conditions for workers will deteriorate. Other analyses suggest that real wages could increase in Europe's German core, benefitting employed workers at the expense of increasing numbers of the unemployed. Alternatively, real wages could increase in particular groups of countries—such as those that presently rely on centrally coordinated wage bargaining or those that are presently poorer and less productive, and therefore have lower nominal wages. Each of these prospects raises the possibility of a significant redistribution of income at the European level and beyond the control of national institutions.

The crucial components of such analyses are the mechanisms. Depending upon the assumptions at work, the impact of EMU on wage bargaining could operate through any one of a number of channels:

- competition in product markets;
- transparency of relative wage rates; and,
- signaling between monetary authorities and wage bargainers.

Increased competition in product markets could encourage trade unions to moderate their wage claims and to accept more flexible contracts and work practices (Danthine and Hunt 1994). Greater transparency in relative wage rates could encourage a convergence in pay scales across countries (Jones 1998). And a change in the pattern of signaling between monetary authorities and wage negotiators could lead to real wage increases in Germany, in countries with centralized wage bargaining institutions, or even across Europe (Hall and Franzese 1998; Iversen 1998; Soskice and Iversen 1998). Such possibilities are contested, and under different assumptions the impact of EMU on wage bargaining can result in a general reduction in unemployment (Grüner and Hefeker 1999). Nevertheless, the prospect of substantial Europe-wide changes in wage bargaining is unsettling.

The evidence from the wage negotiators themselves is equally ambiguous—although, in keeping with the general tenor of this chapter, it is not as exciting as it could be. A July 1999 survey of wage bargaining practices entitled "The 'Europeanization' of Collective Bargaining" produced characteristically ambivalent results (EIRO 1999). Wage negotiators in some countries—such as Ireland—have emphasized national wage bargaining as a means of maintaining competitiveness. Meanwhile, those in other countries have looked at the possibility of coordinating wage bargains across national boundaries: In September 1998, trade union representatives in Belgium, Germany, and the Netherlands agreed to coordinate their activities "in order to prevent possible competition on wages and working conditions, with the prospect it raises of a downward spiral." Moreover, similar diversity can be found at the sectoral level, with some sectors retaining a purely national focus while others—such as the metalworkers—exploring new possibilities for coordination across countries.

The impact of these different strategies of isolation and integration remains to be seen. Although wage negotiators are taking advantage of the single currency as a basis for making comparisons across countries, the role such comparisons play in setting wage claims is indeterminate. Even within multinational enterprises—where the existence of enterprise works councils greatly facilitates wage and benefit comparisons—the attitudes of wage negotiators tend to vary by sector, firm, and region. Even among the representatives of labor, the appropriate balance between the objective of coordination and the constraint of national and regional conditions is undecided. Finally, it is simply too soon to characterize the interaction between national wage negotiators and the European Central Bank. Thus, while there is considerable evidence of adaptation in the political economy of adjustment, the final distribution of costs is unclear. The potential for disruption remains unsettling and the evidence is mixed.

ADJUSTMENT AND THE POLITICS OF EMU

The ambiguous reaction of wage negotiators to EMU reveals a stable hierarchy of institutions for adjustment, with domestic institutions at the top and European institutions much farther down. In this sense, at least, the new political economy of adjustment in Europe is much like the old: What goes on inside the member states is more important than how the black boxes are put together. Of course there are exceptions to the rule. Should EMU result in a sudden strengthening of one domestic group over another—for example, by increasing the power of trade unions across Europe, and therefore within the member states—the resulting distributive conflict would be powerfully disruptive. This is the real concern about the impact of EMU on wage bargaining and, given the danger of rising unemployment or falling living standards, such concern is warranted. Nevertheless, despite the validity of the concern, the evidence of such a sudden shift in domestic coalitions has yet to materialize. Indeed, what is clear at the moment is that the impact of EMU has not been as dramatic as we might have feared.

If anything, the impact of EMU is likely to get even less dramatic. Given time to prepare, domestic groups are unlikely to allow themselves to be outmaneuvered as a result of the single currency. On this point, the verdict of European public opinion is clear. What matters is not that Europe has a single currency, but who pays for it, and how much opportunity there is to avoid paying more than a fair share of the cost. Moreover, the focus for reformist attention lies on the structure of national institutions and not European monetary bargains. If for some reason national institutional reforms are to prove inadequate, and some future constituencies are to complain about having received an inequitable share of the cost of adjustment, then national reform efforts are more likely to be re-doubled than European monetary integration is to be rolled back.

For EMU as for any big policy innovation, institutional reform and popular resistance are closely inter-connected. As national adaptations to EMU progress, national resistance to leaving Europe's monetary union will increase as well. This argument can be developed as a simple extension to Paul Pierson's (1996a) "new politics of the welfare state." Once domestic institutional arrangements have been adapted to operate within EMU, generating the motivation to change them again will be difficult. Auspicious or no, EMU became part of the status quo on 1 January 1999. Both popular resistance and institutional inertia now work in its favor.[17] Following the logic of this claim, EMU has less need for reform than for consolidation. Moreover, such consolidation will be un-dramatic (although welcome). From inauspicious beginnings, EMU will gradually recede into the background of European politics and economics—arguably where it belongs.

NOTES

1. For the record of public statements, see, respectively, "Euro Embarrassing, Says Deutsche Chief," *The Independent* July 17, 1999; "Prodi's Remarks Leave the Euro Bruised and Battered: Soon May Be Worth a U.S. Dollar," *Financial Post* June 22, 1999; and "Euro Warning on IMF Website Sparks Debate," *The Independent* August 2, 1999.

2. Barry Eichengreen (1998, 34) supported Feldstein's argument with the assertion that "there is no shortage of monetary unions which have disintegrated . . . where the decision to file for a political divorce led to the decision to go for a monetary divorce." This may be so. However, his suggestion that the political motivation for such schisms can be equated with a desire for policy autonomy is reductionist. Even had the leaders of multinational countries he cites as examples—Austria-Hungary, the Soviet Union, and Czechoslovakia—been enlightened enough to allow the introduction of sub-national currencies it is highly doubtful (to say the least) that these multinational conglomerations would have continued to exist. See, for example, Goodhart (1995, 448–449).

3. A principal exception to this trichotomy is the literature on the agglomeration effects of industrial activity under a single currency. This is dealt with below.

4. Consider the following citation from the *New Palgrave Dictionary of Money and Finance* under the heading "monetary unions": "Although the international

community tries to observe the rule '*pacta sunt servanda*,' history is full of examples of 'irrevocable commitments' to exchange rates that have broken down. The reason is simple: Assuming that national governments behave rationally, they will evaluate the costs and benefits of the fixed exchange rate union [according to economic criteria]. If the costs become overwhelming with respect to the benefits, the government concerned may be tempted to change the parity, even if this means breaking an international agreement. The evaluation of the costs and benefits, in fact, may vary over time, for example in relation to economic conditions and/or to preference functions of governments" (Gandolfo 1992, 768).

5. Indeed, this is the essence of Martin Feldstein's (1997b) critique of EMU in the *Journal of Economic Perspectives*.

6. This telling of the nominal exchange rate-adjustment story omits a range of complicating factors such as the possibility of price distortions resulting from asymmetric supply shocks and the nature of the demand stimulus. For a more comprehensive and yet still summary treatment, see Kawai (1992).

7. The obvious contrast is with endogenous models of trade protection, where the micro- foundations of firm behavior and political lobbying are more easily established.

8. The short quotation and the "black box" metaphor are taken from Magee, Brock, and Young (1989, 30–31). Two of the best attempts to "endogenize" national preferences for monetary regime types in Europe are Frieden (1996) and Oatley (1997).

9. The case studies are published in Pisani-Ferry, Hefeker, and Hughes Hallett (1997) and Jones, Frieden, and Torres (1998).

10. Indeed, while 62 percent of respondents in the fifteen EU member states believe EMU will reduce business costs and 48 percent believe it will decrease exchange rate volatility, only 37 percent believe it will result in faster growth and 29 percent expect it to create more jobs. See Eurobarometer (1999, 66).

11. Polling of business support for EMU in the UK has been the subject of considerable controversy. See "Pole Axed: The CBI's Survey Undermines Its Position on the Euro." *The Times* July 21, 1999; "The Proof of the Poll Is in the Interpretation." *The Financial Times* July 26, 1999. An interesting result, however, is that 30 percent of respondents could not or did not name what they thought to be "an appropriate competitive exchange rate" for the pound to enter EMU and 57 percent thought the pound should enter at 2.60 Deutschemarks or higher. By comparison, the average daily spot rate for the pound-Deutschemark exchange is 2.63 for the period from December 31, 1994, to August 5, 1999. The CBI poll can be found both on the CBI's own Website (www.cbi.org.uk) and on the MORI Website (www.mori.com).

12. For a comprehensive analysis of this subject see European Commission (1997b).

13. See, for example, "Turning European - The Euro has Brought about a Sector Allocation Approach to the Management of European Equities, but Investors Cannot Afford to Forget Geographical Considerations." *Investors Chronicle* July 23, 1999.

14. In reviewing much the same evidence, Dornbusch, Favero, and Giavazzi (1998) add that the impact of any change in monetary policy on the external value of the euro could compound the regional diversification of effects.

15. Artis and Zhang (1999) provide evidence that a European business cycle is emerging, but are cautious in asserting that this emergence is the result of European monetary integration. For the purpose of this argument, the trend is more important than the causality behind it.

16. In anticipation of this lack of institutional convergence, writers such as Richez-Battesti (1996) have called for the creation of a European welfare state. However, if anything, that prospect is even more remote than the establishment of a minimal union-wide fiscal stabilization mechanism.

17. The logic of the argument can be spelled out more explicitly as follows: Once established, the direct benefits of EMU participation are high and (too a large extent) narrowly concentrated among, for example, large enterprises and tourist associations. The costs of leaving EMU are high and concentrated as well—such as for banks and retailers. Meanwhile, the costs of staying in and the benefits of leaving are diffuse. Apart from the differential effects of European monetary policy changes, the shock-adjustment problems under EMU are difficult for groups to anticipate beforehand and the adjustment to EMU itself has already been incorporated in public attitudes. Indeed, even if we accept that such costs of staying and benefits of leaving are high, because they are diffuse—and because they can be redistributed through existing institutional arrangements—the motivation to avoid or attain them through collective action will be limited.

5

✢

Motivation: Insulation and the Welfare State

The creation of the European Union's economic and monetary union (EMU) is an attempt to provide a zone of macroeconomic stability in Europe. By implication, macroeconomic stability is something that the member states cannot generate individually for themselves. Yet if EMU promises to provide stability, it is relevant to ask at what cost. Implicit in this question is the concern that EMU as a solution may be worse than the challenges it addresses. Just because we can argue that the construction of EMU has promoted a new political economy of adjustment does not mean that it is good value for money.

What is at stake is the autonomy of the welfare state and, by extension, the capacity of Europe's member states to define their own political objectives. These stakes are most evident in reference to the challenges posed by global market forces. The reason for this is simple. "Globalization" as a framework of integrated national markets for goods, services, and (most important) capital has replaced the embedded liberalism that supported the "golden age" of the welfare state (Ruggie 1983; Scharpf 1999). In the process, the natural order of things has somehow become inverted. Where embedded liberalism meant that market integration took place only to the extent to which it did not conflict with the underlying values of separate welfare states, globalization implies that welfare states must operate only to the extent to which they do not hinder the functioning of shared (and integrated) markets (Ruggie 1995; McNamara 1998). The implications for policymakers are clear. Failure to heed this newly established hierarchy invites international financial crisis.

Or does it? Presumably if states could eliminate the threat of exchange rate collapse (and so shore up their attractiveness to foreign investors) then they could enjoy the benefits of liberalized capital markets without sacrificing domestic autonomy. Indeed, following much this sort of reasoning, the links between market liberalization and monetary integration are tight, both analytically and causally. Analytically, liberalized capital markets weaken state control over exchange rates and complicate the task of monetary policy coordination between countries. Causally, recognition of the threat posed by capital market integration to the European monetary system was an important factor in the political drive for monetary union during the late 1980s. As Tomaso Padoa-Schioppa (1987, vi) explained in the introduction to his report to the European Commission: "The success obtained by persuading the Community that efficient allocation of resources and price stability come first is what today makes it necessary to verify the overall consistency of the Community's design for years to come." Padoa-Schioppa's report did not itself call for the creation of EMU. However, it was clear in asserting that if the objective is "to successfully implement, and benefit from, full economic and financial integration," then "monetary union is the first-best solution"(106).

But is monetary integration really part of the solution or part of the problem? Like globalization, EMU is often seen to subvert the basic principles of the national state. Where the state is inherently political, EMU appears wholly technical. Where the priorities of the state are national, the priorities of EMU are international (and internationally imposed). Where the focus of the state lies on institutional arrangements, the focus of EMU lies on market behavior. And where the state promises economic stability, EMU necessitates flexible prices, wages, and incomes. Small wonder, then, that many question whether the member states of Europe can reconcile their diverse social objectives with anything like a credible commitment to EMU and even suggest that monetary integration may be part of some larger neo-liberal agenda (Richez-Battesti 1996; Luttwak 1997; Moss 2000).

The argument in this chapter is that the formation of EMU is about restructuring the financial architecture of Europe in order to enhance—rather than simply diminish—national autonomy. By implication, EMU functions—at least in part—to shore up and insulate Europe's member states during a period of necessary adjustment. The need for adjustment derives from the growing requirement for flexibility in the allocation of economic and political resources (Rhodes and Mény 1998). Such flexibility is necessary for market actors and state agents to meet a range of objectives in the provision of goods and services, private and public. In part, these objectives reflect the requirements of participating in an ever more integrated global economy (Berger 1996). In part, they also reflect the changing values and priorities of diverse European electorates (Inglehart 1997). However, *that* Europe's states require greater flexibility does not necessarily predetermine *how* such flexibility is achieved. EMU represents a common response to the problem of adjustment, but it does not preclude diversity elsewhere. Indeed, given different institutional starting points, it should be expected that Europe's member states will arrive at different formulas for enhancing flexibility at the national and local levels (Pierson 1998; Esping-Anderson 1999; Regini 2000; Scharpf 2000).

This argument is developed in five sections. The first section makes the broad claim that Europe's economic and monetary union effectively reconstitutes the compromise of embedded liberalism at the regional (European) level. The second focuses on the relationship between capital market integration and the development of greater flexibility in the current account. The third places current account flexibility against the background of broader strategies for macroeconomic management. The fourth draws attention to the associated problems of volatility and risk when capital markets are integrated but currencies are not. The fifth section concludes by returning to the problem of reforming the welfare state.

EMU AS EMBEDDED LIBERALISM

The benefit of access to international capital markets is greater macroeconomic flexibility. Countries with access to international capital markets do not necessarily have to worry about the impact of macroeconomic policies on the current account balance—so long as they can borrow sufficient financial resources from abroad. The cost is increased risk and volatility. Countries that rely on capital inflows to finance deficits on the current account must face the prospect that international lending will dry up and so throw the overall balance of payments (and the exchange rate) into crisis. When countries cannot attract sufficient resources from abroad, they face an immediate need for structural adjustment—and one often accompanied by a collapse in the external value of the currency.

The challenge confronting national policymakers in Europe (as elsewhere) is to lower the cost without sacrificing the benefit. The problem is that different countries have different aspirations and confront different costs. At the same time, the existence of such differences constitutes a new problem in its own right. Variation from country to country raises fundamental questions about the equity and even utility of market integration. Finding one solution that fits all cases is difficult to say the least. Nevertheless, it is necessary if market integration is to be sustainable in the long run. And that is what the Europeans have tried to achieve through monetary union.

The founders of Europe's single currency hope to provide much of the flexibility afforded by capital market integration, but at a lower cost. They also intend EMU to serve as a necessary bulwark for the completion of Europe's internal market. Such motivation is political to be sure. However, it is not altruistic and neither is it necessarily federalist. Rather, EMU represents an alternative form of "the compromise of embedded liberalism." Where the architects of the postwar order chose to limit capital markets in order to preserve domestic monetary autonomy while promoting free trade, the architects of Europe have chosen to eliminate national currencies in order to preserve access to international capital markets while laying the basis for a common market. The hierarchy of values is the same in both cases. Domestic diversity predominates over international conformity. All that has changed is the source of flexibility and nature of the constraint.

The interpretation of EMU as a new form of embedded liberalism is consistent with the history of European monetary integration. Countries within Europe have long recognized that differing domestic institutional structures have a powerful influence on the costs of doing business with the outside world. This is particularly true in the context of exchange rates, where the diverse impacts of volatility across member states have become part of the legend of monetary integration. The first serious proposal to create a monetary union in Europe—the Werner Plan of 1970—emerged from the exchange rate crises of the late 1960s and the monumental difficulties of creating a single system to protect French farmers and German manufacturers alike (McNamara 1993). Each subsequent phase has reiterated the importance of monetary macroeconomic stability both in its own right and in order to create a favorable environment for investment.

The argument that EMU operates as a form of embedded liberalism is also consistent with what Jeffry Frieden (1996) has identified as "the impact of goods and capital market integration on European monetary politics." Frieden's argument is that those countries that are most closely integrated have the greatest common interest in stabilizing exchange rates. His reasoning is that closer integration increases the importance of volatility in bilateral exchange rates such as between the member states of Europe. By implication, the relative importance of exchange rate volatility in other bilateral rates is lower. Thus while dollar volatility may be important for Europe as a whole (Belke and Gros 2000), it is less important for Europe's member states than volatility between their national currencies.

Having made the claim that EMU acts as a European compromise of embedded liberalism, however, it is necessary to illustrate two points: first, that EMU offers protection from the problems associated with capital market integration; and second, that member states retain the flexibility afforded by a relaxation of the current account constraint. The first point is most easily demonstrated during the immediate run-up to monetary union. Europe's heads of state and government announced the values for their irrevocably fixed exchange rates in May 1998. Soon thereafter, the financial shockwaves of the Asian, Latin American, and Russian financial crises hit Europe. However, rather than forcing a change in the parities between European countries, the existence of these crises seemingly added to the rationale behind EMU. Even those countries such as Spain and Portugal that have displayed periodic vulnerability to adverse speculation in capital markets were able to retain their currency pegs. Moreover, they were also able to complete the process of interest-rate convergence on European (read German) norms. By December 1998, these countries no longer had to shoulder the burden of risk premiums for their access to international capital (ECB 1999a, 43–48).

The protection afforded by EMU is also evident with reference to countries that remain outside, most notably the United Kingdom. Between January 1999 and September 2000, the exchange rate between the British pound and the euro appreciated by 15 percent while the exchange rate between the pound and the dollar depreciated by 13 percent. In effect, the European and American currencies traded places in their relative value toward the pound—with the British currency being worth $1.66 and 1.41 at the start of the single currency, and $1.45 and 1.63 twenty-one months later. Despite the apparent symmetry of these movements, however, the disparate impacts of this reversal of fortune did not cancel out. Instead large manufacturers, particularly in the automotive sector, began to clamor for rapid British entry into the single currency. They also began to redistribute some of the risks of currency volatility onto their suppliers (Toyota) and onto their workforce (Vauxhall). These actions resulted in a minor political crisis over British membership in EMU during August 2000 and may have contributed to the solidification of divisions within the Blair government over the appropriate timing for membership.[1]

The flexibility afforded by EMU is more difficult to establish. This is true both because monetary integration implies the transfer of monetary policy authority to the supranational level and because it builds on a foundation of integrated capital markets. The constraint implied by ceding monetary policy authority is tautological and therefore impossible to refute. The constraint implied by capital market integration is equally well established. In its simplest form, the argument is that states that choose to remove capital controls must inevitably select between exchange rate policy and monetary policy: Either monetary policy must be directed toward manipulating capital flows in support of exchange rate targets, or exchange rate targets must be allowed to respond to the flows of capital resulting from monetary policy changes (Andrews 1994). In this sense, the impact of capital market integration is both mechanical and direct. The more deeply capital markets are integrated, the more elastic are flows of capital with respect to changes in monetary policy variables and the more influential are international capital movements as determinants of national exchange rates.

CAPITAL MARKET INTEGRATION AND STATE AUTONOMY

Analysis focusing on the constraints implied by market integration poses a problem for most conventional stories about EMU. First, analysts must explain why industrial states chose to eliminate capital controls. The consensus is that while states might have opted for partial liberalization, they soon found themselves unable to prevent a wholesale integration of capital markets (Goodman and Pauly 1993). Second, analysts must explain why European states chose to prioritize exchange rate targeting over domestic monetary policy autonomy. Here the argument is driven by attempts to make the best of a bad situation: Europe's heads of state and government acknowledged the failure of Keynesian demand management as well as the apparent success of Germany, and so opted to pattern their institutions and behavior along German norms (McNamara 1999). Third, analysts question whether monetary integration necessarily follows from capital market integration and—if so—whether any form of monetary policy coordination is sustainable (Cohen 1993, 1994). The apparent consensus around EMU is historically contingent (McNamara 1999), but the constraints implied by liberalized capital markets and monetary unions are permanent.

The relevant question to ask is why Europe's member states have opted for a system from which they cannot opt out. Again borrowing from Padoa-Schioppa (1987), the standard pro-European argument for monetary union is that only a single currency can ensure the benefits of capital market integration. Leaving aside for the moment the general welfare effects arising from the greater efficiency of deeper capital markets, this standard argument places the advocates of EMU in a difficult position: By promoting monetary integration they are also further constraining their room for maneuver in policymaking. This is not a necessary paradox, and policymakers may be capable of (altruistically) pursuing the common good even at their own disadvantage. Alternatively, politicians may be courting favor with the voters precisely by "tying their own hands" (Giavazzi and Pagano 1988). However it seems a difficult assumption to admit at face value—forcing analysts to posit the existence of "political influences" powerful enough to encourage politicians to override their material self-interest (Garrett 2000, 169). Therefore, without denying that capital market integration does impose some constraint on macroeconomic policy choices, it is useful to look for other implications of liberalized capital movements as well.

The focus for this analysis is not constraint but empowerment. While accepting that constraints do exist, the point to note is that international capital mobility increases the range of options available to macroeconomic policymakers. Not only do international capital flows promise to finance current account deficits, but they also provide alternative sources for domestic investment that might otherwise be "crowded out" by government borrowing (or that might fail to be "crowded in" by fiscal consolidation). Hence macroeconomic policymakers with access to international capital markets can afford to overlook important constraints—both external and internal—that policymakers with closed domestic capital markets must accept.

The greater macroeconomic flexibility afforded by integrated capital markets was immediately apparent after the 1973 oil price shock. Confronted with a high dependence on energy imports and a correspondingly low price elasticity of demand for energy, policymakers in advanced industrial societies relied on international capital accounts to finance inevitable current account deficits. The extent of this reliance was so great that already during the period from 1974 to 1976 foreign exchange reserves created in international capital markets took over from U.S. balance of payments deficits as the principal source of international liquidity (McCracken et al. 1977, 129). Meanwhile, the public sector share of gross domestic product increased in most countries, and government borrowing increased as well. As a result, firms too increased their reliance on international capital markets as an alternative source of investment resources as well as opportunities. The volume of international financial transactions—and the macroeconomic flexibility they afforded—grew apace.

The implications of this new flexibility were not all salutary and neither were they easily reversible. Released from the tight confines of national capital markets, firms and other private actors began to whittle away at those restrictions on capital flows that remained in place. Meanwhile, governments benefitting from a relaxation of the short-run current-account constraint confronted the tension between moral hazard and international creditworthiness. Although international capital flows can finance current account deficits, foreign debt must be serviced and ultimately repaid (Corden 1972, 30–34). Therefore, the problem with the liberalized capital markets of the 1970s was not that countries became hugely indebted to foreign lenders but rather that governments did not use the breathing space offered by international capital flows in order to encourage the structural changes necessary to generate current account surpluses in the future (McCracken et al. 1977, 125–126). For many countries, the challenge was to create an environment suitable for investment or investor confidence. And in some cases—most famously Italy and the United Kingdom during the late 1970s—international lending threatened to dry up, facing the governments with an immediate crisis in the balance of payments affecting both the current and capital accounts.

The experience of the 1970s left three important lessons behind. The first two are well-known: Governments can liberalize international capital markets more easily than they can control them, and governments can ignore developments in international capital markets only at their own peril. The third lesson has had more obvious acceptance among economists than elsewhere. Simply, even governments with access to international capital markets cannot disregard the current account over the long run. This third lesson is supported by a powerful body of data and analysis (Razin 1995). Nevertheless, despite the strength of economic argument in favor of a long-run current account constraint, governments seem content to accept (and even encourage) long-term imbalances. Within Europe, some countries have taken advantage of international capital mobility to support consistent current account surpluses, such as Germany before unification, the Netherlands since 1982, and Belgium since 1985. Other countries have run consistent deficits, such as Spain and Italy in the late 1980s and early-to-mid 1990s, and Portugal from the late 1980s onward. There are clear advantages on either side. The surplus countries benefit from an export-led pattern of growth. The deficit countries can draw upon foreign capital for domestic investment. Persistent imbalances also entail costs. For the surplus countries the risk is that capital exports will undercut domestic investment (Bean 1989, 42). For the deficit countries the risk is that capital imports will do little more than fuel consumption. How these benefits and costs add up is a case-by-case consideration. In general terms it suffices to note that current account variability has undergone a steep change at the European level.

Evidence for the change in European current account performance is assembled in Tables 5.1 and 5.2. Both tables contain the average and standard deviation for the balance on current accounts as a ratio to gross domestic product (GDP) for the periods from 1960 to 1973 and from 1983 to 2000 respectively. The period from 1974 to 1982 is omitted because of the powerful influence of the two oil price shocks (1973 and 1979). The countries are ranged from deficit to surplus, and clustered into "large" and "modest" groups. In comparing the 1980s and 1990s with the 1960s and early 1970s, three changes stand out: More countries are running average deficits; the extreme deficits and (particularly) surpluses are greater; and the variability (standard deviation) of national performance has increased in all but three cases—Portugal, Greece, and Spain. What is less apparent from the tables—but can be calculated from the underlying data—is that national performance during the earlier period tends toward balance (zero) while during the later period it tends toward imbalance. The conclusion, then, is straightforward. Under conditions of international capital mobility, the variability of national performance on current accounts has increased.

Table 5.1. European Current Account Performance, 1960–1973 (percent GDP)

Country	Average	Standard Deviation
Large Deficits		
Ireland	−2.3	1.8
Denmark	−1.9	1.0
Greece	−1.9	1.3
Finland	−1.4	1.0
Modest Deficits		
Spain	−0.3	2.2
Modest Surpluses		
Austria	0.0	0.8
Portugal	0.1	3.9
Sweden	0.2	1.0
United Kingdom	0.3	1.0
France	0.6	0.5
Netherlands	0.7	1.5
West Germany	0.8	0.9
Large Surpluses		
Belgium	1.3	1.1
Italy	1.4	1.5

Data Source: European Commission.

Table 5.2. European Current Account Performance, 1983–2000 (percent GDP)

Country	Average	Standard Deviation
Large Deficits		
Portugal	−3.7	3.1
Greece	−2.5	1.2
United Kingdom	−1.1	1.5
Spain	−1.1	1.7
Modest Deficits		
Austria	−0.9	1.2
Germany	−0.6*	0.4*
Denmark	−0.6	2.3
Ireland	−0.3	2.9
Modest Surpluses		
Finland	0.1	4.0
Sweden	0.1	2.4
Italy	0.2	1.6
France	0.4	1.0
Large Surpluses		
Belgium	2.2	2.2
West Germany	2.5**	1.5**
Netherlands	4.4	1.3

* 1991–2000; ** 1983–1994.
Data Source: European Commission.

STRATEGIES AND OUTCOMES

Having established that there has been increasing variation in European current account performance, the next step is to explain how this change relates to macroeconomic policy. My argument is that the most extreme cases of current account imbalance are the result (whether intended or not) of the prevailing macroeconomic policy mix. The level of demonstration at this point is illustrative. Rather than rehearse a variety of policy scenarios under different regimes and using different models, my strategy is simply to establish the existence of policy combinations that (a) are not available in a world of closed national capital markets and (b) can explain the increasing divergence of current account behavior.[2] Because this is a general argument, the examples draw from outside Europe as well as from within.

Consistent Current Account Deficits

Examples of countries with consistent current account deficits include the United States in the 1980s and 1990s under a flexible exchange rate regime and Spain and Portugal in the 1990s under the fixed-but-adjustable regime of the European Monetary System (EMS). In all three cases, the policy mix combines loose fiscal policy with tight monetary policy. The effects of this mix are easiest to describe under a flexible exchange rate regime. The fiscal expansion increases domestic consumption and so draws down on the current account. Meanwhile, tight monetary policy raises interest rates and so attracts an inflow of foreign capital. Despite the deterioration on the current account, this inflow of foreign capital places upward pressure on the exchange rate and so induces an appreciation of the currency. This currency appreciation blocks off the use of relative prices as a means of correcting the current account and so prolongs and even intensifies the deficit. Nevertheless, so long as the country can continue to attract foreign capital, it can also continue to finance a deficit on current accounts. Therefore, over the short-to-medium term the stability of the policy mix is principally dependent upon the international creditworthiness of the country as well as its relative attractiveness to foreign investors.[3] Over the long-run, however, accumulated foreign debts will have to be serviced and ultimately repaid. Therefore the long-run stability of the strategy depends upon the government's willingness to use foreign capital to support domestic investment and restructuring in order to generate current account surpluses in the future.

The advantages of the policy mix are domestic. Loose fiscal policy fuels consumption, tight monetary policy reins in inflation, and an appreciating exchange rate improves the terms of trade (read allows for cheaper and more plentiful imports). In the event that the country also suffers from a shortage of investment capital, an additional advantage is the increase in foreign funds for domestic restructuring. The disadvantages of the policy are both domestic and international. Although the domestic economy experiences a boom in consumption, the lower price of imports ensures that manufacturing faces intense competition from foreign producers. Meanwhile tight monetary policy results not only in attracting capital from across the globe but also in raising real interest rates. Funds for investment may be more available, but they are also likely to be more expensive.

The United States' experience during the 1980s and 1990s illustrates all of the hallmarks of the loose fiscal / tight monetary policy mix. Under the first Reagan administration, both real interest rates and fiscal deficits increased, leading to a massive inflow of foreign capital, a strong appreciation of the dollar, and a dramatic deterioration on current account. This strategy was both surprising and unwelcome. Not only did it seem to encourage a rapid "de-industrialization of America," but it also threatened the stability of the international economic system. As the decade progressed, concern that the U.S. economy would experience a "hard landing" rather than a smooth adjustment increased (Marris 1987). Meanwhile, the presumption was that the ability of the United States to sustain such current account deficits is a function of its unique role in the world economy. It is American hegemony in a less powerful and more decadent guise (Calleo 1992).

The argument here is that the policy mix is less a function of American power than of the integration of capital markets. Therefore it is possible to identify a similar strategy used by smaller countries as well. Spain and Portugal follow the characteristic pattern of the tight monetary/loose fiscal policy mix in the early 1990s: domestic expansion leading to a deterioration on current account financed by capital imports induced through relatively high real interest rates. Evidence for the Spanish and Portuguese policy mixes is assembled in Table 5.3, which provides average data for fiscal balances, current accounts, nominal short-term interest rates, interest rate differentials with Germany, and real interest rates (GDP deflated) for the period from 1988 to 1995. In order to facilitate comparison, Table 5.3 also includes U.S. data from 1982 to 1998. The data support the broad similarities between the policy mixes and current account performance in the United States on the one hand and Spain and Portugal on the other hand. In all three cases, persistent current account deficits were only possible as a result of foreign capital inflows and therefore of capital market integration.

Table 5.3.   Consistent Current Account Deficits

Period Averages	1988–1995		1982–1998
	Portugal	Spain	United States
	percent gross domestic product		
Government Deficit	4.7	5.0	3.9
Current Account Deficit	2.7	2.2	1.6
	percent		
Nominal (Real*) Short Term Interest Rates	14.1 (4.2)	12.2 (5.9)	6.5 (3.4)
Nominal (Real*) Interest Rate Differentials with Germany	7.2 (0.2)	5.2 (1.9)	0.6 (0.1)

* Real interest rates are deflated by GDP.
Data source: European Commission.

Despite the similarities, however, the experience of Spain and Portugal differed from that of the United States in three respects. First, the smaller countries benefitted from capital transfers and so did not rely solely on foreign borrowing as did the United States.[4] Second, the two countries did not undergo such a strong currency appreciation despite their reliance on capital inflows to finance deficits on current account. Third, both Spain and Portugal were subject to periodic currency crises as international lenders questioned whether and how long the tight monetary/loose fiscal policy mix could be maintained. These three differences reflect the importance of America's hegemonic position in the world economy to its ability to maintain current account deficits over the long run. Because of its economic and military might, and because most countries hold dollars as a reserve currency, the United States has a relatively easy time attracting foreign capital and maintaining international creditworthiness. For Spain and Portugal, running consistent current account deficits is more difficult and more volatile. Indeed, it may be possible only because where the United States can benefit from hegemony, Spain and Portugal can rely on their institutional and symbolic association with Europe.

Spanish and Portuguese participation in the European Union and specifically in the fixed-but-adjustable exchange rate mechanism (ERM) of the European Monetary System (EMS) can account for much of the difference between U.S. and Iberian experiences. The European Union represents the source of much of the capital transfers to the Iberian Peninsula—and with the ostensible purpose of stimulating regional and structural reforms. Moreover, for both Spain and Portugal, the demonstration of a willingness to undertake domestic economic reform lent credibility to their participation in the EMS (Torres 1998; Calvet 1996). In turn, EMS participation enhanced the creditworthiness of both countries by reducing exchange rate risk and so made them more attractive to foreign investors. Finally, once foreign capital inflows began to place upward pressure on the peseta and escudo, the intervention requirements of the ERM displaced responsibility for maintaining the system of fixed-but-adjustable exchange rates onto the weaker European currencies.[5]

The combination of macroeconomic policies, capital transfers, and EMS participation was not wholly stable. Both Spain and Portugal experienced sharp depreciations during the 1992, 1993, and 1995 currency crises within the ERM. Nevertheless, both countries were able to sustain persistent deficits on current accounts using foreign capital to stave off a crisis in their balance of payments. Moreover, reliance on capital inflows meant that the escudo and peseta tended to appreciate between crises even in the face of persistent current account deficits. At the same time, this tendency to appreciate was contained despite the strong inflow of foreign capital. Indeed, both currencies remained in the top of their intervention bands against the median EMS currency even during periods of gradual depreciation such as that between 1996 and 1998 (European Commission 1998a, 158–159). Such a performance would not be possible without integrated capital markets.

Consistent Current Account Surpluses

Capital flows can offset consistent current account surpluses as well as consistent deficits. From an intuitive standpoint, however, the alternatives are not symmetrical. If a country is able to outperform its competitors either domestically, in the rest of the world, or both, why would investors—domestic and foreign—prefer to place their money elsewhere? Why would a government not encourage its successful manufacturers to repatriate profits and invest them at home? Alternatively, why should governments not allow current account surpluses simply to translate into ever increasing official holdings of foreign exchange reserves—a mercantilist war chest so to speak? The answer to the first and second questions has to do with relative returns on investment while the answer to the second and third questions concerns the risk of domestic inflation. Capital will flow where the rates of return are relatively higher or the opportunities for investment are greater. By the same token, capital inflows—including repatriated profits and increased foreign exchange reserves—increase domestic liquidity.

If governments confronting a current account surplus do not take action, the likelihood is not only that capital will flow into the country but also that firms and workers will use their increased earnings to bolster investment and consumption. The result will be higher prices coupled with a change in performance on the current account. The logic of this mechanism suggests the paradox that governments hoping to run consistent current account surpluses may have to loosen domestic monetary conditions in order to hold down demand and stave off inflation. More generally, such governments must not only allow but also encourage international capital mobility.

Loosening monetary conditions to dampen demand and control inflation only represents a paradox when monetary policy instruments are directly and consistently assigned to domestic stabilization. When monetary policy instruments are assigned to influence international capital accounts the paradox is eliminated. All that is necessary is that the impact of monetary policy changes on the balance of payments as a monetary influence is greater than the direct impact of those changes on domestic monetary conditions—a point made implicitly in Mundell's (1960) early analysis of international capital mobility. However, the assignment of monetary instruments either wholly or principally to influence the capital account—like the constraint that monetary instruments must accommodate international capital markets—leaves open how the government will control domestic sources of inflation. Once again what is interesting is not so much the assignment of (or constraint on) monetary policy but rather the structure of the policy mix.

Examples of countries that have run consistent current account surpluses include Japan and the Netherlands throughout the 1980s and 1990s, (West) Germany before unification, and Belgium from 1986 onward. The macroeconomic characteristics of these countries are similar in that they combine tight fiscal policy, high domestic savings relative to investment, stable prices, and declining real wages. All four countries also benefit from non-market mechanisms for ensuring wage stability, ranging from direct intervention in wage negotiations (Belgium and the Netherlands), to concerted wage bargaining (the Netherlands and Germany), to institutionalized wage restraint (Japan). Data in support of this characteristic pattern are assembled in Table 5.4, and include the balance on current account, net national savings, the ratio of savings to investment, the average annual price inflation, and the rate of increase in real unit labor costs. Table 5.4 also provides comparable data from the United States as a benchmark for relative comparison. What the data reveal is that the four countries running consistent current account surpluses save more, invest (relatively) less, have lower inflation and more rapidly declining real unit labor costs than the United States.

What the data in Table 5.4 do not indicate is the extent to which the four countries running current account surpluses must manage macroeconomic (and specifically monetary) policy instruments with an eye to their impact on the capital account and on exchange rates. The empirical literature on the subject is substantial (Cooper 1968; Wadbrook 1972; Henning 1994; Kaltenthaler 1998; and Jones, Frieden, and Torres 1998). What it reveals is the complexity of the policy mix both at any given

Table 5.4. Consistent Current Account Surpluses

Period Averages	1986–1998 Belgium	1982–1990 Germany	1982–1998 Netherlands	1982–1998 Japan	1982–1998 USA*
	percent gross domestic product				
Current Account Surplus	2.7	3.2	4.2	2.5	−1.6
Net National Saving	9.0	10.3	9.6	17.2	5.5
	ratio				
Gross Saving/Investment	1.08	1.15	1.17	1.10	0.94
Net Saving/Investment	1.30	1.42	1.59	1.20	0.83
	annual percentage change				
Price Deflator,					
Gross Domestic Product	2.6	2.6	1.8	1.1	2.9
Real Unit Labor Costs	−0.6	−1.0	−0.8	−0.5	−0.2

Note: The United States is a "consistent deficit" country presented here as a benchmark for comparison.
Data source: European Commission.

phase in time and across different time periods. Within the mix, monetary policy is not always and completely ineffective in the management of domestic demand.[6] Nevertheless, its use is not entirely transparent either. For example, Henning (1994, 134–170) outlines five phases in the evolution of Japanese monetary and exchange rate policy during the period from 1980 to 1992. The differences between the phases are categorical, and pivot around whether the yen should be made stronger or weaker, whether capital flows should be regulated or liberalized, whether interest rates should be raised or lowered, and whether the Bank of Japan should intervene in foreign currency markets. In each phase, however, the maintenance of the surplus on current accounts remains a priority and so at least some international mobility of capital remains a necessity.

As with the current account deficit, the advantages of pursuing a surplus are domestic while the disadvantages are both domestic and foreign. The advantages are also relatively concentrated in the tradable goods sector. Export manufacturers benefit from a relatively favorable real exchange rate, from elevated profits, and from enhanced international liquidity. Meanwhile, the non-traded goods sector must labor under unfavorable terms of trade (read fewer and more expensive imports), constrained wages, and a relative lack of investment. Internationally, trade competitors are likely to view sustained current account surpluses as prima facie evidence of unfair trading practices. Such international concern is not wholly misplaced. Armed with access to international capital markets, states are empowered to sustain current account surpluses despite the constraints this may place on the exercise of monetary policy. Moreover, the evidence suggests that they have done so.

RISK, VOLATILITY, AND COST

Integrated capital markets offer the promise of macroeconomic flexibility, but only at a cost. The cost is expressed in terms of risk and volatility. Countries that rely on international capital markets face the risk that lenders will withdraw their credit or borrowers will default on their obligations. They also run the risk that sudden movements of capital between currencies will cause dramatic swings in exchange rates—altering relative prices in complete disregard for "the fundamentals" such as movements in relative costs. Indeed, given that goods markets play so little role in determining the value of exchange rates, countries run the risk that no matter how favorable their cost structures may be relative to their competitors—or how coherent their macroeconomic policy mix—a sudden or long-term movement of exchange rates may obliterate any advantage in relative prices (MacDonald 1999). Finally, countries run the risk that capital market and exchange rate effects will reinforce one-another, with a credit crisis leading to an exchange-rate crisis or the other way around, and so on. The permutations of such risks are vast, and each contributes to the volatility of exchange rates and interest rates.

In turn, this volatility is both self-reinforcing and costly in its own right. Investors estimating relative returns must bring forward their time horizons and so assume shorter positions that focus on shorter-term gains. Industries hoping to protect the value of their capital and output must either accept the cost of exposure to volatility, redistribute the risk onto weaker groups in the marketplace (suppliers, workers, consumers), or engage in financial hedging. The results of such distributive games are "negative-sum": everyone loses. Weaker groups must share in the cost of international exposure even if the focus of their activity is domestic. At the same time, the financial intermediaries that offer hedging contracts must cover their own exposure. In the end, the hedging instruments themselves become a focus for short-term investments and an additional source of volatility (Garber 1999; Watson 1999). The fact that forward markets consistently under-predict the scale of volatility suggests that inefficiency—and therefore cost—is somehow inherent to the system (Rogoff 1999).

The costs of capital market integration are systemic in origin but not in distribution. Institutional arrangements can influence both the allocation of risks and the nature of volatility. Similarly, institutions can influence the economic mechanisms that make risk and volatility important in the first place, changing perceptions or expectations and so moderating behavior. As a consequence, the negative impact of capital market integration is not everywhere the same. This is most obvious in the fact that different countries represent different "risks" for international investors and so must pay different premiums for access to international capital. There are premiums associated with the choice of macroeconomic strategy (sovereign risk), premiums associated with the possibility of sudden movements in the value of the currency (exchange rate risk), and premiums associated with the ease of getting into and out of the national capital market (liquidity risk). In turn, these premiums result in a higher cost of capital for some countries than for others.

The differences in premiums charged by international investors are obvious in any comparison between the industrialized and developing worlds. Where industrialized countries seem to be able to access international capital markets with relative impunity, developing nations do so only at great cost. Moreover, any attempt by developing countries to exercise the type of macroeconomic flexibility described above is likely to meet with disaster, as international investors raise the cost of borrowing exorbitantly or cut off lending altogether. The impact of different institutional arrangements on the cost of participating in international capital markets is less obvious in comparisons between wealthy middle powers like the countries of Europe. It remains important nonetheless.

Moreover, the imposition of premiums on the cost of borrowing is only one manifestation of the "costs" of integrated capital markets. Another manifestation works through the impact of volatility on investment in the real economy. The general claim is that investors confronting volatility in either interest rates or exchange rates will choose to defer their investment until markets calm down (Darby et al. 1999). By implication the expectation is that any relationship between volatility and investment will be negative—more volatility means less investment and the reverse. In more specific terms, the impact of volatility on investment should be influenced by the importance of exchange rates or interest rates to the return on capital and by the ease with which investors can hedge, transform, or eliminate either a specific investment or their exposure to volatility. Thus we should expect investment in some countries to show a greater sensitivity to volatility than in others. This expectation is consistent with the assertion that welfare state institutions help to mitigate or redistribute exposure to risk (Rodrik 1998).

The different sensitivities of national economies to the problem of volatility is even more evident with respect to employment and unemployment. Again, in general terms, the argument is that firms confronting volatile interest rates or exchange rates may delay any decision to expand the workforce and may even be forced into redundancies. Thus, the general expectation is that employment growth will slow—and unemployment may even increase—whenever financial markets become volatile (Gros 1998). Here too, however, national institutions will have a profound effect on the sensitivity of the real economy to volatility in financial markets. Because labor market regulations influence the prospects for hiring and firing, the term structure of wage contracts, and the non-payroll cost of the workforce, they will also have an influence on how firms determine the appropriate strategy for responding to volatility.

CONCLUSION

Discussion of the cost of volatility necessarily returns us to the problem of welfare state reform. Differences in welfare state institutions explain differences in national responses to the problems of integrated capital markets. The greater the problems, the more important these differences become. However, eliminating the differences between countries will not eliminate the problems themselves. All it will achieve is a leveling of the playing field. And, as argued in chapter 2, that is simply not the objective in Europe. Rather the aspiration is to find a common solution to the problem of volatility—one that will preserve the macroeconomic flexibility afforded by capital market integration while at the same time making it possible to ignore substantial institutional differences between the member states. That common solution is EMU.

At this point it is necessary to concede that Europe's member states are all—from richest to poorest—engaged in some process of welfare state reform. However, such reform would be necessary with or without EMU, under segmented capital markets as well as in a globalized world economy. The reasons for reform have been alluded to in the introduction to this chapter and can be related to changes in values, demographics, technology, and a host of other variables. It is also important to reiterate the point made in chapter 2 that the method of reform undertaken in Europe is idiosyncratic—and deliberately so. The buzzwords adopted at the March 2000 Lisbon European Council summit center on "targeting," "benchmarking," and "shared-best-practice." These are terms for individual improvement within a collective process and not for convergence around a common norm.

What is unquestioned in Europe is that reform is necessary. Europe's member states have emerged from the sclerosis of the 1970s and early 1980s only to confront pernicious unemployment in the late 1980s and 1990s. The problem of this unemployment, more than anything else, drives the debate about welfare state reform at both the national and European levels (Jones 1998). Unemployment is also likely to dominate European discussions well into the future. What is clear is that Europe's heads of state and government are insistent that EMU is part of the solution (Jones 2000). What is also clear is that the solution for Europe's unemployment problem is different from one member state to the next (Viñals and Jimeno 1998). For EMU to contribute to resolving Europe's unemployment problem it must be consistent with the wide variety of "solutions" that will be implemented at the national level. The analysis presented in this chapter suggests that it is.[7]

Indeed, if there is a dilemma posed by EMU, it arises from the excess of macroeconomic flexibility monetary integration affords participating countries.[8] The danger is not that countries will be unable to manage their economies. Rather, it is that they will take advantage of their relaxed current account constraints and strengthened creditworthiness to ignore already excessive imbalances. Indeed, evidence from the first two years of EMU suggests that this is likely to be the case.

For those countries in current account deficit, the challenge of attracting sufficient funds for domestic investment remains. However, the significance of this challenge is greatly overwhelmed by the elimination of premiums on the cost of capital. Just as during the early expansion of international capital markets, such deficits could result in enormous future burdens of adjustment. They could also destabilize European macroeconomic performance in the present. Therefore it is small wonder that Europe's heads of state and government would be so adamant about setting down rules to ensure macroeconomic stability under EMU. It is also small wonder that concern in Europe would focus on how such rules could ever be enforced and whether they will actually be obeyed.

For those countries in surplus, the difficulty of eliminating the inflationary potential of capital inflows remains as well. The point to note, however, is that such inflows present an inflationary problem only if Europe as a whole runs a current account surplus. The extremes in this case can balance out.

The point is largely theoretical. If the first 21 months of EMU are any indication, aggregate European current account surpluses are likely to be more than offset by capital flows from Europe to the United States (BIS 2000, 32). The preponderance of these flows explains the collapse of the value of the European currency since its launch in January 1999. Moreover, the flood of capital is so great that it has revived concerns about the differential impact of financial volatility across Europe's member states. EMU is only a partial solution to the problems posed by capital market integration: a regional bulwark within the larger architecture of global capital markets.

The greatest danger at the moment is not that EMU will collapse under the weight of internal division but rather that it will prove inadequate in the face of global forces. The experience of the Bretton Woods system is instructive on this point. The conventional wisdom is that Bretton Woods collapsed under the weight of excessive dollar liquidity. The United States ran balance of payments deficits both to ensure adequate provision of liquidity for international trade and as a symptom of fiscal imbalances resulting from the Vietnam War. In turn these deficits ultimately destabilized the whole of the exchange rate system (McCracken et al. 1977, 12). This conventional wisdom touches on a fundamental conflict between "the conditions for economic growth . . . and the practices of modern governments" (Keohane 1978, 109). Governments do not always exert self-discipline even when it is in their country's long-term self-interest. From the European perspective, the United States is viewed as continuously culpable of falling prey to short-term political pressures. EMU is in many ways not the first-best solution suggested by Padoa-Schioppa but rather a second-best alternative to a broader systemic reform. For most Europeans, any such transformation in the international financial architecture must begin with a reform of the United States.

NOTES

1. Coverage of the political crisis around the automotive industry and EMU can be found in any quality newspaper in August 2000. The stories I relied upon were published in *The Guardian* on August 10. The displacement of exchange rate risk onto the Vauxhall workforce received somewhat less coverage. See, Terry Macalister, Vauxhall Benefits from Sterling's Strength, *The Guardian* (August 24, 2000). The story relates how Vauxhall activated a clause from its 1998 collective bargaining agreement whereby workers would forgo a £100 bonus if the value of the pound "fell below DM 2.70 for two consecutive months." The story also suggests that Vauxhall would continue to include such clauses in its bargaining contracts for the future.

2. Readers interested in deliberating different macroeconomic models are advised to consult Stevenson, Muscatelli, and Gregory (1988) and McKibbon and Sachs (1991).

3. The problem of maintaining creditworthiness (or credibility) is likely to be more easily resolved for rich industrial countries than for poorer developing countries. Hence many of the arguments here may have only limited application outside the privileged membership of the OECD.

4. Capital transfers played a particularly strong role in Portugal, accounting for more than 80 percent of net capital inflows during the 1988–1995 period as opposed to only 20 percent for Spain.

5. Most analyses of the asymmetric intervention requirements of the ERM focus on the privileged position of Germany given the relative strength of the Deutschemark. The point to note is that it is the position of relative strength and not the Deutschemark per se that is privileged by the intervention requirements. For a general analysis, see Gros and Thygesen (1998, 167–178).

6. Pooled cross-section time series analysis of the relationship between real short-term and long-term interest rates in the Group of Seven countries indicates that monetary policy changes have a statistically significant impact on long-term real interest rates (and therefore economic activity) through their impact on short-

term real interest rates. At the same time, this evidence suggests that accumulated current account surpluses have a significant negative impact on long-run real interest rates—as should be expected given the necessity for capital to flow in the opposite direction of the current account. See Sasaki, Yamaguchi, and Hisada (2000).

7. This is not to say, however, that national solutions for Europe's unemployment problem are going to be successful. Indeed, the danger is that the member states will fail and so undermine the legitimacy of EMU. For an elaboration on this point, see Jones (1998).

8. This explains why Germany was so keen to negotiate the "stability pact." See chapter 7.

6

✦

Context: Ambition and Constraint

The need for reform of the global financial architecture suggests a wider motivation for constructing an economic and monetary union (EMU). Europe's single currency is not only an attempt at the depolitization of monetary policy, and neither is it just a response to the problem of exchange rate volatility between member states of the European Union (EU). It is also an attempt to respond to United States management (or manipulation) of the global economy. The question to consider, then, is whether it is realistic to expect Europe's EMU to succeed on all fronts at once—particularly given the dramatic fall in the value of the single currency (the euro) relative to the dollar that was mentioned in chapter 4.

This chapter analyzes the competition between EMU objectives as a constraint on the external performance of the single currency. The argument is that euro-zone politicians must choose between a domestic vision of EMU as a bulwark for macroeconomic stability and an international vision of EMU as an instrument for foreign economic policy. Given the constitutional architecture of the European Union, that choice is more likely to favor the "domestic" than the "international." The usefulness of the single currency as an instrument of foreign economic policy suffers as a result.

This predominance of domestic considerations in the management of EMU is well established both in the Treaty Establishing the European Community (TEC) and in the literature. However, the exchange-rate implications of this focus on domestic macroeconomic stability are less well understood. The conventional wisdom—and the bulk of EU rhetoric—suggests that euro-zone policymakers will regard the external value of the euro with an attitude bordering on "benign neglect."[1] Outside the context of extreme or sustained misalignment, the exchange rate between the euro and third countries can safely be ignored.[2] Counter-intuitively, policymakers operating within a domestic-centered EMU cannot sustain such a laissez-faire approach. For them, the question is not whether they would prefer to stabilize exchange rates with the outside world, but whether they have the instruments to do so unilaterally. By contrast, policymakers operating within a more internationally focused United States have a greater capacity to ignore the value of the dollar whether out of neglect or design. Europe's single currency builds upon an internal focus but retains an external vulnerability.

This argument is developed in four sections. The first sets out the principal objectives behind Europe's monetary union. The second explains how the competition between these objectives results in an exchange rate stability bias with respect to the external value of the euro relative to the dollar. The third examines how this bias toward exchange-rate stability has played out in practice over EMU's first two years of operation not only for the euro, but also for the British pound, which is similarly vulnerable because it is internally focused. The fourth draws out the comparison with the United States and concludes with the implications for the euro as a global currency.

FIVE REASONS FOR A SINGLE CURRENCY

The motives behind the construction of EMU are many and their relative importance depends upon who describes them. Moreover, to pretend that everyone who supports EMU does so for the same reason (or even set of reasons) would be to deny a large and growing body of data suggesting the opposite (European Commission 1999a). Nevertheless, it is possible to aggregate core motivations as they apply to the project as a whole. From this vantage, the broad justifications for EMU are fivefold, and are:

- to symbolize and stimulate European political unity;
- to enhance the efficiency of Europe's internal market;
- to insulate participating economies from world market turbulence;
- to establish a stable macroeconomic framework;
- to provide a viable counterweight to the dollar.

The symbolic argument is ubiquitous and yet poorly delineated. From the start of the project, heads of state and government in Europe have announced that the introduction of a single currency will provide a catalyst for a greater European identification. In making this claim they are supported by a small number of historical precedents—including the introduction of the "Greenback Dollar" during the American Civil War—and a large amount of supposition (Sheridan 1996). As mentioned in chapter 1, the currency union between Great Britain and Northern Ireland has done little to promote common cause. Reciprocally, the fact that private banks are allowed to print notes for circulation in Northern Ireland can hardly be blamed for the troubles between nationalists and unionists. Indeed, what is striking about this objective is that it has less to do with the functioning of the common currency than with its existence. What matters is not whether the currency is better or worse—at least within a large range of variation—but rather that it is.

The efficiency argument is more highly specified but less potent, at least initially. According to the authors of the European Commission's viability study published at the start of preparations for EMU—"One Market, One Money"—the introduction of a single currency will add only a fraction of a percent of gross domestic product in terms of the reduction of transaction costs associated with maintaining multiple currencies (Emerson et al. 1992). Given the size of domestic production across the euro-zone, even a fraction of a percent is considerable. Yet, much of that "efficiency gain" will take the form of an implicit transfer from the banks who forego the commissions they would earn on the exchange of currencies to the importers or exporters who will no longer have to pay such commissions. Other efficiency gains would result from the constitution of a larger, and hence more liquid, market for financial capital. Such liquidity appears to be stimulating more competitive and dynamic financial services as well as greater long-term productive investment. However, once again, the achievement of greater efficiency is tied more closely to the establishment of a single currency than to its operation. It is the fact of not having to change money that counts rather than the name (or constitution) of the money that is actually used.[3]

The symbolic and efficiency objectives of EMU are institutional in the sense that they should be achieved (or their achievement should be set in train) once the single currency is established. By contrast, the insulation objective is only semi-institutional and is at least partly dependent upon the behavior of states and markets. On the one hand, the fact that several national currencies are forged into one means that the participating countries are insulated from fluctuations in their bilateral exchange rates. Neither foreign disturbances nor domestic policies can alter the nominal rate of exchange between one participating country and another. A larger currency also means that international trade is more likely to be denominated in euros, thus insulating the participating countries from exchange-rate induced fluctuations in commodity prices. On the other hand, however, the participating countries may still suffer from the influence of changes in the rate of exchange between the common currency and the outside world.

Here the attitudes of markets and the actions of politicians remain important. Turbulence between the French franc and the Deutschemark may no longer be an issue for France and Germany, but turbulence between the euro and the dollar may well be. Therefore, the insulating property of EMU depends at least in part on how the external value of the single currency is managed even though a good deal of insulation is provided by the fact that the single currency exists.

As with the insulating properties of the single currency, the macroeconomic stability objective is also only partially institutionalized. Here, however, it is not the single currency that is the central institution. Rather it is the European Central Bank (ECB)—and its encompassing European System of Central Banks (ESCB)—which is charged with the "primary objective . . . to maintain price stability" (Treaty Establishing the European Community [TEC], Article 5, Paragraph 1). Because the actions of the ECB are narrowly focused and its management is heavily shielded from political manipulation, there is little reason to doubt but that it will stabilize domestic prices. Nevertheless, the instruments for the conduct of monetary policy cannot by themselves ensure a stable macroeconomic framework. The fact that prices are stable is no guarantee that output, demand, or employment will be stable as well. Not only do the economies of the euro-zone continue to be influenced by the external value of the single currency (as just mentioned), but also—and more important—they are influenced by the fiscal policies of the member states. Despite the strong price stability rule, the establishment of a stable macroeconomic framework remains dependent upon decisions taken by policymakers once the single currency is brought into existence.

If anything, the institutionalization of the macroeconomic stability objective is even weaker than the insulation provided by the single currency. The explanation for this weakness is that while the incentives to disturb the external value of the euro are ambiguous, the incentives to work against the macroeconomic stability of the monetary union are not. Contrary to popular expectations—at least in the British press—the mere existence of a single currency does not impose discipline on macroeconomic policymaking. As chapter 5 has suggested, quite the opposite is in fact the case. By releasing the short-term constraint implied by the need to finance the balance of payments, the construction of a multinational currency actually eases the discipline imposed upon its participants. Should politicians in one or more of the participating countries respond by increasing fiscal spending or by reducing taxation, the resulting inflationary impulse would spread across the monetary union as a whole.

Any relaxation of fiscal discipline would affect not only the stability of macroeconomic conditions within the euro-zone but also the external value of the single currency. The symbolism and efficiency of the euro may not be thus affected, but the insulation it provides vis-à-vis the outside world certainly will. Any change in the expected rate of inflation within the euro-zone will imply a change in the external value of the euro. More important, by undermining the macroeconomic stability of the single currency, those politicians in participating countries who choose to relax fiscal discipline jeopardize investments across the currency area as a whole. Hence the agreement reached at the June 1997 Amsterdam summit of the European Council was to shore up the functioning of EMU through the acceptance of a "Stability and Growth Pact" committing participants to good (i.e., disciplined) behavior.

As chapter 2 has argued, the Stability and Growth Pact institutionalizes a set of norms and procedures for maintaining fiscal discipline. Nevertheless, it is not automatic in the same sense that the existence of a single currency provides a common symbol or an irrevocably fixed internal exchange rate. Indeed, the notion of automatic sanctions on errant behavior was explicitly rejected during the negotiation of the pact. Therefore, it is possible to suggest that—despite the pact—the macroeconomic stability objective of EMU continues to rely almost wholly on the willingness of its participants to act individually in the collective interest. Policymakers in those countries that participate in EMU are expected to set levels of taxation and spending with at least one eye on the macroeconomic stability of the monetary union as a whole. Should any given participant take their eye off the common interest, the European Commission will surely report that fact to the Council of Ministers. However, it is the errant participants—and neither the Council nor the Commission—who are ultimately responsible for making the necessary fiscal corrections.

The objective to use the single currency as a counterweight to the dollar is the most weakly institutionalized of all. The simple facts that a European currency exists or that it benefits from a common monetary policy and a promise of supportive fiscal discipline mean little in terms of the exercise of international monetary power. Such institutions create only potential. They do not engender purpose. To understand the significance of this point, it is necessary to consider that creating a viable counterweight to the dollar implies two different characteristics. The economies of the euro-zone must be made somehow less vulnerable to fluctuations in the value of the dollar. Whether economic agents are directly insulated by the irrevocable fixing of intra-European exchange rates or indirectly compensated for the costs implied by dollar fluctuations through the active use of fiscal policy is less relevant than that movements in the dollar-euro exchange rate should not give rise to domestic political conflict. From this standpoint, the willingness of euro-zone politicians to use fiscal instruments in compensation for changes in the external value of the euro supports and does not undermine the functioning of the single currency (Bayoumi and Masson 1995; Tamborini 2001).

The second characteristic feature of providing a counterweight to the dollar is the capacity for euro-zone politicians to manipulate the external value of the euro in support of other foreign economic (or, more simply, foreign policy) objectives. From this perspective, what matters is not so much the institutions supporting the single currency as the constitution of those agents attempting to wield it as an instrument of economic diplomacy (Kirshner 1995). The pattern of collective action within the euro-zone is different here than for the maintenance of fiscal discipline. Rather than acting separately in the common interest, those politicians in the euro-zone hoping to manipulate the external value of the euro will have to be able to act collectively without regard to their separate interests.

The lack of symmetry in these different patterns of collective action is important. Where politicians looking to impose fiscal discipline can intermediate any conflict over the distribution of costs associated with the policy *ex ante*, as part of the negotiation of the budget, politicians looking to manipulate (or even structure) the external value of the euro will have to manage the distribution of adjustment costs *ex post*. Whether the Council of Ministers chooses to peg the value of the euro to the dollar or to ignore it, some participants will feel the affects of the peg or the float more strongly than others. By the same token, any effort to exercise (or to ignore) global monetary responsibility will affect the insulation EMU provides directly through any change in the external value of the euro. Manipulation of the single currency as an instrument of foreign economic policy may also influence indirectly the objective of establishing a stable macroeconomic framework for investment, as politicians within the member states attempt to compensate those groups that are adversely affected by the policy. Thus not only is the institutionalization of this objective weak, its behavioral characteristics are problematic.

COMPETING RATIONALES AND
THE EXCHANGE RATE STABILITY BIAS

The thumbnail sketches of the five reasons for EMU provided above suggest that these rationales compete on a number of levels—domestic and foreign, institutional and behavioral, national and European. Importantly, however, not all are implicated in such competition to the same degree. The symbolic and efficiency objectives are only seriously threatened once the continued existence of the single currency is brought into question. Although the popularity of the single currency may fluctuate over time, the euro will exist as a symbol and will mitigate transaction costs so long as it functions as a common currency. Therefore, if we can rule out the extreme case of a breakup of EMU, then we can also afford to ignore the symbolic and efficiency reasons for constructing the single currency. As objectives they remain important, but not immediately or problematically so.

The competition between the insulation, stability, and counterweight objectives is less easily put aside. Should the single currency fail to insulate participants from the impact of changes in world market conditions (so-called asymmetric demand shocks), then that failing might also undermine the exercise of fiscal discipline and so work against the goal of macroeconomic stability. Similarly, the prospect that a change in the external value of the currency could adversely affect a participating country—or some politically important constituency within it—could mitigate the use of the euro as an instrument of collective foreign economic policy. And, where policymakers in the euro-zone succeed in exercising foreign economic policy through a manipulation of the external value of the euro, they may also undermine both the insulation that the single currency provides and the fiscal discipline necessary to underpin it. In short, the insulation, stability, and counterweight objectives are deeply interconnected.

The Treaty establishing the European Community (TEC) signed at Amsterdam in 1997 provides a clear hierarchy of objectives. Within that hierarchy, the irrevocable fixing of exchange rates remains at the top of the agenda (Art. 4, Para. 2). Just below that is the provision of a stable macroeconomic framework—both through the conduct of monetary policy according to a price-stability rule (Art. 4, Para. 2) and through the maintenance of requisite fiscal discipline (Art. 4, Para. 3). Management of the external value of the euro whether to insulate participants from fluctuation or as an instrument for foreign economic policy constitutes a distant—and confusing—third (Art. 111). While the treaty recognizes that the European Central Bank may need to respond to changes in the external value of the euro when making monetary policy decisions, it also stipulates that it is the Council of Ministers—and not the ECB—that is responsible for the exercise of foreign economic policy and therefore for the determination of the broad guidelines for the manipulation of the exchange rate. For their part, the Heads of State and Government agreed at the December 1997 Luxembourg summit that such guidelines "will be formulated only in exceptional circumstances" (European Council 1997a, Section 45). Moreover, the treaty stipulates explicitly that any manipulation of the external value of the euro should be made only "after consulting the ECB in an endeavor to reach a consensus consistent with the objective of price stability" or some similar accommodation (TEC, Article 111, Paragraph 1 and passim.).

This hierarchy of objectives makes it clear that the external value of the euro is less important than its domestic stability. By extension, the objective of providing a counterweight to the dollar is less important as well. Nevertheless, the predominance of macroeconomic stability over other objectives should not be taken to imply that the external value of the euro is somehow irrelevant. It is not. Although the precise exchange rate between the euro and any other currency has little significance in its own right, any change in that exchange rate is important in direct and increasing proportion to the size of the change. The larger the fluctuation in the external value of the euro, the more and more broadly important is the change.

The stability bias with respect to the external value of the euro is an implicit function of the competition between the objectives of the single currency. Small fluctuations in the euro exchange rate affect only those sectors or industries not insulated by the irrevocable fixing of exchange rates between participating countries in the euro-zone. In this way, small fluctuations underscore the limitations to the insulation provided by the single currency, but little more. As the size of the fluctuations increases, however, the range of objectives brought into question does as well. Larger fluctuations have a more important impact on exposed groups and begin to affect macroeconomic aggregates for output growth or price inflation directly. Either way, such fluctuations not only undermine the insulation provided by the single currency, they also threaten macroeconomic stability.

This analysis leads to a series of expectations about how the euro-zone will respond to changes in the external value of the euro. If the fluctuation is small or temporary, the response will take place on a case-by-case basis at the industry level—with governments helping firms adjust to the new exchange rate environment or to stave off the need for adjustment. A larger or more prolonged fluctuation will begin to arouse concern from those member states whose industries are most affected as the costs of adjustment assistance or the burden of unemployment become politically salient. Eventually, whether as a function of the size or the duration of the change in the external value of the euro, the ECB will become implicated through its function as guarantor of price stability. The proviso here is that the member states are likely to be less vocal—and the ECB more—in the event of a depreciation in the euro, which will be a boon to exporters but which will also place upward pressure on domestic prices. Reciprocally, the member states will be more vocal—and the ECB less—in the event of an appreciation, which will hurt exports but which will also place downward pressure on domestic prices.

EVIDENCE FROM THE EURO'S FIRST TWO YEARS

The exchange rate stability bias implicit in the constitution of Europe's monetary union is qualitative and not quantitative. Therefore the specification of predicted responses to movements in the exchange rate is weak. Importantly, it is also not unique. Following the logic of the arguments presented above, the expectation is that any monetary union characterized by a domestic stability emphasis will display vulnerability to fluctuations in the exchange rate. In turn, this expectation carries with it the advantage that evidence for the EU's exchange rate stability bias can be found outside the euro-zone as well.

Looking for evidence of exchange-rate vulnerability outside EMU has the advantage that most currencies are smaller than the euro and most currency areas are less well insulated than the euro-zone. Hence not only should we expect to find greater evidence of vulnerability in non-EMU cases, but we should also expect the exchange rate to be subject to a wider variety of influences. Consider, for example, the British pound sterling. In institutional terms, the British currency is very much like the euro. Both currencies are supported by new(ly) independent central banks responsible for prioritizing domestic macroeconomic stability and specifically price stability. The Bank of England was given formal authority over monetary policy in 1998 and the ECB assumed control over the euro in 1999. Both the pound and the euro are widely used in international commerce and finance. And both Britain and the euro-zone have vague pretensions to international monetary power. Nevertheless, it remains true that the euro-zone is much larger than Britain. Britain is more dependent upon external trade as a share of gross domestic product. And where euro-zone politicians worry almost exclusively about the exchange rate with the dollar, British policymakers must keep an eye on the euro as well.

Such differences enhance the usefulness of Britain in comparison with the euro-zone: Not only will the British case demonstrate vulnerability more readily, but also it will allow us to compare the relative importance of appreciation and depreciation as a direction of change in the external value of the currency. Since the launch of the euro on 1 January 1999, the British pound has appreciated against the European currency and depreciated against the dollar at similar rates and in similar magnitudes. Meanwhile (and obviously) the euro has depreciated considerably against both the dollar and (albeit to a lesser extent) the pound. These currency movements are summarized in Table 6.1.

Table 6.1. Euro-Dollar-Pound Exchange Rates, 1999–2001

Period Averages	1999				2000				2001
	Q1	*Q2*	*Q3*	*Q4*	*Q1*	*Q2*	*Q3*	*Q4*	*Q1*
U.S. Dollars per Foreign Currency Unit									
Dollar/Euro	1.12	1.06	1.05	1.04	0.99	0.93	0.91	0.87	0.93
British Pounds Sterling per Foreign Currency Unit									
Pound/Euro	0.69	0.66	0.65	0.64	0.61	0.61	0.61	0.60	0.63
Pound/Dollar	0.61	0.62	0.62	0.61	0.62	0.65	0.68	0.69	0.68

Data source: De Nederlandische Bank.

Following the expectations set out above, we should anticipate that monetary policymakers in both Britain and the euro-zone would express growing concern about the influence of dollar appreciation on domestic prices. Meanwhile, we should also expect British policymakers to draw attention to the impact of euro depreciation on export competitiveness. This asymmetry of concern is both economic and political. The economic asymmetry derives from the fact that Britain trades more with the euro-zone than with the United States. Hence while the pound has tended to follow the dollar in currency markets, the British economy is more widely influenced by movements in the euro. The political asymmetry derives from the fact that firms suffer the loss of competitiveness directly and so have an organic lobby—both in terms of trade unions and sectoral employers associations—to express their concerns. Society as a whole experiences the upward pressure on prices implied by depreciation against the dollar only indirectly through the rising cost of dollar-denominated imports. Meanwhile, far from being organic, societal interests in stable prices are organized administratively in the form of an independent central bank rather than politically in terms of groups ready to complain about the rising cost of imports. Therefore, while the pound's movements against the dollar and the euro are roughly equal and opposite, we should expect the Bank of England to express the balance of interests while British politicians must wrestle with growing cries for a stabilization of the pound-euro exchange rate.

Britain between the Dollar and the Euro

The development of concerns in Britain can be traced through the minutes of the Monetary Policy Committee (MPC), which is responsible for setting the monetary policy of the Bank of England.[4] The offsetting movements of the dollar and the euro against sterling were noted already in March 1999. However, it was the appreciation of sterling against the euro that was regarded as having the more important effect. By May 1999, the MPC considered lowering interest rates in response to sterling's appreciation against the euro and despite concerns that "the market [could reach] the mistaken conclusion that the Committee had a simple rule of thumb for trading off interest rate changes against exchange rate changes." In June, the Committee actually did lower rates, citing the exchange rate as a principal reason behind the decision.

Nevertheless, sterling continued to rise against the euro and so the MPC continued to regard the evolution of the exchange rate with concern. Even as economic indicators began to suggest the need for higher interest rates to stem the growth of inflation, the MPC accepted in September and November 1999 to moderate its rate increases out of concern for their impact on the value of sterling relative to the euro. Such concern dominated MPC discussions in the early months of 2000 and led members of the Committee to question whether the Bank of England should intervene in currency markets to support the euro. A sudden drop in the value of sterling in June 2000 gave some respite, and even had MPC members begin to consider the impact of depreciation on inflation. Yet sterling's secular appreciation against the euro during the summer months provoked another round of intense discussion by early autumn. The September 2000 MPC, meeting two weeks before the coordinated intervention by the Group of Seven leading industrial countries (G7), saw the pound at record lows against the dollar and record highs against the euro. The Committee voted 5–4 against a rise in interest rates in part because "a rise in rates now, at a time when the euro was weak, might strengthen the perceived link between sterling and dollar in an unhelpful way." Thus while the MPC remained resolute that the focus for monetary policy should be on domestic price stability, it is clear that Committee members remained concerned about the relationship between monetary policy decisions and movements in the external value of the pound.

The MPC was not alone in this concern. During the 1999–2000 period, the British manufacturing industry also took a profound interest in the movement of the pound. However, in contrast to the MPC, industry cared little about the depreciation of sterling against the dollar. What mattered for British firms was the loss of competitiveness that they experienced in European markets as a result of the strengthening of the pound against the euro. And the expression of this concern took two forms: efforts to lobby the Bank of England for a more aggressive relaxation of domestic monetary conditions, and efforts to lobby the government in favor of British entry into EMU. Both of these activities find illustration in the welter of events surrounding the collapse of British Rover Group in August 2000. As related in chapter 5, the widespread perception at the time was that the exchange rate between sterling and the euro was damaging the profitability of British automotive production and so either deterring foreign investment or damaging British industry. And while automotive production constitutes only a small fraction of British economic activity, the political implications were obvious both in terms of the need to moderate monetary policy developments and in terms of the need to reconsider arguments in favor of binding sterling to the euro. As already mentioned, the MPC resisted raising interest rates against a weak euro.

Nevertheless, the Blair government did not move to accelerate (or even confirm) British entry into EMU. The preferred political response was to attempt to subsidize car manufacturers through negotiated support mechanisms. That Britain's industrialists considered this strategy to be inadequate was soon apparent. During the winter of 2000–2001, the management of Corus, the Anglo-Dutch steel manufacturer and former British

Steel, decided to lay off more than 6,000 workers citing lack of competitiveness as the principal justification. To the vocal horror of the Blair cabinet, Corus executives took this decision without even bothering to explore the possibility of government aid. As with the automotive industry, steel production is hardly the whole of British economic activity, and the Corus redundancies took place against the backdrop of Britain's lowest unemployment rates in a generation. Yet still the political implications of the external value of sterling were sorely felt by the Labour government which has strong, traditional support from the workforce of heavy industry and was hoping to call a general election within only a few months.

Descent to Intervention in Europe

Policymakers at the European level do not have to worry about appeasing the traditional supporters of the British Labour Party. Moreover, during the first two years of EMU the movement of the euro against the dollar and against sterling was to the benefit of European competitiveness rather than against it. Therefore, the expectation might be that European policymakers would publicly ignore the drop in value of the euro while privately celebrating the boon this provides for manufacturers working in the euro-zone. As suggested in chapter 5, they might deplore the symbolism of a weak currency while at the same time reaping the rewards. Nevertheless, the record of events follows more closely the analysis derived from the contradiction between EMU objectives. Although monetary policymakers initially attempted to downplay the significance of the euro's relative decline, they soon confronted the implications of a weak currency for European macroeconomic performance. Meanwhile, national politicians began to clamor for increasing control over the external value of the single currency. In the ensuing debate, the relative merits of a weak currency for export competitiveness were largely ignored while political consequences of any fluctuation in the external value of the euro moved to center stage. Whether indirectly or directly, the stability bias manifested as clearly with respect to the euro as it did with respect to sterling.

The record of monetary policy decisions can be traced through the press conferences and Euro-parliamentary hearings of ECB President, Wim Duisenberg.[5] The baseline for ECB consideration of exchange rates was set soon after the start of EMU. At his first press conference after the start of EMU, held on 7 January 1999, the ECB President outlined his emphasis on domestic stability:

> we, as the central bank, are interested first and foremost in achieving our statutory aim, i.e. internal price stability. The exchange rate for the central bank is not an explicit aim. It is one of the indicators we will look at . . . together with a broad range of other indicators in determining our policy de-

cisions. But then one cannot repeat often enough that the impact of the exchange rate on the domestic economy is much less than we were used to in the fragmented markets when we were still eleven different markets with ten different exchange rate regimes. As you know, exports account for only 10–11 percent of the combined GDP and which makes the impact of exchange rate variations comparable to those in the United States and Japan. So, most of all, we are interested in stable internal prices and, secondary, we are also interested in a stable exchange rate development. But that is the outcome of policies rather than as the aim.

Duisenberg reiterated this position in response to questions from members of the European Parliament's sub-committee on monetary affairs on 19 January 1999. Speaking to Parliament, Duisenberg made it clear that "the exchange rate vis-à-vis the other big blocks in the world, let's give the animal a name, the dollar and the yen, is the outcome rather than the target of monetary policy." And, while he conceded that the ECB is "very much in favor of . . . as stable a relationship as we can achieve," he also made it explicit that he was strongly opposed to any formal targeting of exchange rate policy objectives.

The immediate decline of the euro against the dollar nevertheless held the question of the external value of the euro on the agenda for the ECB press conferences. By February 1999, Duisenberg noted the decline in the value of the euro with "puzzlement" and yet described it as "not a matter of concern." In March he indicated that the ECB "will closely monitor, and keep monitoring, the exchange rate developments, also with a view to their impact on, or the impact they might have on prices, particularly through import prices." He also signaled that the ECB "would probably react" if it viewed exchange rate developments as "really seriously out of line with the economic fundamentals." The point to note, however, is that the ECB's first policy move in April 1999 was to reduce interest rates in a manner that might have the effect of weakening the value of the euro relative to the dollar. Hence while the ECB noted the decline in the value of the euro, it remained as yet unconcerned. By May 1999, Duisenberg even suggested that the euro was appreciating rather than depreciating.

He was wrong. Already by June 1999, the euro began to approach parity with the dollar. Nevertheless, Duisenberg repeated his mantra about the ECB's emphasis on domestic price stability: "as far as devaluation is concerned, may I repeat what I said: the euro is a currency which is firmly based on internal price stability and therefore has a clear potential for a stronger external value. I think that should be 'crystal clear'." Again in July he insisted: "The view is that the monetary policy of the Eurosystem will safeguard the euro's internal purchasing power and will thereby support its external value. That is what I had to say, what I have to say about the exchange rate. It is all that I am going to say about it."

During the summer months of 1999, the euro appeared to stabilize against the dollar at just above parity. Speculation among financial journalists was that this stabilization was in part due to pronouncements by the ECB that it was developing a bias in favor of monetary tightening and therefore perhaps future increases in the interest rate. Nevertheless, during the September 1999 press conference, Duisenberg doggedly refused any suggestion that monetary policy and exchange rate developments were linked in this manner. Indeed, he refused to mention the exchange rate at all. This refusal to discuss exchange rates continued through the ECB's interest rate rise of November 1999. By December, Duisenberg again began asserting the euro's potential to appreciate over the longer term.

He was wrong again. The secular decline of the euro during the first six months of 2000 had an immediate impact on the considerations of the ECB. Duisenberg conceded the inflationary potential of rising import prices already in February, as the ECB moved to raise interest rates for the second time. In March, the exchange rate "remain[ed] a cause for concern." By May, Duisenberg made an unprecedented appeal to the people of the euro-zone not to lose confidence in their currency. The value of the euro stabilized somewhat during the summer months of 2000, in part perhaps due to the interest rate rise announced in June. However, as autumn approached, the euro again started to decline against the dollar and the pace of decline accelerated. By September, Duisenberg was ready to call for a coordinated intervention in support of the euro.

What is clear from this record is that the ECB cannot afford to ignore the external value of the currency despite the clearest of mandates and the best of intentions. Returning to the analysis posited in the concluding section of chapter 2, the point to note is that the national politicians active in the Council of Ministers have neither clear mandates nor good intentions to restrain their agitation over the exchange rate. Then German Finance Minister Oskar Lafontaine began calling for greater political efforts to stabilize exchange rate fluctuations between the dollar and the euro even before EMU started in January 1999. The force of Lafontaine's critique of EMU was that monetary policy should play a more important role in promoting macroeconomic growth. This frontal assault on the political independence of the ECB and the prioritization of domestic over international stability ultimately (immediately) proved unsuccessful.

Nevertheless, Lafontaine's strong emphasis on the objectives of macroeconomic policy had the effect of diverting attention from the emerging relationship between monetary policymaking within the ECB and economic policy coordination between the members of the euro-zone. And, it was here that the political arguments in favor of greater exchange rate stability gathered momentum. The informal Euro-11 group of Economic and Finance Ministers from the euro-zone countries meeting before the ECOFIN Council noted with growing concern that the impact of euro-depreciation against the dollar was not felt equally in all member states. Put simply, fluctuations in the external value of the euro pose not only macroeconomic problems but also coordination problems. Moreover, these coordination problems work in both directions—fluctuations in the value of the euro complicate the task of coordination between participating countries and the lack of coordination between participants impacts on the external value of the euro.

During the problematic spring of 2000, the Euro-11 made frequent pronouncements expressing their concern over the euro-dollar exchange rate and even joined in supporting Duisenberg's May 2000 direct appeal to the people of the euro-zone. Moreover, during the summer of 2000, the incoming French presidency consolidated the functioning of the Euro-11 under the more generic title "Eurogroup" as a first step in strengthening coordination both in the face of movements in the external value of the euro and as a means of asserting greater control over those movements. The first pronouncements of the (re-branded) Eurogroup were explicit in asserting that "a strong euro is in the interest of the euro area" (11 September). Meanwhile, French Finance Minister Laurent Fabius suggested that "intervention was a 'tool which is available at any moment'" (European Voice 2000).

He was right. On 22 September 2000, the European Central Bank asked its counterparts among the Group of Seven leading industrial countries to intervene in foreign exchange markets in order to support the value of the euro against the dollar. The G-7 finance ministers and central bankers agreed, citing in justification "a shared interest in a strong and stable international monetary system" and "shared concern . . . about the potential implications of recent movements in the euro for the world economy" (G-7 2000, paragraph 5). Nevertheless, the intervention was an unbalanced and lackluster affair. Although the ECB expended significant dollar reserves in purchasing euros, the United States—which obviously holds a far greater volume of dollars—committed only a modest amount. To make matters worse, the U.S. Secretary of the Treasury, Lawrence Summers, reiterated the Clinton administration's view that a strong dollar is in America's interest. This combination of factors confronted currency markets with contradictory signals. As a result, the euro-dollar exchange rate reacted little if at all: While the price of a euro increased from US 85 cents on 21 September to US 89 cents on 22 September, this modest price improvement deteriorated rapidly and by 25 October a euro was worth just 83 cents.

In the aftermath of the September 2000 currency market interventions it became clear not only that the Euro-zone could ill afford to disregard the external value of the single currency but also that this vulnerability derives from the conflict between EMU objectives. Speaking on the record to Lea Paterson and Anatole Kaletsky of the London *Times* (16 October 2000), Duisenberg attempted both to play up the success of the G-7 interventions and to play down the likelihood that the ECB would ask for further assistance in the near future. His comments sparked a further drop in the euro-dollar exchange rate and drew a fire storm of protest from Europe's capitals. Attempts by Duisenberg to recant his position had little immediate effect. As a result, the ECB soon found itself intervening again in currency markets to support the external value of the euro and against a backdrop of ever greater resolve among at least some participants in EMU to strengthen the coordination capacity of the Eurogroup.

Much like Britain's Monetary Policy Committee, the ECB cannot afford to ignore the external value of the euro. However, unlike the MPC, Europe's monetary union confronted the more gentle of the two possible forms of mis-alignment. Although the symbolism of a weak currency is arguably worse than that for a currency that can be touted as being "strong," the economic implications are more easily managed. This is true particularly in relation to the problems of coordination that lie at the heart of the political challenge to Europe's prioritization of domestic price stability over the stability of the external value of the euro. As the British case makes clear, appreciation against the euro is far more important than depreciation against the dollar, whether considered broadly in terms of British macroeconomic performance or narrowly in terms of specific firms or industries. Thus while the depreciation of the euro against the dollar has created a difficult challenge for EMU, an appreciation would likely have been worse (see also Dornbusch and Jacquet 2000). The bias toward stability in the external value of the euro (and the pound) is asymmetric. Nevertheless it is still potent whether the currency moves up or down.

AMERICAN EXCEPTIONALISM AND
THE INTERNATIONAL ROLE OF THE EURO

Europe's sensitivity to changes in the external value of the euro suggests two questions. What can policymakers in the euro-zone do to stabilize the exchange rate? And why is the United States less vulnerable to exchange rate fluctuations? The answer to the first question returns us to the context within which both the ECB and the Bank of England have to operate. The answer to the second question returns us to the constraint.

The context is globalization. And, within a globalized economy there is very little that a central bank or government can do to manage the external value of the currency. This is clear in reading both the MPC minutes at the Bank of England and the press conferences of the ECB. The realization that changes in the external values of sterling and the euro have significant macroeconomic implications is apparent. The relationship between changes in monetary policy instruments and movements in the exchange rates is not. Throughout both forums there is substantial evidence of the frustration felt by monetary policymakers when confronted with exchange rate developments out of line with "the economic fundamentals"—meaning, which cannot be anticipated or explained given standard models for exchange rate determination. That the policymakers in the MPC and at the ECB both considered and, in the European case, attempted direct intervention in the currency market is a sign of their desperation. That ECB President Duisenberg would express reluctance to intervene only reflects his exasperation with the results. At the end of the day, there is very little that policymakers in the euro-zone can do to stabilize the external value of the euro. There is also very little they can do to ignore it.

Yet somehow the United States can afford to operate a policy of "benign neglect" within which the Secretary of the Treasury is reluctant to intervene in currency markets and—when pressed—is even willing to work against the success of his own interventions. This begs the question: What is at the heart of dollar exceptionalism? The answer is not the dollar.

Possession of a single currency does not by itself insulate the United States from fluctuations in world markets and so cannot provide the basis for American monetary power. The U.S. currency is no different in this respect than either the pound or the euro. What is different for the United States is the willingness of the U.S. Federal Reserve to accept a trade-off between domestic price stability and other economic objectives and the capacity of U.S. fiscal authorities to intermediate the costs associated with fluctuations in the dollar both *ex ante* and *ex post*. The dollar is stronger than the euro or the pound because it is supported by mechanisms that act both to ease and to accommodate the conflicting objectives of the U.S. monetary union. Moreover, it is the creation of these flanking institutions at the time of the American Civil War—and not the introduction of the Greenback dollar—that signals the reconstruction of the U.S. monetary union and that marks the nascence of the United States as a global economic player (McNamara 2000).

Neither the euro-zone nor the United Kingdom can compete with the United States in terms of brute monetary power or in terms of the capacity for "benign neglect." Both Britain and Europe lack the willingness to trade off macroeconomic objectives. Moreover, Britain is more dependent upon foreign trade than the United States and therefore is relatively more vulnerable to the influence of world market forces. Given its smaller size and greater openness, Britain simply is not a good contender for American style monetary power. Europe is neither so small nor so open. Nevertheless, in addition to its domestic stability bias, the euro-zone lacks centralized institutions for the redistribution of adjustment costs *ex post*. Given the structure of collective action between Europe's member states, the Eurogroup can at best aspire to coordinate economic policies *ex ante* and so relies on assumptions of stability rather than being able to react to the requirements of change.

The inability of sterling and the euro to have the strength of the dollar whether in terms of purposeful manipulation or in terms of benign neglect should not lead Europeans to question the merits of EMU. Rather it should necessitate a serious consideration of the objective of exercising—or aspiring to the exercise of—monetary power. For Britain, the solution is straightforward: if British policymakers are serious in their desire to stabilize domestic macroeconomic conditions then they should also give more serious consideration to participating in EMU. Any pretension to "monetary sovereignty" through the maintenance of an independent currency not only has the effect of forcing monetary policymakers to place undue emphasis on movements in the exchange rate which ultimately they cannot control but also risks undermining purely domestic objectives.

For Europe the solution is equally straightforward, though harder to accept. If European policymakers are sincere in their desire to establish EMU as a zone of macroeconomic stability then they must accept that some structured relationship with the dollar is prerequisite. No matter how much more insulation from world market forces a European monetary union provides in comparison with a national currency, the potential for external factors to influence domestic macroeconomic performance remains important. Therefore, the dichotomy facing Europe's policymakers is between a relaxation of emphasis on domestic stability coupled with a greater willingness to centralize the intermediation of adjustment (read fiscal authority) on the one hand, and a more coherent relationship with the dollar on the other hand. In this context, exchange rate coordination benefits—and does not come at the expense of—domestic macroeconomic stability.

The European solution is hard to accept because it presents policymakers in the euro-zone with a chicken-and-egg dilemma. In order to abandon the objective of positing the euro as a counterweight to the dollar they must first convince the United States to do likewise. Yet, as Secretary of the Treasury Summers demonstrated, U.S. policymakers are not easy to convince in this regard. For European policymakers, such U.S. reluctance means that either the United States must be forced to participate in exchange rate coordination or it must be ignored. Whatever the case, Europe must first generate the capacity to pressure the dollar or to weather its "benign neglect." The single currency is only a second-best solution to the problem of a wider reform of global financial markets. To reiterate, Europe's single currency builds upon an internal focus but retains an external vulnerability.

NOTES

1. Two examples are Henning (2000a) and (2000b).

2. Second parties in this context are EU member states that choose not to participate in the single currency. These second parties are covered by the obligation to treat the exchange rate between their national currencies and the euro as a matter of common concern. See chapter 2.

3. This exposition perhaps overstates the claim. The creation of a real-time payment clearing mechanism that works across EMU participants—called TARGET—represents a fundamental change in the way Europe does business. Moreover, it is a change for the better, that should have important knock-on effects in terms of future trade and investment.

4. The minutes of the Bank of England's Monetary Policy Committee are available online at www.bankofengland.co.uk/mpc/minutes.htm.

5. The press conferences and parliamentary hearings of the ECB president are available online at www.ecb.int.

7

✛

Determination:
Power and Collective Action

The argument so far is guardedly optimistic. Europe's economic and monetary union (EMU) represents a minor technological innovation in the use of money intended principally to depoliticize monetary policy through the delegation of authority from the member states to the European Central Bank. Given the nature of money and of economic preferences, there is no a priori objection to such a delegation on democratic grounds, and yet it will require an adjustment on the part of economic actors working both within and across the member states. Most of these actors will adjust through the institutions of the welfare state—which is to say, at the national level—and the political consequences of this adjustment across Europe should be expected to be idiosyncratic in character, and dependent upon the structure of prevailing institutions. Such an arrangement is unlikely to challenge the dollar for global supremacy and indeed has an important external weakness. Still, it is better than any attempt by the member states to go it alone. The analysis concludes that EMU should gradually slip into the background of broader European and national concerns.

Nevertheless, EMU has deeply political origins and in many ways it constitutes a political system in its own right. Therefore, it is relevant to ask how EMU will affect the politics of its own creation. This is the other side of Martin Feldstein's (1997) critique as posited in chapter 4, and it is that EMU will so shift the balance of power in Europe as to force some countries to demand the dismantling of Europe's monetary union. Given the predominant role played by France and Germany in the construction of EMU, the most obvious place to look for an unfavorable shift in the balance of forces is within the Franco-German relationship. Moreover, there is strong reason to believe that both the relationship and the balance of forces within it have changed considerably during the 1990s.

Now that EMU has started, the Franco-German relationship remains at the center of European integration but it is Germany, without France, that lies at the center of Europe's economic and monetary union. It is Germany's own monetary institutions that provide the template for those bestowed on Europe; Germany's constitutional court that underscored the essential importance of European price stability; and Germany's Ministry of Finance that elevated fiscal rectitude above other concerns such as growth or employment.[1] This predominance of Germany in EMU poses a problem for the future of the Franco-German relationship. As EMU becomes more important for Europe, will France become less important for Germany? Put another way, does economic integration continue to provide a common basis for Franco-German reconciliation?

The record of economic cooperation between France and Germany in the 1990s is unimpressive. So too is the record of French and German economic performance. Although both countries succeeded in constructing (and joining) Europe's monetary union, they did so only with great difficulty, against a background of controversy, and to initially mixed reviews. Meanwhile, France and Germany ended the decade with slow growth, high unemployment, and the promise of only a gradual recovery. The contrast with the economic accomplishments of the late 1980s and the tight pattern of bilateral cooperation underwriting the Maastricht Treaty negotiations could not be more striking. Economic relations, it would seem, are no longer a Franco-German forte.

The principal argument in this chapter is that economic issues continue to serve as a focal point for relations between France and Germany and that Franco-German economic relations remain important for European integration. Nevertheless, the emphasis within the economic relations of France and Germany has changed fundamentally in the aftermath of the Cold War. Where once France and Germany might have focused on the importance of bilateral exchanges or patterns of convergence, now Franco-German economic relations are rooted more completely and intentionally in processes of collective action. European integration may not be an objective in its own right, but it is much more than a by-product of the Franco-German relationship.

This argument is not entirely unique in the broader literature on recent developments in Western Europe. Among others, Simon Bulmer (1993, 1997), Peter Katzenstein (1997), and Jeffrey Anderson (1997, 1999) have made a similar point about the growing importance of Europe in "taming" German power after unification.[2] Broadly, their claim is that the complex web of institutions, rules, and procedures in Europe have so defined, divided, and restrained German interests that the increase in power resulting from unification could have only a transitory effect on the pattern of German relations. In other words, Germany has become so entangled in Europe that self-extraction is no longer an option. The low points of the 1990s derive from German assertiveness or recalcitrance, the high points from German acceptance of multilateral identities and constraints.

The "tamed power" argument has considerable merit. Nevertheless, the emphasis is misplaced when applied to economic relations between France and Germany. It can explain some of the excesses of German behavior but not those of the French. Therefore a secondary purpose of this chapter is to provide a different perspective on recent analysis of German power. Specifically, I argue that the stability of the Franco-German relationship derives not simply from the fact that European institutions constrain actors or reshape their preferences, but also from the reality that institution-building and institutionalized collective action are mechanisms for generating and exercising national power.[3] Despite (the supposed) French resistance to multilayered identities and federal arrangements, France is also "tamed" because it is also empowered.

This change in emphasis has important implications for the role of the Franco-German couple in Europe. The roots of Franco-German antagonism may stretch back to the dawn of time, but now cooperation between the two countries is the norm and not the exception.[4] Hence, the old emphasis on how European integration has helped to facilitate Franco-German reconciliation should be replaced with a new emphasis on how France and Germany cooperate to achieve a range of objectives both at home and abroad.[5]

Paraphrasing Julius Friend (1991, 98), the question is not whether France is as important as Germany or whether France has anything to offer Germany directly, but whether either France or Germany can manage Europe alone. No matter how central Germany is within EMU, France and Germany remain central to each other and to both countries' strategies in Europe.

The chapter has five sections. The first surveys Franco-German economic relations in the 1990s. The second examines the evidence that France and Germany have less in common—at least from the broad statistical perspective—in the aftermath of German unification. The third analyzes the pattern of Franco-German economic relations in terms of changes in German power and the fourth reinterprets those relations in terms of collective action. The fifth section concludes by re-establishing the Franco-German relationship as the context of monetary integration.

THOSE TROUBLED NINETIES

The record for French and German macroeconomic performance is poor—particularly in comparison with the United States, but also relative to the United Kingdom. Both France and Germany experienced a prolonged slowdown in real economic growth (overall and per capita), rising levels of unemployment, and creeping public debts. Meanwhile, the two countries did succeed in mastering inflation and lowering long-term real interest rates, but not much more impressively than the Anglo-Saxons. Finally, where available, early predictions suggest that any improvements made in the year 2000 will be reversed in 2001–2002 (see Table 7.1).

This mixed bag of macroeconomic performance carried a high price in terms of the Franco-German efforts to form a monetary union. The relative exchange rate stability of the late 1980s was lost, the institutional structure of the European Monetary System had to be changed, the first deadline to form EMU was missed, and speculation that France and Germany would themselves fail to meet the criteria for entry continued right up until the end. In the event, both France and Germany were accused of fudging their national data in order to ensure that they could join (Pierson et al. 1999). If only in symbolic terms, the appearance of incompetence and impropriety was costly.

Allegations of impropriety were not the only failings of France, Germany, or the Franco-German relationship. In addition, the poor record for macroeconomic performance of the French and German economies has been punctuated by a series of economic-related conflicts. Differences between France and Germany emerged repeatedly during the 1990s and covered the gamut of core European issues from agricultural policy, to interest rates, enlargement, fiscal balances, employment, and the relationship between politics and economics. In summary form, these controversies can be grouped around three questions: Who pays for Europe (coupled with what does Europe pay for)? What are the priorities for economic adjustment? How should the broad guidelines for European economic policy be set?

The question about who pays for Europe touches on a range of issues that emerged at the end of the Cold War about the enlargement of the European Union and about the reform of the Common Agricultural Policy (CAP). In reduced form, it concerns the parity of net contributions to EU coffers across member states on the one hand, versus the depth and breadth of European outlays on the other hand. The French position has been that the existing distribution of burdens is roughly equitable, and that European support mechanisms should be deep but narrow. In other words, net contributions should remain much as they have been and so should the CAP. Meanwhile, any enlargement of the EU should be sup-

Table 7.1. Macroeconomic Performance in France and Germany Compared

	1986–1990	1991–1996	1996–1999	2000
Unemployment (percent labor force)				
West Germany				
(unified Germany)	5.9	5.6 (7.3)	9.2	8.1
France	9.7	11.1	11.8	9.5
United Kingdom	9.0	9.5	6.9	5.6
United States	5.9	6.6	4.9	4.0
Real GDP Growth (annual percentage change)				
West Germany				
(unified Germany)	3.3	1.5 (1.2)	1.7	2.9
France	3.2	1.1	2.3	3.1
United Kingdom	3.3	1.6	2.3	3.3
United States	2.8	2.0	3.4	4.9
Real GDP per capita Growth (annual percentage change)				
West Germany				
(unified Germany)	2.6	0.2 (0.7)	1.9	2.8
France	2.6	0.6	1.9	2.7
United Kingdom	2.9	1.2	2.0	2.6
United States	1.9	0.9	2.7	3.7
Price Deflator, Private Consumption (annual percentage change)				
West Germany				
(unified Germany)	1.5	3.5 (3.3)	1.3	1.4
France	2.9	2.3	1.0	1.2
United Kingdom	5.3	4.2	2.4	0.8
United States	4.1	2.9	1.6	2.4
Real Long-term Interest Rates (deflated by private consumption)				
West Germany				
(unified Germany)	5.2	3.7 (3.5)	3.7	5.7
France	6.0	5.4	4.1	4.9
United Kingdom	4.2	4.1	3.7	3.4
United States	4.2	4.0	4.0	3.9
Public Debt (percentage GDP)				
West Germany				
(unified Germany)	43.8*	44.7 (48.0)	61.1	60.3
France	33.8	44.5	58.2	58.0
United Kingdom	45.9	49.7	42.9	

Note: All German data post-1996 are unified Germany, *1990 only.
Data source: European Commission.

ported only to the extent to which it does not disrupt existing financial arrangements. By contrast, the German position has been that the distribution of burdens needs to be re-balanced, and that European support mechanisms should be less generous but more widely spread. The level of German net contributions should be decreased both through an increase in gross benefits and through a decrease in outlays to Europe. Moreover, the financial arrangements of the EU should be made more realistic, phasing out excessive programs (such as the CAP) in order to facilitate European enlargement.

The contrast between these French and German positions is considerable. As a result, France and Germany came into repeated conflict over enlargement, CAP reform, and budgetary reform more generally. The record of outcomes is mixed. France was unable to delay enlargement to Austria, Finland, and Sweden, and has been signally unsuccessful in postponing an Eastward expansion of the EU for the "decades and decades" suggested by François Mitterrand in June 1991 (De la Serre and Lequesne 1993, 156). However, France was able to moderate—but not to prevent— a succession of CAP reforms, first during the Uruguay Round of GATT negotiations, and later during the financial planning surrounding the Commission's Agenda 2000 program for enlargement (Webber 1999; Edwards and Wiessala 1999). For its part, Germany was able to push for an accelerated enlargement and to place a cap on its contributions to Europe. In essence both sides achieved their objectives by shunting the burdens on third parties—principally the applicant countries in Central and Eastern Europe but also, and to a far lesser extent, the so-called "cohesion" countries whose structural and regional funds are most subject to reform. France and Germany were able to agree on the notion that enlargement should not be allowed to undermine existing financial relations within Europe. Hence while the scope of Europe increases, the benefits of European support mechanisms will become ever more focused (O'Neill 1999; Galloway 1999).

The question about the priorities for economic adjustment concerns an equally broad set of issues relating to labor market performance and fiscal balances. In a nutshell, the question is whether there is a necessary trade-off between efforts to reduce unemployment and to stabilize fiscal balances. The French position has been that there is: No matter what the merits of fiscal austerity for price stability, the cost is high in terms of employment. Therefore, on the margin at least, governments should be allowed some flexibility on the fiscal side to pursue non-monetary objectives. The German position is that the causes of unemployment lie principally in the institutions of the labor market—including the relations between employers and trade unions—rather than in the relative austerity of the government's fiscal stance. Indeed, any observable relationship between employment or unemployment and fiscal balances operates only over the short term. Over the long term, fiscal imbalances threaten employment prospects through (*inter alia*) their effects on price stability. Therefore any excess flexibility on the fiscal side is likely to worsen, rather than to benefit, the functioning of the labor market.

Here again the conflicts have been numerous and the outcomes mixed. For its part, Germany succeeded not only in enforcing the criteria for fiscal performance established in the Maastricht Treaty but also in getting the member states to accept a code of fiscal conduct—the "Stability and Growth Pact" outlined in chapter 2—that is even more restrictive. Meanwhile, France was able to push employment issues closer to the center of the European agenda by adding an "employment chapter" during the treaty revision process at Amsterdam. Finally, both parties were able to secure important elements of compromise. France diluted the procedures and sanctions to be applied in enforcing the Stability Pact, and Germany prevented France from tabling an even more ambitious proposal for the financing of job creation (Pierson, Forster, and Jones 1998). In this area, as in the previous one, the French and the Germans were able to find sufficient common basis for ameliorating their differences.

Such relative success was less available with regard to conflict over the political direction of European economic policy. In institutional terms, what is at stake is whether European macroeconomic policy should be guided by rules or discretion. Moreover, the basis for disagreement is predictable, at least in light of the disagreement concerning the relationship between fiscal austerity and unemployment just discussed. The Germans prefer rules and the French would rather see more scope for discretion. The problem is that the dichotomy between rules and discretion is not symmetrical in terms of the symbolic exercise of political influence.[6] If the choice is for discretion, then all parties can exercise influence both at the moment of choice and during any exercise of discretion. In symbolic terms, the actor who prefers rules loses only once but remains in the game as an equal participant. If the choice is for rules, the parties can exercise influence only over the constitution of the rules. Once the rules are in place, the opportunity for political influence is lost and the actor who prefers rules seems to predominate. From the French perspective, what this means is that the alternatives are not rules versus discretion but rather equality versus subordination. And the only way out of this symbolic trap is to find some way to be seen as managing the rules.

The conflicts that have emerged around the political direction of European economic policy have been bitter. On an institutional level, France has repeatedly insisted that the European Central Bank (ECB) take some form of guidance from the European Council, the Council of Economic and Finance Ministers (ECOFIN), or even a consultative body comprising the ECOFIN delegates of those member states participating in EMU. Equally often, the Germans have insisted that the ECB must retain its political independence in order to pursue a rule of absolute price stability. Given the analysis in chapter 2, the compromise between these two positions is relatively easy to anticipate. The ECOFIN delegates of EMU member states do coordinate their positions in a separate group (originally called the Euro-11 and now called the Eurogroup), but this group neither issues instructions to ECOFIN nor does it issue guidance to the ECB. Put another way, no political discretion is permitted to interfere with the functioning of the price stability rule (Pierson, Forster, and Jones 1999).

On a symbolic level, the conflict between France and Germany over the political direction of European economic policy is much harder to reconcile. Thus during the launch of EMU in the spring of 1998, France attempted to place its own candidate, Jean-Claude Trichet, at the head of the ECB. However, the job had already been promised to a Dutch candidate, Wim Duisenberg, who enjoyed considerable German support. Neither France nor Germany could afford to back down because doing so would suggest either that France had lost power or that the ECB was subject to political influence. Even the compromise ultimately reached—that the two candidates will split the eight year term—is symbolically unsatisfactory because it taints both parties. France is still weak and the ECB is still subject to influence. As a result, this conflict is generally regarded as a low-point in Franco-German cooperation (Dinan 1999).

DRIFTING APART WHILE STANDING STILL

These recurrent ups and downs in Franco-German economic relations look decidedly different from the close cooperation in the mid-to-late 1980s. One possible explanation is that the formula that bound the two countries together before German unification has somehow ceased to apply. The difficulty lies in sorting out what exactly that formula was or is. Obviously a huge range of factors should be taken into account: common interests, identities, history, shared experiences, personalities, etc. However, arranging these factors into a framework for analysis is complicated to say the least. Rather than trying to reinvent the wheel, perhaps it is best to start where others have gone before.

From the 1950s through the early 1990s, two perspectives on the Franco-German relationship have predominated. In one, the relationship is based on patterns of exchange. France wants something from Germany, and Germany wants something from France. In the other, the relationship is based on patterns of convergence. Both France and Germany want to become more like the other. These perspectives are not necessarily symmetrical and neither are they mutually exclusive. France can give more or less than Germany, and France can move more or less toward Germany than the other way around. Moreover, the two perspectives can complement each other. France can give something to Germany and, in return, Germany can facilitate the process of French convergence.

As a set of analytic tools, notions of exchange and convergence necessarily restrict the scope of the argument. Nevertheless, they can help to explain many of the most important developments in the Franco-German relationship. Hence, for Willis (1965), the founding of the European Coal and Steel Community represents an exchange of German sovereignty for French economic benefits. For Simonian (1985), the European Monetary System represents a convergence of French macroeconomic preferences on the German model. And for McCarthy (1990), the welter of events surrounding the hardening of the European Monetary System and the relaunching of Europe after 1983 represents a complex combination of exchange and convergence. Implicitly in each case, the stability of the development derives from the terms of the exchange and from the commitment to convergence. So long as these are fair and firm, the Franco-German relationship will remain stable.[7]

Notions of exchange and convergence can also help to locate sources of change. What will happen to the Franco-German relationship if one day France and Germany have less to offer one-another and little or no desire to become more alike? Within the context of the argument, the answer is in many ways more obvious than the question. If for whatever reason France and Germany had little to exchange, or if they no longer sought to converge, then the ardor of their relationship should be expected to cool. Correspondingly, the stimulus for further integration in Europe should weaken. However, economic integration is not assumed to work that way. Countries become more dependent upon one another and not less. Moreover, in the fire of global competition, both macroeconomic strategies and market structures should be expected to look more and more the same.

Europe's economic and monetary union represents a good starting point for analyzing this problem because it combines many of the classic perspectives on the Franco-German relationship: It is almost wholly Franco-German in origin, it builds on some form of an exchange between France and Germany, and it involves a process of convergence with the effect of making the two countries more alike. In characterized form, the origins of EMU can be stated as follows: France was pursuing closer monetary integration with Germany as a means to bring more symmetry into the economic relations of the two countries, but with limited success. Once the Berlin Wall fell, however, EMU became an essential part of the French strategy for binding Germany to the West. Hence, France agreed to support German unification in return for German acceptance of EMU.

This exchange was insufficient to persuade Germany to abandon the Deutschemark and neither was it adequate to ensure that the EMU created would function according to German norms. Therefore, France accepted embedding EMU within a larger reform of the political institutions of the EU and constructing the monetary union around a framework of predominantly German-looking institutions. According to this characterization of events, EMU represents both an attempt to integrate the French and German economies more deeply and to encourage their convergence.

This characterization of EMU is not an accurate reconstruction of historical events, and neither is it meant to be. Indeed, according to at least one account, the events are simply too detailed and complicated to permit easy characterization (Dyson and Featherstone 1999). That said, characterizations are both useful and used. Despite its obvious simplification, this hackneyed telling of the origins of EMU accurately reflects the thumbnail sketches that appear throughout the literature. What it fails to reflect is the actual development of Franco-German economic relations during the run-up to monetary union. And that is precisely the point.

The broad statistical data suggest that France and Germany have grown less dependent upon one another—at least in terms of the trade in goods and services. In the 1990s, France and Germany have tended to trade less with one-another than they have with everyone else. German exports to France have accounted for only a decreasing proportion of total German exports. By the same token, French imports from Germany have accounted for a decreasing share of total French imports. The story with respect to French exports to Germany is much the same. Although French exporters have sent an increasing share of their output to Germany, German importers have come to rely increasingly on suppliers elsewhere.[8] These data can be found in Table 7.2, which gives the averages for bilateral imports and exports as a percentage of the total for the periods from 1984–1990 and from 1991–1998, which is to say roughly for the period from the relaunching of Europe to German unification, and from the signing of the Maastricht Treaty to the start of EMU.

Table 7.2.   Trade Dependence between France and Germany

	1984–1990	1991–1998
German Exports to France		
Percent Total German Exports	12.4	11.8
Percent Total French Imports	18.4	17.6
French Exports to Germany		
Percent Total French Exports	15.4	16.9
Percent Total German Imports	11.4	11.2

Source: International Monetary Fund.

Of course there is some scope to argue that these data are the result of the general downturn in economic activity across Europe. France and Germany trade less with one-another because they trade less full stop. In such an event, the expectation is that—all things being equal—the country with the sharpest decline in imports will also show the sharpest decrease in import penetration. Hence we should expect French import markets to have contracted more than those in Germany, if only with respect to Europe and perhaps not to everywhere else. In fact, the opposite is the case. While French and German import markets do contract in relation to their extra-European partners by roughly equivalent amounts, German import markets contract by considerably more in relation to Europe. At the same time, while German imports into France have declined, the volume of French imports overall has remained much the same (see Table 7.3).

Another possible explanation is that everything has not remained the same from the 1980s to the 1990s. Specifically, German unification has forced a number of dramatic changes on the German economy and, in particular, on German trade patterns. With the incorporation of the five new Länder, Germany also acquired substantial market relations with the countries of Central and Eastern Europe. As a result, Germany trades considerably more with those countries—and, by implication, marginally less with France. The data here are supportive. Between 1991 and 1997, the share of German exports going to the non-EU countries of Europe increased from 8.0 percent to 12.1 percent while the share of German imports coming from that region increased from 7.4 percent to 11.3 percent. The same figures for France show a much lower expansion, at least in absolute terms if not in proportional terms. Between 1991 and 1997, the share of French exports going to non-EU Europe increased from 2.8 percent to 4.9 percent, while the share of imports increased from 2.9 percent to 3.8 percent.[9]

The prospect that trade between France and Germany has been displaced by trade between Germany and the countries of Central and Eastern Europe

Table 7.3. Import Penetration in France and Germany

Percentage gross domestic product	*1984–1990*	*1991–1998*
Imports from within Europe		
France	11.8	11.4
Germany	13.3	11.5
Imports from Outside Europe		
France	7.3	6.9
Germany	9.3	8.8

Source: European Commission.

represents a significant challenge to any conception of the Franco-German relationship based on a binding notion of exchange. Accepting for a moment that one purpose of the Maastricht Treaty—and specifically of EMU—was to bind Germany to the West, the effectiveness of that strategy is open to question: Germany's economic center of gravity appears to have shifted nonetheless. Moreover, the prospect that this movement has not been reflected in a change in Germany's basic approach to commercial policy and that the driving force for accessing eastern markets originates in the old western Länder is more problematic still (Anderson 1999, 72–73). Despite the best of intentions, the possibility exists that whatever France has to offer Germany is not as attractive as that which can be found elsewhere.

Then again, the decreasing intensity of trading relations between France and Germany could signal the success of Franco-German convergence rather than the failure of some pre-existing exchange. As France and Germany become more alike, it is only natural that they should look elsewhere for trading partners. Of course some division of labor would continue to operate between French and German manufacturing—particularly on the level of intra-industry trade—and yet both countries will have to find trading partners specializing in other parts of the product cycle. For Germany, these partners are to the East, and for France to the South. From 1991 to 1997, the share of French imports originating in Italy, Spain, and Portugal increased slightly from 17.1 percent to 17.4 percent, while the share of German imports originating in these countries decreased from 12.9 percent to 12.3 percent.[10]

The problem is that there is little evidence either that France and Germany are still converging on common institutional arrangements, market structures, or levels of productivity, or that they are converging on a common set of preferences—whether microeconomic or macroeconomic—about how the economy should function. There was some convergence during the 1970s and 1980s, but not after. During the 1990s, French and German macroeconomic performance has "converged"—at least as measured according to the criteria for participation in EMU—but the two economies have remained characteristically French and German. Following the logic of this claim, any dispute over the political direction of economic policy is necessarily exacerbated by disputes over how the economy should function.

Evidence of persistent structural differences between France and Germany is relatively plentiful. For example, trade union density declined in both countries by approximately 6 percent during the period from 1990 to 1995. Nevertheless, the level of trade union activity in Germany remains three times that in France. German trade union confederations are larger, more centralized, and more diverse in their membership. French trade union confederations are more numerous, more decentralized, and far more heavily represented in the public sector than anywhere else (Visser 1998). Similarly persistent differences are evident in terms of the distribution of employment across different branches of the economy. During the 1990s, both France and Germany experienced a shift away from agriculture and manufacturing and toward service-sector employment. Within that broad movement, however, the relative importance of French agriculture and of German manufacturing remains apparent (see Table 7.4).

The broader panoply of institutions and policies that constitute the French and German economies is harder to characterize. Nevertheless, a recent study by Andrea Boltho (1996) seems to encapsulate the consensus view: Although the French have made much discussion of adopting Germany as an economic model, French successes at developing German-style institutions or practices has been limited. Indeed, in microeconomic or institutional terms, France appears to be moving more toward the market liberalism of the United States than toward the organized market economy in Germany.

Table 7.4.   Sectoral Composition of German and French Employment

Period averages, percentage total employment.	*1980–1985*	*1986–1990*	*1991–1997*
Agriculture			
West Germany	4.9	3.9	2.9
Unified Germany			3.1
France	7.8	6.3	4.8
Construction			
West Germany	7.5	6.7	6.7
Unified Germany			8.1
France	8.1	7.3	6.8
Services			
West Germany	53.2	56.0	60.6
Unified Germany			60.5
France	59.4	64.3	68.7
Industry (excluding construction)			
West Germany	34.4	33.3	29.8
Unified Germany			28.2
France	24.8	22.1	19.7
Manufacturing			
West Germany	32.5	31.6	28.3
Unified Germany			26.6
France	23.5	20.9	18.6

Note: Industry and Manufacturing are two different aggregations of similar data.

The lack of structural or institutional convergence between France and Germany makes any meaningful convergence of macroeconomic preferences unlikely. Despite the obvious comparisons of macroeconomic indicators such as those for inflation, interest rates, and fiscal balances, the mechanisms at work behind that macroeconomic performance are bound to differ from one country to another. For example, it is one thing to explain that large German trade unions make their wage bargaining claims in anticipation of stable monetary conditions and out of respect for the capacity of German monetary authorities to create unemployment damaging to German union members. This is, in essence, the classic explanation for German wage moderation—and it relies precisely on those characteristic features of German trade unions, their density, diversity, and centralization, that distinguishes them from the French (Hall 1994). There is no analogous explanation for French wage moderation. That it happened is apparent in the data. Why it happened is not (Bazen and Girardin 1999).

Finally, without a common set of mechanisms to underwrite macroeconomic performance the meaningfulness of expressions of similar macroeconomic preferences is surely open to question. Just because France and Germany both claim to value sound money and stable finances cannot be taken to mean that they hold these values for the same reasons and with the same intensity. Indeed, this has been a concern of German monetary policymakers throughout the process of monetary integration, and it explains to a large extent their desire for a "political union" to complement Europe's monetary union. As Bundesbank President Hans Tietmeyer (1994: 58) explains: "A momentary similarity of interests without a lasting political connection hardly forms a sufficient basis for a monetary union." By implication, the mixed record of Franco-German economic relations in the 1990s is a symptom that their "momentary similarity of interests" may be coming to an end.

THE RIDDLE OF GERMAN POWER

At this point it is necessary to arrest the discussion from falling into extreme pessimism. The economic basis for cooperation between France and Germany may have deteriorated, but that is no reason to write off the Franco-German relationship altogether. For example, relations in other areas—such as defense or foreign policy—could strengthen to pick up the slack.[11] The objective of the argument so far has been simply to establish that something has changed and to begin to explain why. And the answer is still only partial. By itself, the decline in the old formulas for the Franco-German relationship is insufficient to explain the mixed record of performance and conflict during the 1990s. It can help to establish the basis for disagreement, but not the motivation for continued good relations.

One possible solution is to change the emphasis in the argument from exchange and convergence to state power. For example, analysts of Germany have tended to assign any blame for the deterioration of Franco-German relations to the change in Germany's power potential as a result of the end of unification. With the end of the Cold War, Germany both regained its sovereignty and acquired a host of new political interests. Germany also became manifestly the largest member of the EU. It is only natural, therefore, that Germany would become more assertive even if such assertiveness brings it into conflict with France (and Europe). Again, what is important to note is that this transformation has not sparked a complete collapse in Franco-German (or Euro-German) relations. This continued cooperation despite the change in German power and interests is attributed to the country's robust institutional structures and to the Germans' "exaggerated multilateralism" (Anderson 1997, 104).

The argument from German power provides a different perspective on the thumbnail sketch of the origins of EMU outlined above than did the arguments about exchange and convergence. In this telling of the story, the economic changes were inevitable. Germany was manifestly going to gravitate toward the East no matter what the institutional configuration of Europe. The "binding" characteristic of the Maastricht Treaty refers to the institutional links that force Germany to dialogue with France (and the rest of Europe) despite the change in its economic center of gravity. From the power perspective, unified Germany is Europe's Ulysses, strapped to the single currency and the other EU institutions and struggling not to succumb to the siren calls of nationalism or narrowly-defined national self-interest.

The strength of this interpretation lies in the attention it draws to the domestic determinants of Germany's policies in Europe. If Germany is becoming more assertive after unification, then it is relevant to ask what it is that Germany wants as well as who is pushing the agenda. Its weakness derives from its reliance on a peculiar notion of German exceptionalism in order to explain cooperation. Continuity, Anderson (1999, 192) suggests, is a "testament to the resilience of [the] core political values [of the Federal Republic of Germany in Europe] and the national framework of institutions that uphold them."

The problem with focusing on changes in German power, interests, and behavior is that it makes it necessary to consider France in the same way. And, once the comparative basis is established, the shortcomings of the argument from German power are apparent: Germany is not so strong, the domestic determinants of German European policy are not so unique, and the institutions of Europe are not so beneficent. Put another way, if unified Germany is even potentially so strong, self-obsessed, and dangerous as it is made out to be, why are the French so eager—and why does Europe provide so many opportunities—to goad the beast?

The claim that Germany is not so strong in comparative terms is the most easily demonstrated of the three. Looking at a range of indicators suggested by Stephen Krasner (1976) as proxies for measuring the economic power potential of states, it is clear that the changes brought about by German unification are undramatic even if still significant. The incorporation of the five new Länder did increase Germany's size both in terms of population and gross domestic product (GDP), but a substantial part of such advances served only to compensate for West Germany's relative decline since the late 1960s. Moreover, the impact of unification on Germany's share of world trade—both including and excluding the European Union—was marginal. By the same token, Germany's relative GDP per capita declined. In essence, then, unification made Germany bigger, but not necessarily more important, and at the cost of taking on substantial socio-economic differences (see Table 7.5). These findings are confirmed through an anecdotal and institutional analysis of Germany's role in Europe and are broadly accepted by those who argue from the position of German power (Bulmer and Patterson 1996).

Germany's new assertiveness derives not from any increase in its aggregate economic power potential, but from a combination of four factors—two of which have changed as a result of unification and two of

Table 7.5.   German Economic Power Potential in a European Context

		Share in EU 12 (percent)		World Trade Share (percent)		GDP p/c*
		Population	Real GDP	Incl. EU	Excl. EU	EU12=100
1960–69	W. Germany	20.1	25.6	8.3	6.1	128
	France	16.7	19.2	5.0	3.8	115
	Italy	17.4	14.8	3.7	3.1	83
	United Kingdom	18.7	21.5	6.8	7.3	116
1970–79	W. Germany	19.9	24.9	10.8	6.1	126
	France	16.9	20.3	6.6	3.7	120
	Italy	17.5	15.6	4.7	2.9	88
	United Kingdom	18.1	18.7	6.4	4.9	104
1980–89	W. Germany	19.1	24.3	9.5	5.1	127
	France	17.2	20.7	5.8	3.2	120
	Italy	17.5	16.7	4.5	2.7	95
	United Kingdom	17.7	18.0	5.6	3.4	102
1991–99	Germany	23.5	28.2	9.7	5.4	115
	France	16.7	18.7	5.6	2.7	117
	Italy	16.5	15.3	4.4	2.3	95
	United Kingdom	16.9	15.7	5.2	3.1	101

Note: *This series has been temporarily discontinued by the Commission–the final panel is 1990–1996.
Data Source: European Commission.

which have remained the same. The factors that have changed are the status of German sovereignty and the diversity of German interests. In contrast with West Germany, unified Germany is fully sovereign but, as mentioned, contains a much wider diversity of socio-economic interests. Moreover, as Jones (1994) establishes, this diversity of economic and social conditions was remarkably persistent.

The factors that have remained the same are its economic reputation and its domestic institutional arrangements. Whether or not France and Germany are actually converging, Germany remains attractive as an economic model at least in rhetorical terms (Dyson 1999b). Germany also remains a federal state, with strong elements of decentralization and powerful institutional checks on the exercise of state power. Taken together, these factors suggest that—on economic grounds at least—not only is it attractive for Europe to strive to become more like Germany, but it is difficult for the German government to make concessions to Europe. Following Bulmer and Patterson (1996, 31), "internal weakness may thus be a source of external strength."

From this standpoint, the argument from German power looks different from that sketched above. Germany is not necessarily stronger as a result of unification, it is just more problematic. But how is this any different from France? If the claim is that unified Germany is now just as problematic as France ever was, then the argument from German power does not actually tell us very much. It can explain why France and Germany would come to loggerheads—for example, because the French state is held sway by the powerful farm lobby and because the German government has little leverage over the Bundesbank. But it cannot explain why either country would be willing to back down or why they retain their special relationship in the first place.

The influence of European institutions might fill the gap in the argument, but only if it is possible to accept that such institutions can impose restraints and influence identities without incurring costs or provoking antagonisms. Of course no-one is arguing that Europe is cost-free or uncontroversial. Equally, however, few are willing to admit that the costs of Europe could come to overpower its beneficial restraints. Nevertheless, the forces are much more balanced than one-sided, and the momentum occasionally shifts.

A specific example of this "clash of institutions"—European versus domestic—relates to what has earlier been referred to as the classic argument for German wage moderation. Because they are large and centralized, trade unions in Germany tend to moderate their wage claims in order to stave off unemployment. In turn, this wage moderation plays an important role in underwriting Germany's capacity to reconcile economic growth and price stability. The paradox is that while the institutions for EMU are patterned on those found in Germany and are guided by a German-inspired absolute price stability rule, the replacement of German institutions with European ones may inadvertently undermine trade union support for wage moderation. Far from establishing German economic norms, EMU may undermine German economic performance and even ignite a conflict between labor and capital in Germany (McNamara and Jones 1996; Hall and Franzese 1998). The point here is not to say that this will happen, but only that it could—which is sufficient to establish the potential of European institutions to generate contradictory economic effects.

A further set of examples can be found in the relationship between rising unemployment and the shift from center-right to center-left in France and Germany. Here the clash between national and European institutions can be understood on two levels. To begin with, European institutions can exacerbate differences between the two countries. Thus, while Germany is decentralized, France is not. By implication, it is relatively easier for German politicians to segment responsibility for macroeconomic instruments and objectives than it is for the French. The German public may be content to hold the Bundesbank responsible for price stability, the minister of finance responsible for government balances, and the minister of the economy responsible for employment. However the French hold their president and prime minister responsible for all of these things. Thus, in the 1995 French presidential election Jacques Chirac campaigned on a platform that economic policy should focus on the objective of reducing unemployment even though this brought him into conflict with many of the German-inspired macroeconomic policy norms embedded in EMU (Pisani-Ferry 1997). The German response was to propose the Stability Pact as a mechanism for strengthening the fiscal requirements for membership. That Chirac recanted, and pledged his support for EMU, certainly contributed to the December 1995 protests in France and may have helped to undermine the position of the right in the 1997 legislative elections as well.

At another level, the impact of European institutions can be to exacerbate differences within countries even as it forges partial alliances between them. Here the example focuses on tension within the post-1998 center-left government in Germany between the newly-elected prime minister, Gerhard Schröder, and his finance minister, Oskar Lafontaine. The conflict between the two men was both personal and ideological. The personal conflict is relevant only as a motivational factor. The ideological conflict was more threatening, both to Schröder and to the German-inspired constitution for EMU. Specifically, as mentioned in chapter 6, Lafontaine argued for increasing political coordination of macroeconomic policymaking as well as more strenuous efforts to target macroeconomic instruments to the reduction of unemployment. This stand put Lafontaine into conflict both with the Bundesbank and with the newly-launched European Central Bank (ECB). However, it put him into alliance with French interests in general and with the French minister of finance, Dominique Strauss-Kahn, in particular. For a while it seemed that Lafontaine "had emerged as the most powerful player in Bonn" and that the emphasis in German economic policy would change accordingly (Dyson 1999a, 205). In the event, Schröder was able to wrestle away control over his own government and Lafontaine resigned. Importantly, not only was Lafontaine able to gain leverage from his opposition to a particular institutional configuration in Europe, but he was able to block the functioning of European institutions as well. Faced with the prospect of being perceived as under German political influence, the ECB held off making an important interest rate reduction until after Lafontaine had left (Campanella 2000).

European institutions may have played a role in taming German power but they have had a range of other and potentially less desirable influences as well. Moreover, the impact of European institutions is much the same for France as well. As a result, our ability to explain the ups and downs of Franco-German cooperation in the 1990s through this particular form of institutional sociology is limited. We can gain some insight on Germany's problematic nature as a "normal" European power and possibly some purchase on why France and Germany prefer some institutional arrangements over others. Nevertheless, the continuity of Franco-German economic relations as a special relationship remains relatively unexplored.

POWER RESTORED: THE INS AND OUTS
OF THE FRANCO-GERMAN COALITION

The solution to explaining the Franco-German economic relationship in the 1990s is institutional empowerment as well as institutional constraint. The argument is that France and Germany cooperate in Europe to achieve a range of objectives that are held both separately and in common. Within this argument, the observation that France and Germany continue to cooperate is simply a function of the fact that their objectives remain to be achieved and that their continued cooperation is necessary to achieve them. For example, without France and Germany there can be no EMU, and without EMU Europe cannot improve the functioning of the single market. What is novel is not the basis for cooperation, but the recognition that power emanates from the Franco-German relationship rather than from France or Germany per se.

This notion of power is borrowed from Michel Crozier's (1973) study of French society in the late 1960s and early 1970s, as well as from the larger corpus of his sociology (see for example Crozier and Friedberg 1977). Essentially, it has three characteristics: All power derives from social relations; within social relations, the distribution of power is a function of each agent's control over the sources of uncertainty in achieving their common purpose; and, any exercise of power is either within the accepted norms of the relationship (control) or contrary to those norms (blackmail). A strength of this notion is that it encompasses both the traditional formula for the Franco-German relationship and the argument about the restraining influence of institutions. Following Crozier and Friedberg (1977, 25, 27) "any relationship between two parties requires a measure of exchange and mutual adjustment" the terms of which "create compulsory hurdles and opportunities for manipulation for the players, and therefore determine their strategy." Crucially, for collective action to arrive at its desired outcome, the behavior of the participants must be made predictable and transparent.

The notion of predictability is a recurrent theme in Crozier's identification of power within social relations. To the extent to which predictability can be equated with the process of institution-building, Crozier's conception of power can help to explain why France and Germany cooperate within Europe and indeed rely on Europe as a focus for their economic cooperation. Nevertheless, saying that France and Germany create institutions for common purpose does not help in understanding the dynamics of the relationship—at least beyond the *European Rescue of the Nation-State* type of argument forwarded by Milward (1992). Therefore it is necessary to focus attention on three further aspects of Crozier's theory of power: control, blackmail, and integration.

For Crozier, the exercise of control and the resort to blackmail represent a manipulation of uncertainty. They correspond to agents exercising power. However, where control is relatively easily translated into institution-building, blackmail must first be accepted as legitimate. Only once it is accepted within the rules for collective action, can blackmail be relied upon as the basis for institution-building. In the parlance of European integration, the empty chair crisis was blackmail. However, the Luxembourg compromise legitimated national vetoes and so institutionalized unanimous voting procedures in the Council.

In turn, successive rounds of institution-building constitute integration. Moreover, as more and more different (and different types) of agents come into contact with one-another, power tends to become more diffuse, and the institutional requirements for transparency and predictability tend to increase. In other words, so far Crozier's theory of power tends to conform to the patterns of relations in Europe today, starting perhaps with a narrow focus on Franco-German reconciliation, but soon broadening and deepening to engage a much wider range of member states and subnational interests.

What Crozier adds to our understanding of the Franco-German relationship is the notion that control and blackmail both play a role in national strategies for collective action. The ups and downs do not signal a flaw in the Franco-German relationship. They are the Franco-German relationship in the sense that they reflect the ins and outs of French and German strategies within that relationship. This point can be made formally through the observation that players can maximize their voting power by starting from within the winning coalition (Winkler 1998). It can also be made anecdotally: both the conflict over CAP reform at the start of the 1990s and the conflict over the ECB president at the end of the 1990s originated in a French defection from a common Franco-German position. In the first case, the French strategy was successful. In the second it was not. The point is simply that such defections cannot signal a desire to end the Franco-German relationship because, as a strategy, they could not function without the relationship.

The Franco-German controversy surrounding the institutional reforms agreed at the December 2000 Nice summit powerfully illustrates this dynamic at work. As president of the European Council, France broke with convention and introduced a number of strong national claims into the negotiations. First among these was the insistence that any reform of the voting weights used in the Council of Ministers must retain parity between Germany and France. Although this strategy created considerable scandal, it also succeeded not only in reasserting symbolic equality within the Franco-German relationship but also in strengthening the capacity of larger states to control decisionmaking within the Council of Ministers (Jones 2001).

THE PROSPECTS FOR THE FUTURE

Franco-German economic relations have progressed from exchange and convergence to collective action. In doing so, they have become embedded in institutions that both empower and constrain that relationship. Where once Franco-German reconciliation was the context and EMU was the innovation, now EMU is the context and the innovations lie in the Franco-German relationship.

Within EMU, France and Germany should be expected to rely on strategies of cooperation and defection best designed to pursue their national interests. In turn those strategies are informed by national actors who make use of domestic institutions and relationships to further their own agendas. Where these actors can leapfrog their own member states to appeal either to Europe or to the other half of the Franco-German couple, that is to be expected as well. Blackmail is not the sole purview of the nation-state, and neither is the exercise of power under its monopoly control. Moreover, while it is possible that France and Germany have succeeded in ruling the political manipulation of macroeconomic instruments to be out of the bounds of good behavior, the rule of thumb remains that some rules are made to be broken.

The emphasis in this interpretation is that both France and Germany have too much to lose from abandoning EMU or from undermining it. Put another way, no matter how complicated the pattern of integration becomes, Franco-German economic relations will continue to lie at the center of Europe and their economic self-interest will remain a primary motivation for EMU. The question, then, is not whether EMU will upset the balance of power between France and Germany but whether EMU will actually empower France and Germany sufficiently to achieve their objectives. By implication, it is important to consider what exactly those objectives are, and the extent to which they are shared beyond the Franco-German couple and by the other member states of EMU. Such questions extend beyond the conduct of bilateral relationships and into the nature of EMU as a policy regime. Membership in EMU not only provides a bulwark against the vagaries of world markets, but it also reveals the existence of a new "generative grammar" through which the exercise of power at the European level is fused with a sense of legitimate social purpose.[12]

NOTES

1. Three excellent books have recently been published surveying Germany's monetary role in Europe: Heisenberg (1999); Kaltenthaler (1998); and Loedel (1999).

2. The notion of "tamed power" appears most prominently in the title of Katzenstein's (1997) book, but also emerges in the final sentence of Bulmer's (1993) essay. For a generalized version of the argument, see Pierson (1996b).

3. Katzenstein (1997) omits France from his collection of essays and instead focuses attention on relations between Germany and the smaller countries. Nevertheless, he seems to be pushing the argument in the direction of empowerment when he states that: "Only when we move institutional power to center stage can we hope to understand why Germany is willing to give up its new sovereign power or why institutional inefficiency has not stopped European integration (3)." He returns to this theme again to claim that: "The answers this book offers derive from the premise that we can adequately understand the world of power and interest in Europe only when we see power and interest not simply as attributes of distinctive actors, Germany *and* Europe, but as aspects of relationships that place Germany *in* Europe, through institutions that tame power (6)." However, the rest of the introduction focuses on the role of Europe in constituting, shaping, and constraining national interests.

4. Patrick McCarthy (1999, 157) makes much the same point somewhat differently in suggesting that "today, the French and the Germans take conflict for granted."

5. This argument parallels the conclusions made by Szukala and Wessels (1997: 78, 95), but from a different basis.

6. This point is made previously in the argument as well.

7. Here it is useful to note that while Moravcsik (1998, 232) takes issue with McCarthy about the structure of the exchange underwriting the 1983 turnaround in France, he does not challenge the presumption that some exchange was necessary to support the relaunching of Europe. See also McCarthy (1999).

8. The period averages do not reveal the full extent of the trend. Thus, for example, the share of French exports to German peaks in 1991 at just over 18 percent of total French exports and then declines for five of the next seven years.

9. These data are from the Direction of Trade Statistics of the IMF.

10. These data are from the Direction of Trade Statistics of the IMF.

11. This appears to be the assessment of Edwards and Wiessala (1999, 3–4).

12. The term "generative grammar" is borrowed from Ruggie (1983, 196) as is the general conception of policy regimes. This conception broadly complements Crozier's sociology of institutions. According to Ruggie: "we know international regimes not simply by some inventory of their concrete elements, but by their generative grammar, the underlying principles of order and meaning that shape the manner of their formation and transformation. Likewise, we know deviations from regimes not simply by acts that are undertaken, but by the intentionality and acceptability attributed to those acts in the context of an intersubjective framework of meaning."

8

✛

Symbolism: Expectations and Idiosyncrasies

The European Union's economic and monetary union (EMU) is more than an exchange rate regime. It is more than a technology for the depoliticization of monetary policy. It is more than a set of rules and institutions. It is more than a bulwark against the world economy. It is more than a framework for bilateral and multilateral relations between countries. And, somehow, it is more than all these things put together. EMU is a "regime" in the purest and vaguest sense of the term—which is to say that it surely has elements that extend beyond the positive and the rational and into the normative and the inter-subjective.[1] The challenge is to identify both what those normative and symbolic elements of EMU are and what they are not.

That task is easier said than done. The difficulty with such normative or symbolic analysis is to choose appropriate levels of aggregation and abstraction. Does EMU reconstitute norms, rules, and conventions regarding behavior between member states and so emerge as a symbol of a radical transformation in interstate relations? Does the single currency imply some convergence of expectations about what is appropriate (and possible) in state society relations? Does the construction of the euro somehow consummate a new relationship between European individuals and European governance? Should we understand EMU to be a federalist project, a neoliberal project, or an exercise in state-building on a continental scale? These are all important questions, but they are devilishly difficult to answer in anything more than a suggestive manner.[2]

My own suggestions are that EMU reconstitutes the historical compromise of embedded liberalism at the European level (chapter 5) and that it also provides a new basis for collective action (chapter 7). These claims are modest in that they suggest EMU is less of a radical break with the past than it is an improvement on the status quo.

In this chapter, my objective is to extend those suggestions by focusing on symbolism within the context of relations between individuals and political authority. The argument is that the normative and symbolic characteristics of the single currency differ from national currencies generally and also from one national context to the next. In broad terms, this argument parallels that made earlier about the distributive consequences of monetary integration. However, the underlying logic of the claim is stronger in terms of norms and symbols than it is in terms of economic outcomes. Given the wide differences between processes of national integration and the process of European integration, it would be hard to imagine that currency could hold the same symbolic or normative content in both contexts. By the same token, it is hard to imagine that the replacement of a national currency with a European currency could have the same importance or meaning from one place to the next. Hence, while it is possible to identify a group of countries where public opinion is broadly skeptical about participation in the single currency, it is more difficult to characterize the motivations for skepticism across the group. By focusing too much attention on opposition to the euro as a symbol, we risk losing sight of the many and different concerns that the euro has come to represent.

This argument is made in five sections. The first contrasts the role of money in national and international integration. The second examines the convergence of expectations and divergence of concerns across the European Union (EU). The third analyzes opposition to the single currency as it relates to attitudes toward EU membership more generally. The fourth considers why the euro becomes politically important in some countries but not in others. The fifth section concludes.

MONEY AND INTEGRATION

Money, it is often asserted, constitutes one of the core elements of statehood and one of the founding symbols of nationhood. To paraphrase Margaret Thatcher, the very idea that a nation-state would sacrifice its currency is, for many, simply repulsive. However, such assertions have more empirical than analytic worth, and such repulsion should not be taken to mean that money and statehood or nationhood are somehow intrinsically intertwined.

In analytic terms, currency is a technology that can exist with or without states and nations. States are institutional arrangements that can function without control over money. Nations are social constructs that have no necessary connection to currency. The evidence for this set of propositions is straightforward: On my bookshelves at the moment, I have a number of volumes on state theory, nationalism, and monetary- or macroeconomics. All of the state theory books have index entries on nations, nationalism, or nation-states. All of the nationalism books have index entries on states or nation-states. None of the state theory and nationalism books contain index entries on currency or money. By the same token, none of my books on monetary economics contain index entries to the state, the nation, or nationalism.

The connection between state, nation, and currency, is empirical and not essential. During the rise of nationalism and national state-building in the 19th century, national currencies helped reinforce the linkage between the geography of the state, the market, and the nation. Such reinforcement was needed to correct for the fact that most nations in Europe were not culturally homogenous at the start of the 19th century and yet most "nationalists" recognized that a nation had to achieve a certain economic (and therefore geographic and demographic) critical mass in order to survive. The challenge was to combine the ideology of nationalism with the symbols of the state in order to bind culturally diverse groups of citizens to common feelings of identity and patriotism. Hence, states adhered to the gold standard and yet nevertheless took advantage of the symbolism of money in order to reinforce national identity and to encourage national integration. While gold provided the basis for a world economy, the translation of gold into national currencies encouraged the fragmentation of the European polity.[3]

The use of money as an instrument for national integration increased in the period from 1870 to 1939. In symbolic terms, currency provided a vehicle for reinforcing the founding principles of the political community as well as a constant reminder of the essential role of the state.[4] For governments confronting an ever broadening electorate, at the end of the 19th century such support was more than welcome. That said, however, the influence of currency on national identity formation should not be overestimated. Popular media, including newspapers, books, and public spectacles, arguably assumed the lion's share of the burden in constructing nations as "imagined communities."[5]

In more instrumental terms, control over the currency provided an additional means to protect the national economy from world markets and foreign creditors. Governments could force down the value of the national currency relative to gold and so increase the competitiveness of domestic manufactures in world markets. Alternatively, they could restrict the exchange of domestic currency for foreign and so force foreign creditors to spend their interest income on domestic production. The results of such competitive devaluations and exchange restrictions were temporary, they had important distributive consequences, and they were ultimately harmful. Yet currency manipulation remained an option for governments looking to meet domestic demands with state action.[6] In this way, money became an instrument for economic nationalism as well as a symbol for political nationalism. As Polanyi (1944, 202, 205) explains:

> The new crustacean type of nation [that emerged between 1879 and 1929] expressed its identity through national token currencies safeguarded by a type of sovereignty more jealous and absolute than anything known before . . . . Politically, the nation's identity was established by the government; economically it was vested in the central bank.

The link between national identity and national currency was not disrupted by the experience of World War II. It was reinforced. Governments that emerged from the war, whether victors or vanquished, soon turned to control over money creation as a source of political legitimacy as well as economic stability. Whether through aggressive stabilization policies, the nationalization of central banks, or the wholesale replacement of the currency, governments struggled to demonstrate that they "perform an important social function which could not be discharged in [their] absence."[7] The role of currency reform implemented in the western zones of occupied Germany is illustrative in this regard. The introduction of the new German mark in 1948 served both to stabilize the economy of western Germany and to create distinctions between new and old, West and East. That the Deutschemark would emerge from this context as a powerful symbol of the new West Germany is hardly surprising (Bark and Gress 1993, 198–209; Krieger 1987, 374–381).

The euro has almost none of the symbolic association with state-building that is attached to national currencies. The European currency does not encompass the whole of the European Union. And, while universal participation remains an aspiration, the rules for joining the single currency are explicit in stating that member states must qualify economically first. None of the national currencies of the 19th or early 20th centuries was ever founded on the basis of such criteria. Moreover, no nationalist state-builder would have dreamt of inventing obstacles to extending the boundaries of the currency to the boundaries of the state.

Even within the euro-zone, the symbolic function of the single currency has little to do with the fusion of national identity and patriotic loyalty. One of the goals of EMU is to foster a common identity, to be sure. However, this sense of European-ness should complement and not replace national identities and state loyalties. As chapter 2 explains, the member states remain in control of the content of their economic policies and the structure of their market institutions. Moreover, while European institutions control the direction of monetary policy, such control is explicitly removed from political influence. Far from creating a direct linkage between political authority and the individual, the single currency is meant to create a disjuncture. This disjuncture is evident in instrumental terms as well as symbolic terms. Combining the arguments in chapters 5 and 6, the euro is a bulwark shielding Europe's economies from the vagaries of global market forces, but it is not a tool to be manipulated in the interests of economic nationalism on a European scale.

Finally, no-one in Europe is under the illusion that only the European Union can perform the important social function of maintaining a viable currency. Participation in the euro may be better than going it alone, but that is not the same as saying that the euro is the only option available. National currencies have worked reasonably well since the end of the World War II—particularly in comparison with the period from 1870 to 1939. And if the traumatic volatility of national currencies during that earlier period has not succeeded in eliminating the symbolic significance of the state-money axis, then there is no reason to believe that the marginal improvements offered by the euro will be sufficient to undermine the symbolic force of national currencies in the near future.

CONVERGENT EXPECTATIONS AND DIVERGENT CONCERNS

The euro is characteristically different from national currencies in symbolic terms. Yet it still plays an important symbolic and constitutive role both in its own right and as part of the European Union. The difficulty is that we have no solid way of identifying what the contents of that symbolic and constitutive role are.[8] We cannot be sure what such contents imply about the evolution of political authority in Europe. And we cannot say how such contents are likely to influence the development of European societies. We can suggest that the construction of the euro—like the construction of the European Union—will have an effect on the peoples and states of Europe, but we cannot predict what effect it will have.

The limits to our insight on the constitutive and symbolic roles of the euro derive from the limits to our understanding of political regimes. The central lesson from regime theory is that political actors who participate in regimes experience a convergence of expectations. Following Krasner (1983, 2):

> Regimes can be defined as sets of implicit or explicit principles, norms, rules, and decisionmaking procedures around which actors' expectations converge in a given area of international relations. Principles are beliefs of fact, causation, and rectitude. Norms are standards of behavior defined in terms of

rights and obligations. Rules are specific prescriptions or proscriptions for action. Decisionmaking procedures are prevailing practices for making and implementing collective choice.

Taken at face value, this understanding of regimes denies any easy assumption that the euro can play the same role at the European level that national currencies played at the national level. Even ignoring the arguments put forward in the previous section, the likelihood that money would play the same symbolic and constitutive role for two and a half centuries is small. As regimes, 19th century money and 21st century money rely on different rules, norms, and decisionmaking procedures. As political actors, both elites and masses within the European Union are subject to widely different environmental influences, life experiences, and educational endowments than their predecessors. Hence, even accepting that expectations converge in both cases, it is hard to believe they would converge in the same way, on the same issues, and with the same intensity or durability.

Regime theory tells us that expectations will converge within a regime and—by extension—that expectations differ outside a regime. What it does not specify is the basis for differences between actors' expectations prior to convergence, the scope for covergence; or the focus for convergence. The differences between expectations may have many origins such as actors' participation in other (overlapping) regimes, original endowments, or environmental influences. The scope of convergence is bounded both by time and competence: If we can assume that expectations diverged before the regime then arguably they should diverge beyond the competence of the regime as well. Finally, the focus for convergence can be influenced by whether all rules, norms, and procedures will receive equal attention from political actors, and by how actors resolve ambiguity or contradiction within the regime. Once again, regime theory suggests where to look and what to look for, but it does not predict what will be found.

Knowing what to look for is enough to begin mapping the European Union as a regime. For example, if expectations are convergent within the European Union, then we should look to find little variation across countries in the correlation between national and European attitudes concerning EU policies—where "European" attitudes are the average of national attitudes weighted by member state populations.[9] The same can be said for the correlation between national and European attitudes about whether a particular policy area should be decided at the national or European level and about whether given policies in this area should be considered priorities for European action. These three sets of attitudes constitute separate dimensions of the regime—what should be decided (policies), by whom (competencies), and with what importance (priorities)—and so they should also constitute areas of convergence across the European Union. The point is not that all policies should be expected to receive support, to be elevated to the European level, or to be accorded priority. Rather, it is that the balance of support and opposition, EU and national decisionmaking, priority and not, should be roughly the same in any member state as it is across Europe as a whole. And it is.

The evidence in support of a convergence of expectations across the European Union can be found in the responses to biannual Eurobarometer public opinion surveys. In those surveys, the pollsters for Eurobarometer ask members of the public whether they are for or against seven policies, whether they believe decisions should be taken at the national or European level in twenty-five policy areas, and whether they would assign priority or not in twelve areas of EU activity. The responses from one country to the next sometimes differ widely. However, the correlation of responses between any one country and Europe as a whole is tight—averaging above 0.8, at least for attitudes surveyed in November-December 2000.[10]

As a regime, the European Union promotes a convergence of expectations. The question to consider, then, is what role is played by popular attitudes toward the euro. Should we consider EMU to be part of the European Union as a regime or does it remain outside? Such consideration relies on the analysis of relationships between attitudes or expectations across issue areas rather than across member states.

The balance of evidence seems to suggest that EMU is part of the regime. First, popular support for EMU correlates strongly with support for EU membership, with belief in the benefits of European integration, and with satisfaction with European democracy. Second, popular opposition to EMU correlates strongly with opposition to EU membership, with beliefs that European integration provides little benefit, and with dissatisfaction with European democracy. Finally, as expected, general attitudes toward Europe are all highly correlated. Countries where respondents believe membership is a good thing are also likely to contain respondents who believe they benefit from membership and who claim to be satisfied with EU democracy. By the same token, countries where respondents believe membership is a bad thing are likely to contain respondents who believe they do not benefit from membership and who claim to be dissatisfied with EU democracy.[11] These data are summarized in Table 8.1.

The tight correlation between attitudes about the European Union is consistent with the convergence of expectations we would expect to find within a regime. But the EU as a regime is not all encompassing. Put another way, the tightness of the correlation between national and European expectations is relative as well as absolute. The correlation is not only

Table 8.1. Popular Attitudes toward Europe and the Single Currency

Correlates of Support				
	A	B	C	D
A. EU membership is a good thing		0.88	0.71	0.83
B. EU membership is beneficial	0.88		0.68	0.69
C. Very or fairly satisfied with EU democracy	0.71	0.68		0.69
D. Support the creation of a single currency	0.83	0.69	0.69	
Correlates of Opposition				
	E	F	G	H
E. EU membership is a bad thing		0.88	0.77	0.89
F. EU membership is not beneficial	0.88		0.69	0.75
G. Not very or not at all satisfied with EU democracy	0.77	0.69		0.66
H. Oppose the creation of a single currency	0.89	0.75	0.66	

Note: All coefficients are significant at the 0.01 level.
Source: Author's calculations based on data from Eurobarometer (2001).

strong, it is also stronger within the regime than without. To demonstrate this point it is necessary to consider attitudes that are unlikely to be structured by the regime as much as those concerning policy, competence, or priority.

The Eurobarometer currently provides only one series of questions that potentially touches on this area. The question is whether or not the respondent is currently afraid of any of eleven possibilities for the future (Eurobarometer 2001, B.50, emphasis in original):

Some people may have fears about the building of Europe, the European Union. Here is a list of things which some people say they are afraid of. For each one, please tell me if you—personally—are currently afraid of it or not?

- A loss of power for smaller Member States
- An increase in drug trafficking and international organized crime
- Our language being used less and less
- Richer countries paying more for the others
- Other countries joining the European Union will cost member countries too much money
- The loss of social benefits
- The loss of our national identity and culture
- The end of (NATIONAL CURRENCY)
- The transfer of jobs to countries which have lower production costs
- More difficulties for (NATIONALITY) farmers
- Less subsidies from the European Union for (OUR COUNTRY).

What is striking in the analysis of the responses to these questions is how much fears expressed in any one country differ from those expressed

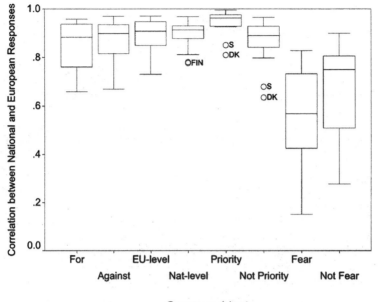

Figure 8.1.   Converging Expectations, Diverging Concerns
Source: Eurobarometer (2001).

across Europe as a whole. This difference is presented in Figure 8.1 as a box-and-whisker diagram, and includes the data previously summarized for convergent expectations for purpose of comparison. In the diagram, fear is more varied than its absence, and both are more varied than attitudes about priority, competence, or policy. While expectations converge within the European Union, concerns within the member states diverge.

MAPPING OPPOSITION TO THE EURO

The single currency is both part of the European Union as a regime and part of the fear expressed in the member states. It is part of the convergence of expectations and part of the divergence of concerns. Therefore, while we can generalize about the existence of opposition to and support for the euro, we must also admit that attitudes toward the euro differ from one country to the next. This claim is supported by three different lines of argument:

- that despite the strong correlation between attitudes about the desirability of integration, the division of member states into groups of Euro-pessimists and Euro-optimists is influenced by the introduction of the single currency as a consideration;

- that the concerns of member states about the future correlate as easily across Euro-optimists and Euro-pessimists as within either group in a manner that suggests the existence of structural (and economic) cleavages that cut across opposition to and support for integration; and,
- that the clustering of concerns suggests a deep intermingling of economic and symbolic issues both among the Euro-pessimists and Euro-optimists and across the European Union as a whole.

The division of European member states into Euro-optimists and Euro-pessimists is a two-step process. The first step is to use a hierarchical clustering technique to see if it actually makes sense to speak of two groups with respect to European integration both generally and including popular support for the single currency.[12] The general analysis builds on the percentage of respondents by member state who claimed that they support European integration, that they benefit from membership in the European union, and that they are satisfied with democracy at the EU level. The additional data line is the percentage of respondents by member state who support the construction of the single currency. The second step is to use a slightly different clustering technique (k-means-squared) to adjust the membership of the two groups in order to ensure that they are as far apart as possible on all issues.[13] As with the hierarchical clustering, the technique is used both for general attitudes, and for attitudes including support for the single currency. In turn, the clusters of optimists and skeptics are reported in Table 8.2.

The separation of member states into groups of Euro-optimists and Euro-pessimists both in general and including support for EMU provides two useful pieces of information. First, the classification of specific countries changes depending upon the importance of the single currency as an issue in comparison with benefits of membership, satisfaction with Euro-democracy, and general support for European integration. Specifically, the single currency makes the difference between optimism and pessimism in Denmark, pessimism and optimism in Italy, and pessimism and ambivalence in France.[14]

The second point to observe from the classification is that, no matter how the clusters are calculated, the optimists and pessimists include both old and new member states that are small and large in terms of population size. This suggests that whatever the statistical validity of the classification used, the clustering of member states into optimists and pessimists obscures differences within the groups and similarities between them. The assignment of groups is "right" in terms of the data. However, that tells us little about why countries are in the groups to which they are assigned.

At this stage it is useful to return to the divergence of concerns between individual member states and the European Union as a whole. The ques-

Table 8.2. Euro-optimists and Euro-pessimists

Hierarchical Clustering			
Attitudes toward the EU		Attitudes toward the EU and EMU	
Optimists	Pessimists	Optimists	Pessimists
Belgium	Germany	Belgium	*Denmark*
Denmark	France	Greece	Germany
Greece	*Italy*	Spain	France
Spain	Austria	Ireland	Austria
Ireland	Finland	*Italy*	Finland
Luxembourg	Sweden	Luxembourg	Sweden
Netherlands	UK	Netherlands	UK
Portugal		Portugal	
Two-means Squared Clustering			
Attitudes toward the EU		Attitudes toward the EU and EMU	
Optimists	Pessimists	Optimists	Pessimists
Belgium	Germany	Belgium	*Denmark*
Denmark	France	Greece	Germany
Greece	*Italy*	Spain	Austria
Spain	Austria	*France*	Finland
Ireland	Finland	Ireland	Sweden
Luxembourg	Sweden	*Italy*	UK
Netherlands	UK	Luxembourg	
Portugal		Netherlands	
		Portugal	

Note: Member states in italics change group assignment from one clustering to the next. This analysis is based on the percentage of respondents in each member state who: (a) supports participation in the EU; (b) believes they benefit from EU membership; (c) is very or fairly satisfied with EU democracy; and (d) supports the single currency. Attitudes toward the EU include only the first three lines of data. Attitudes toward the EU and EMU include all four.
Source: Author's calculations based on data from Eurobarometer (2001).

tion to ask is not whether fear of any or all of the elements surveyed is tied to opposition to European integration or even to the euro. Rather, the question is whether Euro-pessimists or Euro-optimists express similar concerns for the future that are at the same time different from one group to the other. The answer is that they do not.

Among the pessimists, the concerns expressed within the United Kingdom do not correlate with any other member state apart from Italy—which moves from pessimist to optimist once support for the single currency is included. The same point applies to Germany, where the only correlations are with France (which itself is ambivalent after accounting for support for the euro) and with Belgium (an optimist). Concerns expressed in the smaller pessimists—Denmark, Austria, Finland, and Sweden—are closely correlated. However, they are also closely correlated with concerns expressed in Belgium. Denmark and Sweden correlate with

Ireland. Finland and Sweden correlate with Portugal. These results are unaffected if the question concerning the loss of the national currency is omitted from the analysis. The correlations between the smaller countries actually improve in the absence of the question about small state power.

The conclusion to draw from this tangled web of similarities is that the general position of a country's population as Euro-optimist or Euro-pessimist sheds little light on the structure of concerns within the country. By the same token, the structure of concerns within the country tell us little about whether it should be regarded more generally as an optimist or a pessimist with respect to European integration.

That said, it is worth considering whether the structure of concerns across countries can shed light on the nature of concerns associated with the euro. Using the same data about fears within the member states it is possible to ask whether the loss of the national currency clusters more tightly with the loss of language or culture, or whether it arises more closely in the context of economic concerns about expenditures and benefits. Is fear for the loss of national currency a cultural issue, an economic issue, or both?

Here the answer is more complicated. It is possible to map the combination of concern for the loss of the national currency with other concerns using the same hierarchical clustering technique that was used to separate Euro-optimists and Euro-pessimists. However, interpreting the map (or dendrogram) is not exactly straightforward. The fact that two issues emerge close together in the process of combination means only that they are statistically associated and not that they are necessarily conceptually interconnected. Therefore rather than display the maps, and risk giving the false impression of precision, it is perhaps best simply to summarize what they report. Whether the group of countries includes only optimists, only pessimists, or the whole of the European Union, fear for the loss of the national currency emerges consistently within a mixed cluster of economic issues as well as cultural issues. Concerns about the cost of enlargement, the loss of social benefits and subsidies, the loss of language, identity, and culture, all intermingle in the cluster. Concerns about crime, unemployment, agriculture, and small state power all lie elsewhere.[15]

THE POLITICS OF IDIOSYNCRASY

EMU is part of the European Union as a regime, and yet it also remains outside. Meanwhile, attitudes toward the single currency differ from one country to the next and are somehow embedded in a jumbled nest of economic and cultural issues. This combination of factors brings us to the central puzzle concerning popular attitudes toward the euro within the member states. Why is the single currency so controversial in some countries but not in others? Although the question is explicitly comparative, the answer differs idiosyncratically from one country to the next.

Idiosyncrasy is easier to illustrate than it is to prove. Consider, for example, three pairs of member states: Belgium and Denmark, Italy and the United Kingdom, France and Germany. As mentioned earlier, the structure of concerns expressed by respondents to the Eurobarometer polling is correlated in each of these pairs. The political significance of the euro is not. EMU is a positive symbol in Belgium and Italy, but a negative symbol in Denmark and the United Kingdom. And, while it is true that EMU is a problematic symbol in both France and Germany, there is little basis for believing that the single currency is problematic for the same reasons or with the same effect.

The contrast between attitudes in Belgium and Denmark is useful to highlight the difficulty of making generalizations about member state size or influence within the single currency. Both Belgium and Denmark are smaller member states with high levels of exposure to world trade, extensive dependence on exports to and imports from other countries in the single currency, and with strong traditions of using their monetary policies to stabilize exchange rates between their national currencies and the Deutschemark. Within this context, politicians in Belgium succeeded in claiming that membership in the single currency is the only means of safeguarding the country's influence in Europe and providing a necessary bulwark for welfare state reform (Jones 2002). Meanwhile, politicians in Denmark failed to convince voters along similar lines and instead fell prey to concerns that EMU membership would lead to the country's domination by the European Union and would undermine the Danish welfare state. In September 2000, almost 90 percent of the Danish electorate participated in a referendum on the euro and more than 53 percent voted against joining.[16]

The contrast between Italy and the United Kingdom illustrates the contingent basis of symbolic politics. Both countries faced considerable difficulties in joining the single currency. For Italy, the difficulties centered on large public debts and deficits. For the United Kingdom, they centered on the inappropriate pegging of the pound within the exchange rate mechanism (ERM) of the European monetary system (EMS). During the 1992 exchange rate crisis, both the pound and the lire were ejected from the ERM. And, voices in both countries claimed this exchange-rate volatility to be symbolic of the mismanagement of the economy by political elites. The difference between the two cases is that where subsequent Italian governments made Herculean efforts to achieve EMU membership, subsequent British governments sought to maintain distance from the process of monetary integration. In Italy, as in Belgium, the euro has emerged as a symbol of economic competence and political progress. In the United Kingdom, it has become a symbol of economic incompetence and political reticence. To attribute this difference to the strength of British as opposed to Italian nationalism is simply to admit that it is idiosyncratic to these two extremes of identity (see for example Mancini 2000).

The comparison between France and Germany illustrates the symbolic complexities of great power politics. Public reluctance to surrender the Deutschemark in Germany reflects an underlying suspicion that the new European currency will come under foreign influence and so will not be as strong as the German one it replaces. By the same token, public reluctance to surrender the franc in France reflects an underlying suspicion that the new European currency will serve as an instrument for enhancing Germany's power in Europe.[17] These concerns emerged repeatedly during the 1990s and into the 21st century. Their imprint is on the 1992 French referendum on the Maastricht Treaty, the 1993 German Constitutional Court decision, the "Stability and Growth Pact," the debate over whether Wim Duisenberg or Jean-Claude Trichet should be the first governor of the European Central Bank, the constitution of the Euro-11 Group, the Nice summit and so on. The fact that these concerns compete with one another is irrelevant. What matters is not so much that both sets of concerns cannot be true at the same time. Rather what is important is that they cannot both be addressed at the same time.

THE SYMBOLISM OF EMU

The European Union's single currency exists both inside and outside the EU as a regime. It is a familiar institution around which expectations can converge. And it is an unfamiliar change which can be used to invoke fear as an instrument of politics. It is a technology and it is a talisman.

This dual aspect of EMU is as unfortunate as it is unavoidable. The to-and-fro between France and Germany has done much to elaborate the constitutional architecture of EMU. However, it is unclear that such developments could not have been agreed to more easily without concern that the distribution of power within the single currency is a zero-sum-game within the Franco-German couple. Moreover, for every Belgium or Italy, where the symbolic force of participation in the single currency has been matched with heroic efforts, there is a Denmark or United Kingdom, where the symbolism of the euro has done little to promote public debate and much to arouse public concern.

Still it remains true that the single currency is more than a manifestation of economic technology. As much as the designers who laid the foundations for EMU might have hoped to minimize the symbolic associations with the project, their refusal to consider politics per se was more part of the problem than part of the solution. Analysts who insist on bringing the politics, norms, and symbols back in are right to do so. The point to keep in mind, however, is that there is no one politics of EMU, no single set of norms that underwrites the single currency, and no coherent iconography of the euro.[18] The symbolism of EMU is every bit as varied as are the distributive consequences of participating in a monetary union. In turn, managing that symbolism will require an equally varied approach. Analysts looking to generalize about the normative or symbolic content of the single currency can perhaps afford to overlook this diversity. However, as experience has shown in France and Denmark, politicians who ignore diversity of meanings attached to the euro are likely to confront some unpleasant surprises.[19]

NOTES

1. For an early discussion of the conceptual problems surrounding regime types, see Young (1980). See also Krasner (1983).

2. Far and away, the most persuasive argument along these lines is McNamara (1998). Siedentop (2000) sets the opposite end of the spectrum, with a incredible set of assertions about the motivations behind and implications of the establishment of the single currency. McKay (1999) provides a federalist perspective on EMU. Dyson (1994) and (2000) makes arguments both about the reconstitution of interstate relations and about emergent relations between the individual and the European Union. The essays in Moss and Michie (2000) either argue or assume the neo-liberal perspective.

3. See, for example, Carr (1945, 16–17); Hobsbawm (1990, 14–45). This use of money to reinforce national identity was unexpected by most economists of the period. As Polanyi (1944, 203) explains: "The constitutive importance of the currency in establishing the nation as the decisive economic and political unit of the time was as thoroughly overlooked by writers of the liberal Enlightenment as the existence of history had been by their eighteenth century predecessors."

4. For a summary of the mechanisms behind monetary symbolism, see Cohen (1998, 36).

5. Here the allusion is to Anderson (1991).

6. Pollard (1981, 304–305). For a more general treatment of the tension between national integration and international disintegration, see Myrdal (1956).

7. The citation is from Gerschenkron (1966, 28–29) and is taken only slightly out of context. Gerschenkron's point is that an unpopular government such as the Soviet Union must convince the people of its necessity in order to establish its legitimacy. He goes on to suggest that "industrialization provided such a function for the Soviet government." My paraphrase is that monetary stabilization and reform provided such a function for the Western governments involved in World War II.

8. This is hardly a unique situation for analysis in the study of regimes or of social constructivism more generally. See, for example, Wendt (1999) and particularly his struggle to generalize the notion of homogeneity (353–357). See also the comments on Wendt by Keohane (2000) and Krasner (2000).

9. My argument makes a little bit of a leap here that students of international relations may or may not accept. Krasner's definition is explicit in identifying regimes as part of the realm of international relations. The actors in that realm are states, and not the electorates that support state governments. Hence it would be fair to argue that the convergence of expectations should take place at the level of government and not at the level of public opinion. My leap is to suggest that regimes extend all the way down.

10. These calculations are based on data found in Eurobarometer (2001). The correlations are displayed in Figure 8.1.

11. The claim here is correlative and not causal. For a causal argument linking some of these variables, see Gabel and Palmer (1995).

12. The hierarchical clustering technique used here takes the sum of the square of the difference in responses between any two countries as a measure of the distance between them (squared Euclidean distance). It then combines those cases that are closest, averages their positions, and recalculates the distances between member states and clusters. This process is repeated until only two clusters are left. These clusters are tested using an analysis of variance (ANOVA) on all dimensions in order to ensure that they are statistically different, one from the other. In this case, it was possible to reject the hypothesis that the two groups were really the same on all dimensions at the 0.01 percent level.

13. The principal difference between the hierarchical and k-means-squared techniques lies in the prior assumption of the number of clusters.

14. The French are "ambivalent" insofar as they sit on the boundary between hierarchical clusters and those optimized for difference.

15. These data are available upon request.

16. For a summary analysis of the Danish referendum, see Downs (2001).

17. See the essays in McCarthy (2001), and particularly Guerot (2001).

18. The difference between an icon and a symbol is that while an icon has consistent (communally shared) meaning, a symbol is subject to the interpretation of the person exposed to it (the interpretant). See Hawkes (1997, 128–129).

19. The June 2001 referendum on the Nice Treaty in Ireland suggests that such symbolic pluralism is not unique to the single currency.

✛

Conclusion:
The Politics of EMU

Economic and Monetary Union (EMU) means different things in different contexts. Far from rushing Europe toward the creation of a centralized superstate, EMU is ushering in new forms of diversity while underscoring the importance of old differences—differences between peoples, sectors, regions, states, cultures, and opinions. At the same time, EMU is not itself a monolithic entity. EMU is a mix of technologies, some of which—like the notes and coins—are centuries old, and others of which—like the real-time payment clearing facilities—are at the cutting edge of the information revolution. EMU is a cluster of rules, some tightly constraining, others less so, and others specifically empowering. EMU is a construct of institutions, some centralized and others not. EMU is a set of aspirations, not all of which can be achieved at the same time. EMU is an arena for collective action—both constitutive (and evolutionary) and distributive (and static). And EMU is a symbol, which can be interpreted as meaning all of these things, any of these things, or something different altogether.

The functioning of EMU is equally varied. The economists who designed the rules and institutions for economic and monetary union failed to lay the foundations for a formulaic or deterministic system—if that indeed was their objective. The politicians and policymakers who adapted, amended, and added onto the original designs have fared no better. As illustration, it is only necessary to point to the fact that the world awaited an appreciation of the single currency (the euro) against the dollar after the formal launch of EMU in January 1999. The subsequent, secular, and prolonged fall in the value of the euro left virtually everyone scratching their heads in dismay. On a finer level of detail, it is also possible to note that the European Central Bank (ECB) has missed both of the indicators it claims to follow in the determination of monetary policy—often without responding, and then usually without explaining the absence of a response. To their credit, what the representatives of the ECB have said, do say, and will probably continue to say, is that EMU is a new environment for policymaking. As a result, it will take some time to figure out how things actually work.

The same common sense should be applied to the politics of EMU as well. If the economics fails to conform to predictions, why should we assume the politics will do any better. Rather than structuring political hypotheses as specific covering-law type if-then relationships, we should acknowledge that the politics of EMU is varied, unpredictable, and at times it even defies conventional notions of rationality. EMU is a new political environment—or, perhaps more accurately, it is a new feature in an old political environment—and so it will take some time to figure out how it works.

The purpose of this conclusion is to sketch out what we can determine about the politics of EMU in broad brush. My goal is not to repeat what I have said before, at least not in any detail. Rather, I hope to suggest answers to what are surely the most important questions for the future: What will the maintenance of EMU require in the form of political adaptation in Europe? Is the construction of a single currency really worth the effort? And, even if EMU is worth the effort, will political elites and their electorates actually support the necessary adaptations?

My argument is that the hyperpluralism that is the hallmark of the politics of EMU—whether assessed in terms of distributive consequences or in terms of symbolic interpretations—is both a strength and a weakness for the system. The strength is that most necessary adaptations will be in response to contextually specific or idiosyncratic concerns, and therefore need only require action at the national or local level. The weakness is that further adaptation of EMU at the European level will be complicated by the need to assuage the interests and concerns of numerous different constituencies.

Institutional or behavioral modifications within the member states will be much easier than any changes to the European architecture of the single currency. Moreover, this is likely to be the case no matter how desirable it is or becomes to change the constitution of EMU. If anything, arguments that EMU must be reformed at the European level in order to survive will be greeted by demands within the member states for withdrawal from the single currency. Far from being the start of some grand adventure in European state-building, this analysis of the politics of EMU suggests we will have plenty of time to figure things out before moving on from here.

The argument is made in three sections. The first sets out the relationship between idiosyncrasy and adaptation, value and effort. The second looks at the cost of support. The third section concludes on a cautionary note.

IDIOSYNCRASY AND ADAPTATION, VALUE AND EFFORT

Most analyses of EMU, whether they focus on politics or economics, start from the single currency and work outward from there. Nowhere is this more true than when analysis turns to the stability of the system. The implicit question is why would political or economic actors choose to move from a situation where there is only a single currency to a situation where there are two or more currencies. Once the conditions are identified, all we need to do is adapt the institutions of EMU to prevent those conditions from coming about and we can ensure the stability of the system.

The problem with this pattern of deduction is not only that it assumes that most people will think about the single currency in something like a predictable way, but also that it assumes that we can identify who will think about the single currency in a predictable way before the fact. These are highly problematic assumptions if we accept that the distributive outcomes of monetary policy changes are contingent upon domestic institutional factors and that the symbolic meaning of the single currency is contextually contingent as well. People may be thinking about the euro from a standpoint of distributive rationality, but we will need a lot of information about their institutional environment in order to anticipate what exactly they will be thinking. Then again, people may not be thinking about the euro from a recognizable standpoint of distributive rationality. They may not know enough about their own institutional environment or they may apply some symbolic rationality that is altogether different. How can we assume the capacity to predict attitudes in such an environment before the fact?

Consider the reasoning often provided for refusing to leave one currency regime to join another. For example, I live in the Midlands of Britain, where the exchange rate consequences of the Bank of England's monetary policy have been disastrous for local industry. Nevertheless, when I speak to local businessmen about joining the euro, one of the concerns they invariably express is that monetary policy set in Frankfurt will not be taken in the British interest. No doubt at some level they are right. But whatever the British interest, the monetary policy decisions taken in London are surely not in the interests of small businesses in the Midlands. So what is the rational basis for their concern about shifting monetary authority from London to Frankfurt?

The simple conclusion to draw from this is that we really cannot make many strong assumptions about why people would actually choose to leave a situation defined by a single currency in order to move into a situation defined by many currencies or by a different currency. We can make assumptions about why people might choose to change their currency regime, but we can never safely assume what rationality will actually lie at the basis of such a hypothetical choice. More important, if our interest is to ensure the stability of EMU as a system, we do not need to make such assumptions.

The problem is not to identify when or why people would choose either for or against a currency regime. Rather it is to identify why people would even consider it necessary or useful to think about changing the currency regime in the first place. Here two questions are relevant:

- Is the currency regime fulfilling the basic functions of money as technology?
- What alternative forms of adaptation are available in response to any particular problem?

Clearly if the currency regime is not fulfilling the basic functions of money—means of exchange, store of value, unit of account—then some other regime is required. Hence, when there is a collapse in the value of the currency or a sharp contraction in the supply of money, we should expect people to look for a change in the currency regime. In immediate postwar Germany, people used cigarettes as currency. During the wars in Yugoslavia, the currency of preference was the Deutschemark. But these are extreme cases, where few alternatives present themselves.

If the problem is not a breakdown in the functioning of money as technology, then the issue of changing currency regimes is not a matter of necessity so much as a question of degrees. We do not have to know very much about local institutions or culture to assume that people will move from a bad currency to a good one.[1] As the functional difference between one currency regime and another decreases, however, the likelihood that some form of redress can be found short of changing the currency regime increases. Here again, we can assume that once the cost of changing the currency regime exceeds the cost of seeking some other form of redress, then the alternative will become the adaptation.

This chain of reasoning is more satisfying than the standard deduction for two reasons. First, it acknowledges both the essential role of money and the limits to that role. Having access to money as technology is important, but it is not everything and often it is not the most important or most obvious thing. Second, this chain of reasoning emphasizes the trade-offs between the cost of achieving a marginal improvement in the technology and the cost of doing something else. In other words, it more accurately mirrors the political calculus that led to the promotion of EMU in the first place. The heads of state and government of the European Union agreed to the construction of EMU because they wanted to improve the functioning of money as technology and because they could not realize these improvements with the same cost-effectiveness through other means. Of course it is true that *some* heads of state and government had other designs in mind when they agreed to move to EMU. But it is not true that *all* of them had such designs, that they all had the *same* designs, or that they *only* had such designs. By the same token, it is unlikely that anyone would ever change currency regimes with only one set of concerns. The point is not why they acted, but why they chose currency as the area in which to act.

Here is not the place to introduce an angels-and-pins debate about the motivations for EMU. Rather, and more simply, it is to suggest that no matter what the calculus behind the single currency, there is little likelihood that a similar or equivalent congruence of factors will come along to force its unmaking. Given the idiosyncrasy of distributive outcomes and symbolic interpretations it should almost always be possible to provide a means of redressing any concern that might arise under EMU that is easier and cheaper than changing the currency regime. Moreover, the greater the degree of idiosyncrasy on either or both accounts, the easier and cheaper the alternative form of redress is likely to be.

Of course there are two obvious counters to this line of argument. The first is that money will never be ignored because it is inherently central to the political control over the economy. Even before researching alternative forms of redress, people are likely to blame their economic adversity on the state's powerlessness to control the currency. Alternatively, the state will shift blame from itself onto the ECB. In either case, political pressure will come to bear on the need to return to the national currency as an essential means of redress, no matter how costly.

The second counter argument dovetails with the first. The claim is that the rules for fiscal probity embodied in the Stability and Growth Pact have so constrained government action as to cut off alternative forms of redress within the single currency. Hence, not only will governments have fewer resources with which to respond to local economic concern, but they will also have greater need to displace blame onto the ECB.

Both of these points have some merit, but it is not universal and it is short-lived. To begin with, the fiscal rules in the Stability and Growth Pact are problematic only in those member states that have high levels of outstanding public debt. Once that public debt is paid down, the capacity to run periodic deficits as part of a counter-cyclical fiscal policy will increase. Moreover, it remains possible (although admittedly difficult) to transfer resources across budget lines without actually affecting the surplus. And, as a last resort, it is even possible for states to ignore the pact. Second, the symbolic allure of national currencies is not a universal feature of political life and it must surely diminish as a result of participation in EMU. Once it becomes clear that the nation-state is not the only political authority capable of providing a functional currency, then the historic link between currency and statehood described by Polanyi (see chapter 8) will have been weakened—if not lost altogether.

The conclusion at the point is that adaptation under EMU is more likely to be localized than to be generalized, and so should not constitute a threat to the stability of EMU as a regime. And, while the regime may be vulnerable in more general terms, this vulnerability is unlikely to show up outside of extreme situations, it is unevenly spread across the member states, and it is likely to diminish over time. This conclusion is supported not only by the preceding analysis, but also by the functioning of the institutions within EMU. The three clusters of rules outlined in chapter 2 allocate the greatest flexibility to national governments in their efforts to make structural adjustments, somewhat less flexibility in fiscal matters, and considerably less in terms of monetary instruments.

COST AND SUPPORT

The principal argument for a necessary change in the constitution of EMU has little or nothing to do with the problems of adaptation under the regime. Rather it derives from the desire to imbue the regime with greater political force. EMU should have a political authority that is equal in stature to its monetary authority, it should have a single voice to represent the single currency in world affairs, and it should have a political union to support its monetary union. These are all claims that have been made repeatedly in the welter of suggestions for reforming the constitution of EMU. However, they have more bearing on the desirability of the economic and monetary union in normative terms, than on its stability in positive terms. They relate to whether we actually get an EMU that does what we want, rather than just one that "works." In turn, however, the desirability of EMU may have a direct bearing on its stability. If the economic and monetary union cannot deliver what "Europe" wants, then how can it be legitimate? If it is not legitimate, then how can it sustain popular support?

At the heart of this set of propositions lie three assumptions: there is a Europe; this Europe wants something; and that something can be provided through the political management of macroeconomic policy instruments at the European level. Each of these assumptions represents an uneasy blend of normative and positive elements. As a result, it is often unclear what is the direction of causality, how we could test any of the resulting propositions, and whether we should even try.

Consider the notion that there is a Europe. Throughout this book, I have tended to use the term Europe interchangeably with the term European Union. Among people who write on European Union affairs, it is a convenient shorthand. The European Union's single currency is Europe's single currency, and so forth. However, one of my research students, a Dane, has objected to this shorthand vociferously. Her point is that such a use of the term Europe suggests something concrete that is actually highly contested. More important, the concept of Europe is contested particularly by my own analysis. If it is true that both distributive and symbolic politics are highly contingent depending upon local institutions and culture, then how can we speak in meaningful terms about Europe doing or wanting anything.

The answer lies in the intermediation of competing interests. If there is a Europe, then it is a negotiated construct. And what it wants is whatever is the outcome of the negotiations across local idiosyncrasies. This is not a surprising situation. All politics is about the intermediation of interests at some level. Nevertheless, it is an important concession in the context about claims to legitimate EMU through careful examination of Europe's wants. Who is the holder of legitimacy in this notion of Europe? Is it Europe itself, or is it the duly appointed representatives of local interests? In positive terms, I have argued that the heads of state and government are the duly appointed representatives of local interests and that they are also the only essential holders of legitimacy. This argument is consistent with the notion of Europe. However, it leaves it unclear why anyone would care what Europe wants rather than what the member states want or what their electorates want.

The answer is that somehow only collective action between the member states can satisfy the individual desires of the member states or their constituencies. More specifically, only collective action between the member states in guiding and representing the instruments of macroeconomic policy can satisfy those wants. And even more specifically, such action must take place beyond the degree of macroeconomic coordination that is already present in the constitution of the EMU.

This chain of reasoning suggests the existence of a Europe that transcends the simple intermediation of the member states and constitutes a political entity in its own right—one capable of demanding sacrifices from some of its members so that others can benefit. The difficulty is that it is unclear whether such a Europe actually exists. Although the member states have shown some willingness to make national concessions in the national interest, they have shown remarkable reluctance to institutionalize the practice of making national concessions in the collective interest. It is even more unclear how anyone could ever determine what this Europe wants apart from surveying the heads of state and government. Most important, however, it is unclear that anything such a Europe wants could be addressed only through coordinated macroeconomic action at the European level (rather than through the coordination of macroeconomic actions taken at the national level as already takes place).

Of course this thinking could also be the wrong way around. A different perspective on the argument is that only the construction of a European macroeconomic authority can effectively conjure Europe into being. Only a single macroeconomic representative can come to symbolize the essential significance of macroeconomic policymaking at the European level. And only the combination of a single currency, a single fiscal authority, and a single political voice can support the construction of a political union that is commensurate in size and scale to EMU. Following this line of thought, the existence of Europe is not the assumption. It is the goal.

It is at this point that the normative and the positive become inextricably intertwined. We need to create institutions to serve Europe. And these same institutions will also have the effect of creating Europe. Because Europe is the goal, the institutions are not only good but essential. Hence, Europe should want them. The circularity of the reasoning is self-evident.

If we return to first principles, however, such circularity is easily avoided. A Europe constituted of heads of state and government is unlikely to agree to a centralization of economic policy authority or even to the appointment of anything more than a token representative for EMU unless there is some compelling advantage to such an arrangement that cannot be had in any other way. The reason for this reluctance is that open-ended fiscal commitments at the European level can only serve to constrain the capacity of member states to satisfy their constituents at the domestic level. In turn, such constituents are likely to express their unhappiness with national political elites.

The growing concern for the costs of enlargement and for the levels of net contributions to EU coffers in countries such as the Netherlands, Sweden, Denmark, and Germany all signal that the limits of member state commitment in fiscal terms are close at hand and may already have been reached. Hence, even if we were to accept the proposition that some form of economic government is necessary, it is unlikely to be forthcoming. More important, the Irish veto of the Nice Treaty—coming, as it did, on the heels of the Council of Ministers' decision to reprimand the Irish government for its fiscal position—suggests the likelihood of further retrenchment in the future.

THE *FORBIDDEN PLANET*

The surprise decision of the Irish electorate is a useful place to conclude an argument about the politics of EMU that stretches from technology to symbolism. That decision was arguably unrelated to the single currency, although to be sure the Council's reprimand did play a role. The Irish are strong supporters of EMU. Moreover, the symbolism of joining the single currency actually reinforces rather than detracts from notions of Irish sovereignty and economic modernization.

The Irish government used participation in the exchange rate mechanism of the European monetary system (EMS) as a means of severing the link between the Irish punt and the British pound in the late 1970s and early 1980s. EMS participation also encouraged a redirection of Irish trade from Britain to the Continent, not only enhancing the country's economic independence from its former colonial masters but also strengthening the technological base for Irish manufacturing. Membership in EMU is a culmination of these developments and not a rejection of Irish statehood.

The Irish referendum is important because it illustrates the power of idiosyncrasy to overwhelm the self-confidence of predictive analysis in specific cases. If the Irish government made an overwhelming mistake, it was to assume that the referendum was a foregone conclusion. By extension, the mistake was to take economic self-interest and symbolic interpretation for granted, to assume a particular rationale, and to ignore the alternatives.

Of course critics of this book will argue that I do much the same. They will claim that my reliance on idiosyncrasy masks analytic complacency. They will suggest that my unpicking of assumptions only serves to hide my own dependence on hidden claims. And they will conclude that I fail to grasp the transcendent importance of the issues at stake in constructing an economic and monetary union in Europe. In this sense, they will argue that I should be held just as culpable as those economists and policymakers who failed to foresee the complexities of the Maastricht ratification process, who underestimated the role of symbols or of politics, and who aspired to construct a technocratic Europe that was ultimately and inherently out of touch with political reality.

My only counter to such criticisms is to suggest that they ask too much from EMU. And, in asking too much from EMU, they assume too little about the politics of its construction. The single currency is a minor technological improvement over the alternatives that promises to offer significant rewards over a long period of time. As a policy change it was carefully considered, well planned, and cautiously implemented. As a political matter it was only rarely oversold. And yet it was in the infrequent overselling of EMU that the trouble started.

The point is that a minor technological improvement is easily adapted into an environment of highly contingent distributive and symbolic politics. A major revolution in the practice of government is not. The more people focus their attention on the scale of the adaption that is suggested, the more it is likely to appeal to their fears rather than to their expectations. And the more hyperbolic the rhetoric becomes, the greater is the threat of backlash.

My point is not to say that EMU should have been slipped in through the back door. Rather it is that EMU is the back door, at least in technological terms. Most people in Europe use money for vanishingly few transactions. Instead, they use bits and bytes. EMU simply changed what the bits and bytes are called and who created them. Since no-one can tell how the process of creation will affect them directly at any specific point in time, and since strict rules have been agreed as to how the creation will work over time, this should not be such a big issue. It certainly should not be sold as the founding moment of a European super-state.

The Irish referendum—like two of the three Danish referendums that preceded it—demonstrates the danger involved in trying to make something out of nothing. Like the thought machine on the *Forbidden Planet*, these referenda made the nightmares of European political elites a reality. The only thing that could make matters worse at this point, would be to reflect that same fearsome generative power through the electorate of a larger member state. The good news is that Europe's heads of state and government seem to have learned this lesson from the 1992 referendum in France. The politics of EMU will settle down over time. Over time, we may even figure precisely how it works. For now, though, it may be best simply to leave it alone.

NOTE

1. The point to note here is that Gresham's Law, which states that cheap money drives out the dear, assumes that cheap and dear currencies are functionally equivalent as a means of exchange and yet different as stores of value (the dear being better). Cheap money drives out the dear as a means of exchange, and yet dear money drives out the cheap as a store of value.

References

Alesina, Alberto. 1987. Macroeconomic Policy in a Two-Party System as a Repeated Game. *Quarterly Journal of Economics* 102:3 (August) 651–678.

———. 1989. Politics and Business Cycles in Industrial Democracies. *Economic Policy* 8 (April) 55–98.

Alesina, Alberto, Nouriel Roubini, and Gerald D. Cohen. 1997. *Political Cycles and the Macroeconomy.* Cambridge: MIT Press.

Anderson, Benedict. 1991. *Imagined Communities.* London: Verso.

Anderson, Jeffrey. 1997. Hard Interests, Soft Power, and Germany's Changing Role in Europe. In Peter J. Katzenstein, ed. *Tamed Power: Germany in Europe.* Ithaca: Cornell University Press, 80–107.

———. 1999. *German Unification and the Union of Europe.* Cambridge: Cambridge University Press.

Andrews, David M. 1994. Capital Mobility and State Autonomy: Toward a Structural Theory of International Monetary Relations. *International Studies Quarterly* 38:2 (June) 193–218.

Arrow, Kenneth J. 1985. The Economics of Agency. In John W. Pratt and Richard J. Zeckhauser, eds. *Principals and Agents: The Structure of Business.* Boston: Harvard Business School Press, 37–51.

Artis, Michael J., and Wenda Zhang. 1999. Further Evidence on the International Business Cycle and the ERM: Is There a European Business Cycle? *Oxford Economic Papers* 51 (January) 120–132.

Bacchetta, Philippe, and Eric van Wincoop. 1998. Does Exchange Rates Stability Increase Trade and Capital Flows? Manuscript. New York: Federal Reserve Bank of New York (July).

Backus, David, and John Driffill. 1985. Inflation and Reputation. *American Economic Review* 75:3 (June) 530–538.

Bailey, Martin J. 1956. The Welfare Cost of Inflationary Finance. *The Journal of Political Economy* 64:2 (April) 93–110.

Bank for International Settlements. 2000. *70th Annual Report, 1 April 1999–31 March 2000*. Basle: Bank for International Settlements (June 5).

Bark, Dennis L., and David R. Gress. 1993. *A History of West Germany, Volume 1: From Shadow to Substance, 1945–1963*. Oxford: Blackwell.

Barrell, Ray, and Nigel Pain. 1998. Real Exchange Rates, Agglomerations, and Irreversibilities: Macroeconomic Policy and FDI in EMU. *Oxford Review of Economic Policy* 14:3 (autumn) 152–167.

Barro, Robert J., and David B. Gordon. 1983. Rules, Discretion, and Reputation in a Model of Monetary Policy. *Journal of Monetary Economics* 12 (July) 101–121.

Bayoumi, Tamim, and Barry Eichengreen. 1998. Exchange Rate Volatility and Intervention: Implications of the Theory of Optimum Currency Areas. *Journal of International Economics* 45, 191–209.

Bayoumi, Tamim, and Paul Masson. 1995. Fiscal Flows in the United States and Canada: Lessons for Monetary Union in Europe. *European Economic Review* 39, 253–274.

———. 1998. Liability-creating Versus Non-liability Creating Fiscal Stabilization Policies: Ricardian Equivalence, Fiscal Stabilization, and EMU. *The Economic Journal* 108 (July) 1026–1045.

Bazen, Stephen, and Eric Girardin. 1999. France and the Maastricht Criteria: Fiscal Retrenchment and Labor Market Adjustment. In David Cobham and George Zis, eds. *From EMS to EMU: 1979 to 1999 and Beyond*. London: Macmillan, 95–128.

Bean, Charles. 1989. Capital Shortages and Persistent Unemployment. *Economic Policy* 8 (April) 11–53.

Beck, Nathaniel. 1987. Elections and the Fed: Is There a Political Monetary Cycle? *American Journal of Political Science* 31:1 (February) 194–216.

Belke, Ansgar, and Daniel Gros. 1999. Estimating the Costs and Benefits of EMU: The Impact of External Shocks on Labor Markets.*Weltwirtschaftliches Archiv* 135:1, 1–47.

———. 2000. Designing EU–US Monetary Relations: The Impact of Exchange-Rate Variability on Labor Markets on Both Sides of the Atlantic. Manuscript. Brussels: Centre for European Policy Studies (April).

Berger, Suzanne. 1996. Introduction. In Suzanne Berger and Ronald Dore, eds. *National Diversity and Global Capitalism*. Ithaca: Cornell University Press, 1–25.

Bergman, Michael, and Jan-Erik Lane. 1990. Public Policy in a Principal-Agent Framework. *Journal of Theoretical Politics* 2:3, 339–352.

Berman, Sheri, and Kathleen R. McNamara. 1999. Bank on Democracy: Why Central Banks Need Public Oversight. *Foreign Affairs* 78:2 (March/April) 2–8.

Bernhard, William. 1999. A Political Explanation of Variation in Central Bank Independence. *American Political Science Review* 92:2 (June) 311–327.

Berthold, Norbert, Rainer Fehn, and Eric Thode. 1999. Real Wage Rigidities, Fiscal Policy, and the Stability of EMU in the Transition Phase. *IMF Working Paper WP/99/83*. Washington, D.C.: International Monetary Fund (June).

Blanchard, Olivier, and Justin Wolfers. 1999. The Role of Shocks and Institutions in the Rise of European Unemployment: The Aggregate Evidence. *NBER Working Paper No. 7282*. Cambridge: National Bureau for Economic Research (August).

Bleaney, Michael. 1996. Central Bank Independence, Wage-Bargaining Structure, and Macroeconomic Performance in OECD Countries. *Oxford Economic Papers* 48:1 (January) 20–38.

Boltho, Andrea. 1996. Has France Converged on Germany? Policies and Institutions Since 1958. In Suzanne Berger and Ronald Dore, eds. *National Diversity and Global Capitalism*. Ithaca: Cornell University Press, 89–104.

Brunner, Karl. 1975. Comment [on Gordon (1975)]. *Journal of Law and Economics* 18:3 (December) 837–857.

Bulmer, Simon. 1993. Germany and European Integration: Toward Economic and Political Dominance? In Carl F. Lankowski, ed. *Germany and the European Community: Beyond Hegemony and Containment?* New York: St. Martin's Press, 73–99.

———. 1997. Shaping the Rules? The Constitutive Politics of the European Union and German Power. In Peter J. Katzenstein, ed. *Tamed Power: Germany in Europe*. Ithaca: Cornell University Press, 49–79.

Bulmer, Simon, and William E. Patterson. 1996. Germany in the European Union: Gentle Giant or Emergent Leader? *International Affairs* 72:1, 9–32.

Calleo, David P. 1992. *The Bankrupting of America: How the Federal Budget Is Impoverishing the Nation*. New York: William Morrow and Company.

Calmfors, Lars. 1998. Macroeconomic Policy, Wage Setting, and Employment—What Difference Does EMU Make? *Oxford Review of Economic Policy* 14:3 (autumn) 125–151.

Calmfors, Lars, and John Driffill. 1988. Centralization of Wage Bargaining: Bargaining Structure, Corporatism, and Macroeconomic Performance. *Economic Policy* 6 (April) 13–61.

Calvet, Josep González. 1996. Le cas de l'Espagne. In Philippe Ponchet and Otto Jacobi, eds. *Union économique et monétaire et négotiations collectives*. Brussels: Observatoire social européen, 99–115.

Campanella, Miriam. 2000. The Battle between ECOFIN 11 and the European Central Bank: A Rational Choice Perspective. In Maria Green Cowles and Michael Smith, eds. *The State of the European Union: Risks, Reforms, Resistance, and Revival, Vol. 5.* Oxford: Oxford University Press, 110–126.

Carlino, Gerald, and Robert DeFina. 1998a. The Differential Regional Effects of Monetary Policy. *The Review of Economics and Statistics* 80:4 (November) 572–587.

———. 1998b. Monetary Policy and the U.S. States and Regions: Some Implications for the European Monetary Union. *Working Paper No. 98–17*. Philadelphia: Federal Reserve Bank of Philadelphia.

Carr, Edward Hallett. 1945. *Nationalism and After*. London: Macmillan & Co., Ltd.

Centre for European Policy Studies (CEPS). 1999. *Macroeconomic Policy in the First Year of Euroland: 1st Annual Report of the CEPS Macroeconomic Policy Group*. Brussels: CEPS.

Cohen, Benjamin J. 1993. The Triad and the Unholy Trinity: Lessons for the Pacific Region. In Richard Higgott, Richard Leaver, and John Ravenhill eds. *Pacific Economic Relations in the 1990s: Cooperation or Conflict?* St. Leonards, Australia: Allen and Unwin, 133–158.

———. 1994. Beyond EMU: The Problem of Sustainability. In Barry Eichengreen and Jeffry Frieden, eds. *The Political Economy of European Monetary Unification*. Boulder: Westview Press, 149–165.

———. 1998. *The Geography of Money*. Ithaca: Cornell University Press.

Commission of the European Communities (CEC). 1975. Rapport du groupe de re-flexion "Union Èconomique et monétaire 1980." Brussels: Commission of the European Communities (March).

———. 1989. Report on Economic and Monetary Union in the European Community. Brussels: Commission of the European Communities.

Cooper, Richard N. 1968. *The Economics of Interdependence: Economic Policy in the Atlantic Community*. New York: McGraw-Hill.

Corden, W.M. 1972. Monetary Integration. *Essays in International Finance* No. 93. Princeton: Princeton University (April).

Council of Ministers. 1998. Meeting of the Ministers for Economic Affairs and Finance, Governors of Central Banks, European Commission and European Monetary Institute. Brussels: Council of Ministers (May 3) 9173/98 (Press 126) C/98/126.

———. 2000. *Broad Guidelines of the Economic Policies 2000*. Brussels: General Secretariat of the Council.

———. 2001. 2329th Council Meeting—ECOFIN—Brussels, February 12 2001. Brussels: Council of Ministers, 5696/01 (Presse 35).

Cowles, Maria Green, and Michael Smith. 2000. Risks, Reform, Resistance, and Revival. In Maria Green Cowles and Michael Smith, eds. *The State of the European Union Vol. 5: Risks, Reforms, Resistance, and Revival*. Oxford: Oxford University Press, 3–16.

Crozier, Michel. 1973. *The Stalled Society*. New York: The Viking Press.

Crozier, Michel, and Erhard Friedberg. 1977. *L'acteur et le système*. Paris: Éditions du Seuil.

Dahl, Robert A., and Charles E. Lindblom. 1976. *Politics, Economics, and Welfare: Planning and Politico-economic Systems Resolved into Basic Social Processes*. Chicago: University of Chicago Press.

Danthine, Jean-Pierre, and Jennifer Hunt. 1994. Wage Bargaining Structure, Employment, and Economic Integration. *The Economic Journal* 104 (May) 528–541.

Darby, Julia, et al. 1999. The Impact of Exchange Rate Uncertainty on the Level of Investment. *The Economic Journal* 109 (March) C55-C67.

De Haan, Jakob. 1997. The European Central Bank: Independence, Accountability, and Strategy—a Review. *Public Choice* 93, 395–426.

De la Serre, Françoise, and Christian Lequesne. 1993. France and the European Union. In Alan W. Cafruny and Glenda G. Rosenthal, eds. *The State of the European Community Vol. 2: The Maastricht Debates and Beyond*. Boulder: Lynne Rienner, 145–157.

Dinan, Desmond. 1999. Governance and Institutions: A Transitional Year. In Geoffrey Edwards and Georg Wiessala, eds. *The European Union Annual Review 1998/1999*. Oxford: Blackwell, 37–61.

Dornbusch, Rudiger, Carlo A. Favero, and Francesco Giavazzi. 1998. The Immediate Challenges for the European Central Bank. In David Begg et al., eds. *EMU: Prospects and Challenges for the Euro*. Oxford: Blackwell, 15–64.

Dornbusch, Rudiger, and Pierre Jacquet. 2000. Making EMU a Success. *International Affairs* 76:1, 89–110.

Downs, Anthony. 1957. *An Economic Theory of Democracy.* New York: Harper and Row.

Downs, William D. 2001. Denmark's Referendum on the Euro: The Mouse that Roared . . . Again. *West European Politics* 24:1 (January) 222–226.

Dyson, Kenneth. 1994. *Elusive Union: The Progress of Economic and Monetary Union in Europe.* London: Longman.

———. 1999a. Benign or Malevolent Leviathan? Social Democratic Governments in a Neo-liberal Euro Area. *The Political Quarterly* 70:2 (April-June) 195–209.

———. 1999b. The Franco-German Relationship and Economic and Monetary Union: Using Europe to "Bind Leviathan." *West European Politics* 22:1 (January) 25–44.

———. 2000. *The Politics of the Euro-Zone.* Oxford: Oxford University Press.

Dyson, Kenneth, and Kevin Featherstone. 1999. *The Road to Maastricht: Negotiating Economic and Monetary Union.* Oxford: Oxford University Press.

EAPN Ireland. 1999. *The Social Consequences of EMU for Marginalized and Socially Excluded Groups in Ireland.* Dublin: Irish Chapter of the European Anti-Poverty Network.

Edwards, Geoffrey, and Georg Wiessala. 1999. Editorial: Plus ça changes . . . ? In Geoffrey Edwards and Georg Wiessala, eds. *The European Union Annual Review 1998/1999.* Oxford: Blackwell, 1–8.

Eichengreen, Barry. 1998. European Monetary Unificiation: A Tour d'Horizon. *Oxford Review of Economic Policy* 14:3 (autumn) 24–40.

Eichengreen, Barry, and Charles Wyplosz. 1993. The Unstable EMS. *Brookings Papers on Economic Activity* 1, 51–143.

———. 1998. The Stability Pact: More than a Minor Nuisance? In David Begg, et al., eds. *EMU: Prospects and Challenges for the Euro.* Oxford: Blackwell, 67–104.

EIRO. 1997. Social Partners Reach Agreement on EMU Buffer Funds. www.eiro.eurofound.ie/1997/11/features/FI9711138F.html (November).

———. 1999. The "Europeanization" of Collective Bargaining. www.eiro.eurofound.ie/1999/07/study/TN9907201S.html (July).

Elgie, Robert. 1998. Democratic Accountability and Central Bank Independence: Historical and Contemporary, National and European Perspectives. *West European Politics* 21:3 (July) 53–76.

Emerson, Michael, et al. 1992. *One Market, One Money: An Evaluation of the Potential Benefits and Costs of Forming an Economic and Monetary Union.* Oxford: Oxford University Press.

Esping-Anderson, Gøsta. 1999. *Social Foundations of Postindustrial Economies.* Oxford: Oxford University Press.

Eurobarometer. 1998. *Public Opinion in the European Union, Report Number 49.* Brussels: European Commission.

———. 1999. *Public Opinion in the European Union, Report Number 50.* Brussels: European Commission.

———. 2001. *Public Opinion in the European Union, Report Number 54.* Brussels: European Commission.

European Central Bank. 1999a. *ECB Annual Report, 1998.* Frankfurt: European Central Bank.

———. 1999b. *Possible Effects of EMU on the Banking System in the Medium to Long Term.* Frankfurt: European Central Bank (January).

European Commission. 1997a. Amsterdam European Council, 16 and 17 June 1997: Presidency Conclusions. Brussels: European Commission (June 17) SN 150/97.

———. 1997b. Le passage à l'euro: assurer l'acceptation et la confiance des consummateurs. Brussels: European Commission, DG XXIV (November 27).

———. 1998a. Convergence Report 1998. Brussels: European Commission (March 25).

———. 1998b. Growth and Employment in the Stability-Oriented Framework of EMU: Economic Policy Reflections in View of the Forthcoming 1998 Broad Guidelines. Brussels: Directorate General II, Economic and Financial Affairs. II/33/98-EN.

———. 1999a. European Public Opinion on the Single Currency. *Monitoring Europinion.* Special Edition. Brussels: European Commission, DG X (January).

———. 1999b. Presidency Conclusions: Cologne European Council, June 3 and 4, 1999. Brussels: European Commission (June 4) SN 150/99.

European Council. 1997a. Extraordinary European Council Meeting on Employment, Luxembourg, November 20 and 21, 1997: Presidency Conclusions. Luxembourg: European Council (November 21) C/97/300.

———. 1997b. Luxembourg European Council, December 12 and 13, 1997, Presidency Conclusions. Luxembourg: European Council (December 13) C/97/400.

———. 2000. Presidency Conclusions—Lisbon European Council, March 23 and 24, 2000. Brussels: Council of Ministers (March 24) C/00/900.

European Voice. 2000. 8–10 September ECOFIN Informal. *European Voice* 6:13 (September 14).

Feldstein, Martin. 1997a. EMU and International Conflict. *Foreign Affairs* 76:6 (November/December) 60–73.

———. 1997b. The Political Economy of European Economic and Monetary Union: Political Sources of an Economic Liability. *Journal of Economic Perspectives* 11:4 (fall) 23–42.

Forder, James. 1998. Central Bank Independence—Conceptual Clarifications and Interim Assessment. *Oxford Economic Papers 50*, 307–334.

Frenkel, Jacob A., and Assaf Razin. 1987. *Fiscal Policies and the World Economy.* Cambridge: MIT Press.

Frieden, Jeffry 1996. The Impact of Goods and Capital Market Integration on European Monetary Politics. *Comparative Political Studies* 29:2 (April) 193–222.

———. 1998. The Political Economy of European Exchange Rates: An Empirical Assessment. Manuscript. Cambridge: Harvard University, Department of Government (August).

Frieden, Jeffry, and Erik Jones. 1998. The Political Economy of European Monetary Union: A Conceptual Overview. In Jeffry Frieden et al., eds. *The New Political Economy of EMU.* Lanham, Md.: Rowman & Littlefield, 163–186.

Friedman, Milton. 1969. *The Optimum Quantity of Money and Other Essays.* London: Macmillan.

———. 1977. Nobel Lecture: Inflation and Unemployment. *Journal of Political Economy* 85:3 (June) 451–472.

Friend, Julius W. 1991. The Linchpin: French-German Relations, 1950–1990. *The Washington Papers, No. 154*. New York: Praeger for CSIS.

G-7. 2000. State of G-7 Finance Ministers and Central Bank Governors (Prague. Press Release LS-910, Office of Public Affairs, Department of the Treasury. Washington, D.C.: United States Treasury (September 23).

Gabel, Matthew, and Harvey D. Palmer. 1995. Understanding Variation in Public Support for European Integration. *European Journal of Political Research* 27:1 (January) 3–19.

Galloway, David. 1999. Agenda 2000—Packaging the Deal. In Geoffrey Edwards and Georg Wiessala, eds. *The European Union Annual Review 1998/1999*. Oxford: Blackwell, 9–35.

Gandolfo, Giancarlo. 1992. Monetary Unions. In Peter Newman, Murray Milgate, and Jeahn Eatwell, eds. *The New Palgrave Dictionary of Money and Finance*. London: Macmillan, 765–770.

Garber, Peter M. 1999. Derivatives in International Capital Flows. In Martin Feldstein, ed. *International Capital Flows*. Chicago: University of Chicago Press, 386– 407.

Garrett, Geoffrey. 2000. Capital Mobility, Exchange Rates and Fiscal Policy in the Global Economy. *Review of International Political Economy* 7:1 (spring) 153–170.

Gerschenkron, Alexander. 1966. *Economic Backwardness in Historical Perspective: A Book of Essays*. Cambridge: The Belknap Press of Harvard University Press.

Giavazzi, Francesco, and Marco Pagano. 1988. The Advantages of Tying One's Hands: EMS Discipline and Central Bank Credibility. *European Economic Review* 32, 1055–1082.

Goodhart, Charles A. E. 1995. The Political Economy of Monetary Union. In Peter B. Kenen, ed. *Understanding Interdependence: The Macroeconomics of the Open Economy*. Princeton: Princeton University Press, 448–505.

Goodman, John B., and Louis W. Pauly. 1993. The Obsolescence of Capital Controls? Economic Management in an Age of Global Markets. *World Politics* 46:1 (October) 50–82.

Gordon, Philip. 1995. *France, Germany, and the Western Alliance*. Boulder: Westview.

Gordon, Robert J. 1975. The Demand for and Supply of Inflation. *The Journal of Law and Economics* 18:3 (December) 807–836.

Gourevitch, Peter. 1986. *Politics in Hard Times: Comparative Responses to International Economic Crises*. Ithaca: Cornell University Press.

Gros, Daniel. 1998. External Shocks and Labor Mobility: How Important Are They for EMU? In Jeffry Frieden et al., eds. *The New Political Economy of EMU*. Lanham, Md.: Rowman & Littlefield, 53–81.

Gros, Daniel, and Erik Jones. 1997. Does EMU Need to Converge on the US Model? Manuscript. Brussels: Centre for European Policy Studies (May).

Gros, Daniel, and Niels Thygesen. 1998. *European Monetary Integration: From the European Monetary System to Economic and Monetary Union*. New York: Addison Wesley Longman, 2nd Edition.

Grüner, Hans Peter, and Carsten Hefeker. 1999. How Will EMU Affect Inflation and Unemployment in Europe? *Scandinavian Journal of Economics* 101:1, 33–47.

Guerot, Ulrike. 2001. Ten Years After the Fall of the Wall: France's New View of Germany. In Patrick McCarthy, ed. *France-Germany in the Twenty-First Century*. London: Palgrave, 35–56.

Hall, Peter A. 1986. *Governing the Economy: The Politics of State Intervention in Britain and France.* Oxford: Oxford University Press.

———, ed. 1989. *The Political Power of Economic Ideas: Keynesianism across Nations.* Princeton: Princeton University Press.

———. 1994. Central Bank Independence and Coordinated Wage Bargaining: Their Interaction in Germany and Europe. *German Politics and Society* 31 (spring) 1–23.

Hall, Peter A., and Robert J. Franzese, Jr. 1998. Mixed Signals: Central Bank Independence, Coordinated Wage Bargaining, and European Monetary Union. *International Organization* 52:3 (summer) 505–535.

Hallerberg, Mark. 2001. EU Institutions and Fiscal Policy Coordination, 1991-2001. Paper presented at the 2001 European Community Studies Association Meetings in Madison, Wis. (May 29–July 3).

Harrison, Andrew. 2001. The European Central Bank: Transparency, Accountability, and Monetary Policy Success. *Working Documents in the Study of European Governance No. 8.* Nottingham: Centre for the Study of European Governance, University of Nottingham (May).

Hawkes, Terence. 1997. *Structuralism and Semiotics.* London: Routledge.

Heisenberg, Dorothee. 1999. *The Mark of the Bundesbank: Germany's Role in European Monetary Cooperation.* Boulder: Lynne Rienner Publishers.

Henning, C. Randall 1994. *Currencies and Politics in the United States, Germany, and Japan.* Washington, D.C.: Institute for International Economics.

———. 2000a. External Relations of the Euro Area. In Robert Mundell and Armand Clesse, eds. *The Euro as a Stabilizer in the International Economic System.* London: Kluwer Academic Publishers, 35–46.

———. 2000b. U.S.-EU Relations after the Inception of the Monetary Union: Cooperation or Rivalry? In C. Randall Henning and Pier Carlo Padoan, eds. *Transatlantic Perspectives on the Euro.* Washington, D.C.: Brookings Institution Press for the European Community Studies Association, 5–63.

Hibbs, Douglas A. 1977. Political Parties and Macroeconomic Policy. *American Political Science Review* 71:4 (December) 1467–1487.

Hobsbawm, Eric J. 1990. *Nations and Nationalism since 1780: Programme, Myth, Reality.* Cambridge: Cambridge University Press, Second Edition.

Inglehart, Ronald. 1997. *Modernization and Postmodernization: Cultural, Economic, and Political Change in 43 Societies.* Princeton: Princeton University Press.

Italianer, Alexander. 1993. Mastering Maastricht: EMU Issues and How They Were Settled. In K. Gretschmann, ed. *Economic and Monetary Union: Implications for National Policy-Makers.* Maastricht: European Institute for Public Administration, 51–113.

Iversen, Torben. 1998. Wage Bargaining, Central Bank Independence, and the Real Effects of Money. *International Organization* 52:3 (summer) 469–504.

Jones, Alun. 1994. *The New Germany: A Human Geography.* Chichester: John Wiley and Sons.

Jones, Erik. 1998. Economic and Monetary Union: Playing with Money. In Andrew Moravcsik, ed. *Centralization or Fragmentation? Europe Facing the Challenges of Deepening, Diversity, and Democracy.* Washington: Brookings, 59–93.

———. 1999. Is "Competitive" Corporatism an Adequate Response to Globalization? Evidence from the Low Countries. *West European Politics* 22:3 (July) 159–181.

———. 2000. The Politics of Europe 1999: Spring Cleaning. *Industrial Relations Journal: European Annual Review 1999* 31:4 (October/November) 248–261.

———. 2001. The Politics of Europe 2000: Unity through Diversity. *Industrial Relations Journal: European Annual Review 2000* 32:4 (October/November) 362–379.

———. 2002. Consociationalism, Corporatism, and the Fate of Belgium. *Acta Politica* (in press).

———. Forthcoming. *Economic Adjustment and Political Transformation in Small States*. Lanham, Md.: Rowman & Littlefield.

Jones, Erik, Jeffry Frieden, and Francisco Torres, eds. 1998. *Joining Europe's Monetary Club: The Challenges for Smaller Member States*. New York: St. Martin's Press.

Kaltenthaler, Karl. 1998. *Germany and the Politics of Europe's Money*. Durham: Duke University Press.

Katzenstein, Peter J. 1997. United Germany in an Integrating Europe. In Peter J. Katzenstein, ed. *Tamed Power: Germany in Europe*. Ithaca: Cornell University Press, 1–48.

Kawai, Masahiro. 1992. Optimum Currency Areas. In Peter Newman, Murray Milgate, and Jeahn Eatwell, eds. *The New Palgrave Dictionary of Money and Finance*. London: Macmillan, 78–81.

Kenen, Peter B. 1969. The Theory of Optimum Currency Areas: An Eclectic View. In Robert A. Mundell and Alexander K. Swoboda, eds. *Monetary Problems of the International Economy*. Chicago: University of Chicago Press, 41–60.

Kennedy, Ellen. 1991. *The Bundesbank: Germany's Central Bank in the International Monetary System*. London: Pinter Publishers for the Royal Institute for International Affairs.

Keohane, Robert O. 1978. Economics, Inflation, and the Role of the State: Political Implications of the McCracken Report. *World Politics* 31:1 (October) 108–128.

———. 2000. Ideas Part-Way Down. *International Studies Review* 26:1 (January) 125–130.

Kirshner, Jonathan. 1995. *Currency and Coercion: The Political Economy of International Monetary Power*. Princeton: Princeton University Press.

Krasner, Stephen D. 1976. State Power and the Structure of International Trade. *World Politics* 28 (April) 317–347.

———. 1983. Structural Causes and Regime Consequences: Regimes as Intervening Variables. In Stephen D. Krasner, ed. *International Regimes*. Ithaca: Cornell University Press, 1–21.

———. 2000. Wars, Hotel Fires, and Plane Crashes. *Review of International Studies* 26:1 (January) 131–136.

Krieger, Wolfgang. 1987. *General Lucius D. Clay und die amerikanische Deutschlandpolitik, 1945–1949*. Stuttgart: Ernst-Klett Verlage.

Krueger, Anne O. 1990. Economists' Changing Perceptions of Government. *Weltwirtschaftliches Archiv* 126:3, 417–431.

Krugman, Paul. 1994. Competitiveness: A Dangerous Obsession. *Foreign Affairs* 73:2 (March/April) 28–44.

Kruse, D. C. 1980. *Monetary Integration in Western Europe: EMU, EMS, and Beyond*. London: Butterworth Scientific.

Kydland, Finn E., and Edward C. Prescott 1977. Rules Rather than Discretion: The Time-Inconsistency of Optimal Plans. *The Journal of Political Economy* 85:3 (June) 473–492.

Levitt, Malcolm, and Christopher Lord. 2000. *The Political Economy of Monetary Union*. London: Macmillan.

Loedel, Peter Henning. 1999. *Deutsche Mark Politics: Germany in the European Monetary System*. Boulder: Lynne Rienner Publishers.

Lohmann, Susanne. 1992. Optimal Commitment in Monetary Policy: Credibility versus Flexibility. *American Economic Review* 82:1 (March) 273–286.

———. 1998. Federalism and Central Bank Independence: The Politics of German Monetary Policy, 1957–1992. *World Politics* 50 (April) 401–446.

Ludlow, Peter. 1982. *The Making of the European Monetary System: A Case Study of the Politics of the European Community*. London: Butterworth Scientific.

Luttwak, Edward. 1997. Central Bankism. In Peter Gowan and Perry Anderson, eds. *The Question of Europe*. London: Verso, 220–233.

MacDonald, Ronald. 1999. Exchange Rate Behavior: Are the Fundamentals Important? *The Economic Journal* 109 (November) F673–F691.

Magee, Stephen P., William A. Brock, and Leslie Young 1989. *Black Hole Tariffs and Endogenous Policy Theory: Political Economy in General Equilibrium*. Cambridge: Cambridge University Press.

Magnifico, Giovanni. 1973. *European Monetary Unification*. London: Macmillan.

Mancini, Frederico G. 2000. The Italians in Europe. *Foreign Affairs* 79:2 (March/April) 122–134.

Marris, Stephen. 1987. *Deficits and the Dollar: The World Economy at Risk—Updated Edition*. Washington, D.C.: Institute for International Economics.

Masson, Paul R., and Mark P. Taylor. 1993. Fiscal Policy within Common Currency Areas. *Journal of Common Market Studies* 31:1 (March) 29–44.

Mayes, David G. 2000. Independence and Coordination—The Eurosystem. Paper presented at the 30th Anniversary UACES research conference, Central European University, Budapest, 6–8 April.

McCarthy, Patrick. 1990. France Faces Reality: Rigueur and the Germans. In David P. Calleo and Claudia Morgenstern, eds. *Recasting Europe's Economies: National Strategies in the 1980s*. Lanham, Md.: University Press of America, 25–78.

——— ed. 1993. *France-Germany, 1983–1993: The Struggle to Cooperate*. New York: St. Martin's Press.

———. 1999. The Grand Bargain: A New Book Demystifies European Integration. *Foreign Affairs* 78:5 (September/October) 150–157.

——— ed. 2001. *France-Germany in the Twenty-First Century*. London: Palgrave.

McCracken, Paul W. 1973. The Practice of Political Economy. *The American Economic Review* (papers and proceedings) 63:2 (May) 168–171.

——— et al. 1977. *Towards Full Employment and Price Stability*. Paris: OECD.

McKay, David. 1999. *Federalism and the European Union: A Political Economy Perspective*. Oxford: Oxford University Press.

McKibbon, Warwick J., and Jeffrey D. Sachs. 1991. *Global Linkages: Macroeconomic Interdependence and Cooperation in the World Economy*. Washington, D.C.: Brookings.

McKinnon, Robert I. 1963. Optimum Currency Areas. *American Economic Review* 53:4 (September) 717–725.

McNamara, Kathleen R. 1993. Systems Effects and the European Community. In Robert Jervis and Jack Snyder, eds. *Coping With Complexity in the International System*. Boulder: Westview Press, 303–327.

———. 1998. *The Currency of Ideas: Monetary Politics in the European Union*. Ithaca: Cornell University Press.

———. 1999. Consensus and Constraint: Ideas and Capital Mobility in Monetary Integration. *Journal of Common Market Studies* 37:3 (September) 455–476.

———. 2000. State Building and the Territorialization of Money: The American Greenback. Manuscript. Princeton: Princeton University.

McNamara, Kathleen R., and Erik Jones 1996. The Clash of Institutions: Germany in European Monetary Affairs. *German Politics and Society* 14:3 (fall) 5–30.

Miller, Richard. 1987. *Fact and Method: Explanation, Confirmation and Reality in the Natural and Social Sciences*. Princeton: Princeton University Press.

Milward, Alan. 1992. *The European Rescue of the Nation-State*. London: Routledge.

Moe, Terry M. 1984. The New Economics of Organization. *American Journal of Political Science* 28:4 (November) 739–777.

Moravcsik, Andrew. 1993. Preferences and Power in the European Community: A Liberal Intergovernmentalist Approach. *Journal of Common Market Studies* 31:4 (December) 473–524.

———. 1998. *The Choice for Europe: Social Purpose and State Power from Messina to Maastricht*. Ithaca: Cornell University Press.

Moses, Jonathon. 2000. *OPEN States in the Global Economy: The Political Economy of Small-State Macroeconomic Management*. London: Macmillan.

Moss, Bernard. 2000. Is the European Community Politically Neutral? The Free Market Agenda. In Bernard H. Moss and Jonathan Michie, eds. *The Single European Currency in National Perspective: A Community in Crisis?* London: Macmillan, 141–167.

Moss, Bernard, and Jonathan Michie, eds. 2000. *The Single European Currency in National Perspective: A Community in Crisis?* London: Macmillan.

Mundell, Robert A. 1960. The Monetary Dynamics of International Adjustment under Fixed and Floating Exchange Rates. *Quarterly Journal of Economics* 74:2 (May) 227–257.

———. 1961. A Theory of Optimum Currency Areas. *American Economic Review* 51:4 (September) 657–665.

———. 1963. Capital Mobility and Stabilization Policy under Fixed and Flexible Exchange Rates. *Canadian Journal of Economics and Political Science* 29:4 (November) 475–485.

Myrdal, Gunnar. 1956. *An International Economy: Problems and Prospects*. New York: Harper & Brothers.

Nordhaus, William D. 1975. The Political Business Cycle. *The Review of Economic Studies* 42:2 (April) 169–190.

Oatley, Thomas. 1997. *Monetary Politics: Exchange Rate Cooperation in the European Union*. Ann Arbor: Michigan University Press.

Okun, Arthur M. 1973. Comments on Stigler's Paper. *The American Economic Review* (papers and proceedings) 63:2 (May) 172–177.

Olson, Mancur. 1971. *The Logic of Collective Action: Public Goods and the Theory of Groups*. Cambridge: Harvard University Press.

———. 1982. *The Rise and Decline of Nations: Economic Growth, Stagflation, and Social Rigidities*. New Haven: Yale University Press.

O'Neill, Patrick H. 1999. Politics, Finance, and European Union Enlargement Eastward. In James Sperling, ed. *Two Tiers or Two Speeds? The European Security Order and the Enlargement of the European Union and NATO*. Manchester: Manchester University Press, 81–99.

Padoa-Schioppa, Tomaso 1987. *Efficiency, Stability, and Equity: A Strategy for the Evolution of the Economic System of the European Community*. Brussels: European Commission, II/49/87 (April).

———. 1994. *The Road to Monetary Union in Europe: The Emperor, the Kings, and the Genies*. Oxford: Clarendon Press.

Philip Morris Institute (PMI). 1994. *Is European Monetary Union Dead?* Brussels: Philip Morris Institute (April).

Pierson, Christopher, Anthony Forster, and Erik Jones. 1998. The Politics of Europe: (Un)Employment Ambivalence. In Brian Towers and Michael Terry, eds. *Industrial Relations Journal: European Annual Review, 1997*. Oxford: Blackwell, 5–22.

———. 1999. Changing the Guard in the European Union: In with the New, Out with the Old? *Industrial Relations Journal: European Annual Review 1998*. 30:8 (December) 277–290.

Pierson, Paul. 1996a. The New Politics of the Welfare State. *World Politics* 48:2 (January) 143–179.

———. 1996b. The Path to European Integration: A Historical Institutionalist Analysis. *Comparative Political Studies* 29:2 (April) 123–163.

———. 1998. Irresistible forces, immovable objects: Post-industrial Welfare States Confront Permanent Austerity. *Journal of European Public Policy* 5:4 (December) 539–560.

Pisani-Ferry, Jean. 1997. France and EMU: Economic and Political Economy Issues. In Jean Pisani-Ferry, Carsten Hefeker, and A. J. Hughes Hallett. *The Political Economy of EMU: France, Germany, and the UK*. Brussels: Centre for European Policy Studies, CEPS Paper No. 69, 5–38.

Pisani-Ferry, Jean, Carsten Hefeker, and A. J. Hughes Hallett. *The Political Economy of EMU: France, Germany, and the UK*. Brussels: Centre for European Policy Studies, CEPS Paper No. 69 (May).

Polanyi, Karl. 1944. *The Great Transformation: The Political and Economic Origins of Our Time*. Boston: Beacon Hill Press.

Pollard, Sidney. 1981. *Peaceful Conquest: The Industrialization of Europe, 1760–1970*. Oxford: Oxford University Press.

Posen, Adam S. 1993. Why Central Bank Independence Does Not Cause Low Inflation: There Is No Institutional Fix for Politics. In Richard O'Brien, ed. *Finance and the International Economy 7*. Oxford: Oxford University Press for the *AMEX Bank Review*, 41–65.

Ramaswamy, Ramana, and Torsten Sløk. 1998. The Real Effects of Monetary Policy in the European Union: What Are the Differences? *IMF Staff Papers* 45:2 (June) 374–399.

Razin, Assaf. 1995. The Dynamic-Optimizing Approach to the Current Account: Theory and Evidence. In Peter B. Kenen, ed. *Understanding Interdependence: The Macroeconomics of the Open Economy*. Princeton: Princeton University Press, 169–198.

Regini, Marino. 2000. Between Deregulation and Social Pacts: The Responses of European Economies to Globalization. *Politics and Society* 28:1 (March) 5–33.

Rhodes, Martin, and Yves Mény. 1998. Introduction: Europe's Social Contract Under Stress. In Martin Rhodes and Yves Mény, eds. *The Future of European Welfare: A New Social Contract?* London: Macmillan, 1–19.

Richez-Battesti, Nadine. 1996. Union Économique et monétaire et État-providence: la subsidiarité en question. *Revue Études internationales* 27:1 (March) 109–128.

Rodrick, Dani. 1998. Why Do More Open Economies Have Bigger Governments? *Journal of Political Economy* 106:5 (October) 997–1032.

Rogoff, Kenneth. 1985. The Optimal Degree of Commitment to an Intermediate Monetary Target. *Quarterly Journal of Economics* 100:4 (November) 1169–1189.

———. 1999. Perspectives on Exchange Rate Volatility. In Martin Feldstein, ed. *International Capital Flows*. Chicago: University of Chicago Press, 441–453.

Rowthorne, R. E. 1992. Centralization, Employment, and Wage Dispersion. *The Economic Journal* 102:412 (May) 506–523.

Ruggie, John Gerard. 1983. International Regimes, Transactions, and Change: Embedded Liberalism in the Postwar Economic Order. In Stephen D. Krasner, ed. *International Regimes*. Ithaca: Cornell University Press, 195–231.

———. 1995. At Home Abroad, Abroad at Home: International Liberalization and Domestic Stability in the New World Economy. *Millennium: Journal of International Studies* 24:3 (winter) 507–524.

Sasaki, Hitoshi, Satoshi Yamaguchi, and Takamasa Hisada. 2000. The Globalization of Financial Markets and Monetary Policy. *International Financial Markets and the Implications for Monetary and Financial Stability: Conference Paper No. 8*. Basel: Bank For International Settlements, 57–78.

Scharpf, Fritz. 1999. *Governing in Europe: Effective and Democratic?* Oxford: Oxford University Press.

———. 2000. The Viability of Advanced Welfare States in the International Economy. *Journal of European Public Policy* 7:2 (June) 190–228.

Sekkat, Khalid. 1998. Exchange Rate Variability and EU Trade. *Economic Papers No. 127*. Brussels: European Commission, DG II (February).

Servet, Jean-Michel, et al. 1998. Summary of Experts Report Compiled for the Euro Working Group / European Commission DG XXIV on Psycho-Sociological Aspects of the Changeover to the Euro. Manuscript. Brussels: European Commission, DG XXIV.

Sheridan, Jerome. 1996. The Déjà Vu of EMU: Considerations for Europe from Nineteenth Century America. *Journal of Economic Issues* 30:4 (December) 1143–1161.

Siedentop, Larry. 2000. *Democracy in Europe*. London: Penguin.

Simmel, Georg. 1978. *The Philosophy of Money*. Translated by Tom Bottomore and David Frisby. London: Routledge and Kegan Paul.

Simonian, Haig. 1985. *The Privileged Partnership: Franco-German Relations in the European Community, 1969–1984*. Oxford: Clarendon Press.

Smith, Adam. 1983. *The Wealth of Nations*. New York: Penguin.

Soskice, David, and Torben Iversen. 1998. Multiple Wage-bargaining Systems in the Single European Currency Area. *Oxford Review of Economic Policy* 14:3 (autumn) 110–124.

Stevenson, Andrew, Vitantonio Muscatelli, and Mary Gregory. 1988. *Macroeconomic Theory and Stabilization Policy*. Oxford: Philip Allan.

Stigler, George J. 1973. General Economic Conditions and National Elections. *The American Economic Review* (papers and proceedings) 63:2 (May) 160–167.

Szukala, Andrea, and Wolfgang Wessels. 1997. The Franco-German Tandem. In Geoffrey Edwards and Alfred Pijpers, eds. *The Politics of European Treaty Reform: The 1996 Intergovernmental Conference and Beyond*. London: Pinter, 74–95.

Tamborini, Roberto. 2001. Living in EMU. *Journal of Common Market Studies* 39:1 (March) 123–146.

Tavlas, George. 1993. The "New" Theory of Optimum Currency Areas. *The World Economy* 16:6 (November) 663–685.

Thorlakson, Lori. 2000. Government Building and Political Development in Federations: Applying Canadian Theory to the German Case. *Regional and Federal Studies* 10:3 (autumn) 129–148.

Thygesen, Niels. 1979. Exchange Rate Experiences and Policies of Small Countries: Some European Examples of the 1970s. *Essays in International Finance* No. 136. Princeton: Princeton University (December).

Tietmeyer, Hans. 1994. Europäische Währungsunion und politische Union—das Modell mehrerer Geschwindigkeiten. *Europa Archiv* 49:16 25 (August) 457–460.

Torres, Francisco. 1998. Portugal toward EMU: A Political Economy Perspective. In Erik Jones, Jeffry Frieden, and Francisco Torres, eds. *Joining Europe's Monetary Club: The Challenges for Smaller Member States*. New York: St. Martin's Press, 171–202.

Tsoukalis, Loukas. 1977. *The Politics and Economics of European Monetary Integration*. London: Allen and Unwin.

Verdun, Amy. 1996. An "Asymmetrical" Economic and Monetary Union in the EU: Perceptions of Monetary Authorities and Social Partners. *Journal of European Integration* 20:1 (fall) 59–81.

———. 1998. The Institutional Design of EMU: A Democratic Deficit? *Journal of Public Policy* 18:2, 107–132.

Viñals, José, and Juan Jimeno. 1998. Monetary Union and European Unemployment. In Jeffrey Frieden, Daniel Gros, and Erik Jones, eds. *The New Political Economy of EMU*. Lanham, Md.: Rowman & Littlefield, 13–52.

Visser, Jelle. 1998. European Trade Unions in the Mid-1990s. In Brian Towers and Michael Terry, eds. *Industrial Relations Journal: European Annual Review, 1997*. Oxford: Blackwell, 113–130.

Von Hagen, Jürgen, and George W. Hammond. 1998. Regional Insurance Against Asymmetric Shocks: An Empirical Study for the European Community. *The Manchester School* 66:3 (June) 331–353.

Wadbrook, William Pollard. 1972. *West German Balance of Payments Policy: The Prelude to European Monetary Integration*. New York: Praeger.

Walsh, James. 1999. Political Bases of Macroeconomic Adjustment: Evidence from the Italian Experience. *Journal of European Public Policy* 6:1 (March) 66–84.

Watson, Matthew. 1999. Rethinking Capital Mobility: Reregulating Financial Markets. *New Political Economy* 4:1 (March) 55–75.

Webber, Douglas. 1999. Franco-German Bilateralism and Agricultural Politics in the European Union: The Neglected Level. *West European Politics* 22:1 (January) 45–67.

Wendt, Alexander. 1999. *Social Theory of International Politics*. Cambridge: Cambridge University Press.

Willis, F. Roy. 1965. *France, Germany, and the New Europe: 1945–1963*. Stanford: Stanford University Press.

Winkler, G. Michael. 1998. Coalition-Sensitive Voting Power in the Council of Ministers: The Case of Eastern Enlargement. *Journal of Common Market Studies* 36:3 (September) 391–404.

Wyplosz, Charles. 1997. EMU: Why and How It Might Happen. *Journal of Economic Perspectives* 11:4 (fall) 3–21.

Young, Oran R. 1980. International Regimes: The Problem of Concept Formation. *World Politics* 32:3 (April) 331–356.

Zysman, John. 1983. *Governments, Markets, and Growth: Financial Systems and the Politics of Industrial Change*. Ithaca: Cornell University Press.

Index

accountability, 37, 43, 52, 59, 72, 78; monetary union without political union, 54–55, 156, 188

Agenda 2000, 148. *See also* enlargement

Amsterdam Treaty, 36, 123, 129; economic provisions of, 39–40; employment provisions of, 41; and ESCB, 44; exchange rate policy provisions of, 56n1, 129; monetary provisions of, 37–38, 53

Anderson, Jeffrey, 144

asymmetric shocks, 83, 86–87, 129

Bank of England, 19, 131–134, 141n5, 185

benign neglect, 123, 139

Berlin Wall, 151

Blair, Tony, 105, 133

Blum, Leon, 33n11

Boltho, Andrea, 155

Bretton Woods system, 6, 119–120; and dollar convertibility, 5, 107

Breuer, Rolf, 82

Broad Economic Policy Guidelines (BEPGs). *See* Council of Ministers

Bulmer, Simon, 144

Bundesbank, 75, 159–161

capital markets, 10, 116; crises in, 11, 89, 105; integration of, 12, 93, 101; international creditworthiness in, 112. *See also* financial actors

central bank independence, 11, 26, 66, 73; consensus about, 67–68; democratic legitimacy of, 59–62, 72, 143; and distributive conflict, 74, 96; ESCB provisions for, 45–47, 59

Chirac, Jacques, 160

Clinton, William Jefferson, 137

Common Agricultural Policy (CAP), 146–148, 163

Corus (formerly British Steel), 133–134

Council of Ministers, 36, 43; broad economic policy guidelines of, 47–49; economics and finance ministers (ECOFIN), 45, 55, 137, 149–150; influence over monetary policy, 59; Irish reprimand, 50, 53–54; voting in, 163

credibility, 74

Crozier, Michel, 161–163

culture of price stability, 60, 62, 75

currency; electronic, 18, 31; functions of, 20, 91, 186; metallic, 17; proxy

for utility, 69; role in state-building, 170; single (*see* euro)
current account, 103, 108; consistent deficits, 110–113; consistent surpluses, 113–115; long run constraint, 108

delegation, 60, 78, 78n2. *See also* accountability
Delors, Jacques, 9
Denmark, 176, 179; referendums, 10, 179, 182n16, 192
Deutchemark, symbolic importance of, 170, 180, 186
distributive coalitions, 25, 28, 30, 54, 71, 94, 96; absence at European level, 55, 77, 94; and conflict, 73–74. *See also* economic preferences, monetary policy
Downs, Anthony, 63, 64, 68–69, 70, 78n4
Duisenberg, Wim, 53, 55, 57n28, 134–138, 150, 180

ECOFIN. *See* Council of Ministers
economic adjustment, 25, 26, 84; and exchanges rates, 86, 88; political economy of, 82, 91; political reaction to, 30
Economic and Financial Committee (EFC), 48
economic and monetary union (EMU), 1, 37; beginning of, 2, 11, 105, 152; benefits of, 28–29, 85; constraint on European democracy, 12, 56, 59, 72, 76–77; definition of, 97–98n4; Delors proposal for, 9, 15n15; economic adjustment in, 89, 91; and insulation, 31, 102; institutional design of, 11; Maastricht plan for, 10; as political system, 32, 59, 99n17; reasons for choosing, 3, 124; stability of, 12, 77, 84; and unemployment, 82, 88, 118–119
Economic Policy Committee (EPC), 51
economic preferences, 60–62, 67–68, 70. *See also* monetary policy

Eichengreen, Barry, 97n2
electoral business cycle, 64–65, 67
embedded liberalism, 101, 103–104, 167
employment policy, 35, 40–42, 51, 94, 149; open method of coordination, 51–52
enlargement, 146–148
epistemic communities, 68, 79n9
euro, 1, 83, 91, 170; exchange rate with the U.S. dollar, 11, 13, 81, 104, 123, 127–128, 134–138, 183; external value of, 130
Euro-11. *See* Eurogroup
Eurobarometer, 82, 173–175. *See also* public opinion
Eurogroup, 55, 136–137, 140, 180
"Europe," 189
European Central Bank (ECB), 38, 126, 141n4, 149; Executive Board of, 45; president of, 163, 180. *See also* European System of Central Banks; Duisenberg, Wim
European Coal and Steel Community (ECSC), 151
European Commission, 7, 127; *One Market One Money* report, 125
European Community. *See* European Union
European Council, 5, 51; Amsterdam summit, 40, 127; Cardiff summit, 41; Cologne summit, 41; Lisbon summit, 51, 54, 118; Luxembourg summits, 40, 41, 129; Nice summit, 163, 180
European Parliament (EP), 43; oversight of ESCB, 46, 53, 55, 57n26, 57n28, 59, 134
European monetary system (EMS), 2, 4, 7, 146, 179, 191; currency realignments, 8–9; Franco-German relationship, 7–9, 151; negotiation of, 15n10
European Rescue of the Nation-State, 162
European System of Central Banks (ESCB), 36, 38, 43; communications strategy of, 44, 50, 57n17; exchange-

rate policy, 130; General Council of, 46; monetary policy of, 93, 126, 150, 184; national central banks and, 45. *See also* central bank independence

European Union, 8

Europessimism, 175–178

Eurosclerosis, 118

excessive deficits procedure. *See* fiscal policy

exchange rate mechanism (ERM), 10, 112, 120n5, 179

exchange rate regimes, 2–3; commitment to, 26–27; devaluation and, 26, 85–86; "fixed but adjustable," 31; "irrevocably fixed," 2, 31, 37, 84–85, 89; reasons for choosing, 3–4, 90; volatility in, 123

federalism, 104, 159, 167, 192

Feldstein, Martin, 81, 83, 98n5, 143

financial actors, 43. *See also* capital markets

Finland, response to asymmetry, 88

fiscal policy, 35, 93; democratic legitimacy of, 78; rules for, 39, 49

France, 6; convergence on U.S. model, 155; economic turnaround (1982–1983), 8, 151, 165n7; elections in, 160; qualification for EMU, 50; referendum in, 180, 192

Franco-German relationship 7–9, 13, 143, 154, 180; balance of power within, 144, 150; Elysée Accords, 8; EMS, 7–9; and exchange rates, 126; trade interdependence, 152

French franc, 6

Frieden, Jeffrey, 87, 104

Friedman, Milton, 33n7, 67

Friend, Julius, 145

"generative grammar," 164, 165n12

Germany, 6, 157, 186; constitutional court decision, 144, 180; cost of capital in, 92; economic power potential, 158; preference for price stability, 6, 75; qualification for EMU, 50; as "tamed power,"

144–145, 164n3; trade with Central and Eastern Europe, 153; unification of, 145, 152–153, 158–159; wage bargaining in, 95, 156, 159

German mark. *See* Deutschemark

Gerschenkron, Alexander, 181n7

Giscard-d'Estaing, Valéry, 7

globalization, 77, 101, 138

Gresham's Law, 192n1

Group of Seven leading industrial nations (G-7), 120n6, 137

Hibbs, Douglas, 65, 67, 70

identity, 57n26. *See also* culture of price stability

"imagined communities," 169

income; distribution of, 27, 74; and justice, 28, 77; stabilization of, 27, 33n13, 85, 88, 90

Inquiry into the Wealth of Nations. See Adam Smith

institutions, constitutive effect of, 68, 75, 82, 87, 90, 159; and monetary transmission, 93; and risk, 116–117, 118

International Monetary Fund (IMF), 81, 82

Ireland, 88, 95, 190; referendum, 182n19, 191–192; reprimand of by Council of Ministers, 50, 53–54, 190–191

Italy, 107, 179–180

Japan, 114–115

Jenkins, Roy, 7

Katzenstein, Peter, 144, 164n3

Kenen, Peter, 90

Keynesianism, 6, 24, 37, 106

Krasner, Stephen, 158, 182n9

labor theory of value, 17

Lafontaine, Oskar, 53, 136, 160–161

Lakatos, Imre, 79n6

Luxembourg compromise, 162

Maastricht Treaty, 9–11, 77–78, 144, 149, 152, 154, 180
Marjolin Report, 5, 14n5
McCarthy, Patrick, 151, 165n4, 165n7
Mitterrand, François, 8
monetarism, 24
monetary policy; instruments, 21; left-right preferences for, 33n6; manipulation of, 23; one size fits all, 93; political cleavages around, 21–22; rules for, 23–26, 35; and time inconsistency, 22, 66
Monetary Policy Committee (MPC). *See* Bank of England
multilateral surveillance procedure. *See* Council of Ministers
Mundell, Robert, 85, 90, 114

nationalism, 157, 169–170, 187–188
neo-liberalism, 102, 167
Netherlands, 76
Nordhaus, William, 64, 67
North Atlantic Treaty Organization (NATO), 9
Noyer, Christian, 57n26

oil price shock, 5, 107
Olson, Mancur, 33n9
open method of coordination. *See* employment policy; European Council
optimal inflation tax, 63, 64, 65–66, 69, 71
optimum currency areas, 29, 84, 89
Organization for Economic Cooperation and Development (OECD), 120n3

Padoa-Schioppa, Tomaso, 14n3, 106, 120
partisan business cycle, 65, 67
Philips curve, 62, 64, 69, 74, 86, 88
Pierson, Paul, 97
positive economics, 63
pound sterling. *See* United Kingdom
principal-agent relationship. *See* accountability; delegation

Prodi, Romano, 81
public opinion, 3, 91–92, 94, 171–175

Reagan, Ronald, 111
regimes, 167, 171–172; expectations convergence within, 172
risk, 105; calculation of, 91; as a cost of capital market integration, 103, 116–118; currency, 92, 117; geographic, 92; investment, 92; liquidity, 117; sovereign, 117
Rover Group, 133
rules versus discretion, 73, 149

Schmidt, Helmut, 7
Schröder, Gerhard, 160–161
Smith, Adam, 17
Soviet Union, 181n7
Stability and Growth Pact, 40, 77–78, 121n8, 127, 149, 160, 180, 187. *See also* fiscal policy
Strauss-Kahn, Dominique, 161
Summers, Lawrence, 137
symbolism, 13, 128, 149, 169, 180–181, 187–188; and exchange rates, 26–27, 82, 138

Thatcher, Margaret, 168
Toyota, 105
Treaty establishing the European Community (TEC). *See* Amsterdam Treaty
Treaty on European Union (TEU). *See* Maastricht Treaty; Amsterdam Treaty
Trichet, Jean-Claude, 150, 180

United Kingdom, 19, 107, 131–134, 179–180; business attitudes in, 98n11, 185; Conservative Party, 83; economic preferences in, 65; Labour Party, 134; press attitudes, 126; pound sterling, 105, 124, 131–134
United States, 2, 111, 119–120, 123–124, 137–141; civil war in, 32n3, 83, 125, 139; distribution of income in, 33n13; economic preferences in, 65;

exceptionalism, 138–141; hegemony of, 111–112; monetary performance of, 75, 93, 139

Uruguay Round, 148

Vauxhall, 105, 120n1
Vietnam War, 120

wage bargaining, 6, 60–61, 76, 88, 95–96; as complement to central bank independence, 74

welfare state, 30, 77; autonomy, 101, 105; reform of, 118
Werner, Pierre, 5
Werner Plan for EMU, 5–7, 104; economist-monetarist division over, 6
West European Union, 8
Wilson, Harold, 33n11
World War II, 170–171, 181n7

Yugoslavia, 186

About the Author

Erik Jones is Reader in Political Science and Jean Monnet Chair in European Integration at the University of Nottingham and Professorial Lecturer at the Bologna Center of the Johns Hopkins University. He is coeditor of *Disintegration or Transformation? The Crisis of the State in Advanced Industrial Societies* (1995), *Joining Europe's Monetary Club: The Challenges for Smaller Member States* (1998), *The New Political Economy of EMU* (1998), and *Developments in West European Politics 2* (2002). He is also author of *Economic Adjustment and Political Transformation in Small States*, which is forthcoming from Rowman & Littlefield.